SOME GRAVER SUBJECT

By the same Author

✱

POETIC LOVE

Mansell-Anderson

I Raphael

Adam and Eve (1510)

SOME GRAVER SUBJECT

AN ESSAY ON PARADISE LOST

By

J. B. BROADBENT

Fellow of King's College
University Lecturer in English
Cambridge

'Yet I had rather if I were to chuse,
Thy service in some graver subject use.'

1967

CHATTO & WINDUS

LONDON

PUBLISHED BY
CHATTO & WINDUS LTD
42 WILLIAM IV STREET
LONDON W.C.2

*

CLARKE, IRWIN & CO. LTD
TORONTO

First Published 1960
Second Impression 1967

PRINTED PHOTOLITHO IN GREAT BRITAIN
BY EBENEZER BAYLIS AND SON, LTD.
THE TRINITY PRESS, WORCESTER, AND LONDON

For F. J. L.

Not content with neutral ground for its development, it was attracted by the sublimity of divine subjects to ambitious and hazardous essays.

NEWMAN

At once delight and horrour on us seize.

MARVELL

Abbreviations

Standard for Bible. Those for Milton's work will become apparent by reference to the index. *EC: Essays in Criticism* (Oxford); *ELH: ELH, A Journal of English Literary History*; *HLQ: Huntington Library Quarterly*; *MLN: Modern Language Notes*; *MP: Modern Philology*; *PMLA: Publications of the Modern Language Association of America*; *SP: Studies in Philology*; *UTQ: University of Toronto Quarterly*.

Preface

I FIRST tried to read Milton for myself in the Flying Scotsman. I am grateful to Miss Winifred Maynard of Edinburgh University for helping me over this false start; and to Dr Tillyard for constant help and encouragement. My thanks are due to colleagues and pupils for many suggestions; especially the Rev. Gurney Gutekunst of Union Seminary, New York, for theological prompting, and Prof. J. H. Summers for reading the MS. I was enabled to write this book in the first place by a scholarship from the Carnegie Trust for the Universities of Scotland, and subsequently by research fellowships at St Catharine's College and King's College, Cambridge. I should like to say how much I appreciate the personal interest which the then secretary and treasurer of the Carnegie Trust, Dr J. R. Peddie, took in all the Trust's beneficiaries.

I use the *Poetical Works of Milton* edited by H. C. Beeching in the Oxford Standard Authors series (1904): i.e. 1667 edition of *Paradise Lost*, with occasional reference to 1674 variants and common emendations; and the Bohn *Prose Works* edited by J. A. St John (5 vols. 1848); but one letter is quoted from the first volume of the Yale *Prose Works*, edited by D. M. Wolfe (New Haven, 1953) and others from the *Private Correspondence and Academic Exercises* translated and edited by P. B. and E. M. W. Tillyard. There are references to the Commonplace Book, which is included in the Yale edition, and to the Cambridge Manuscript which is reprinted in facsimile in *Milton's Minor Poems* edited by W. Aldis Wright (Cambridge, 1899). I quote the Bible in the Authorised Version to emphasise by familiarity its pervasion of the poem, and the Old Testament Apocrypha from the edition of R. M. Charles (2 vols. Oxford, 1913). Details of other works are given in the notes, usually at the first quotation. Place of publication is London unless otherwise stated.

Parts of Chapter II have appeared as "Milton's Hell" in *ELH, A Journal of English Literary History*, 1954; of Chapter VI as "Milton's Paradise" in *Modern Philology*, 1954, and as "Landscape with Figures", a talk on the B.B.C. Third Programme produced by Mr D. S. Carne-Ross on 28th December 1956. Some minor points are taken up from "Links between Prose and Poetry in Milton" published in *English Studies*, 1956, from "Milton and Arnold" in *Essays in Criticism*, 1957, and from "Milton's Rhetoric" in *Modern Philology*, 1959. I am grateful for permission to use this material again.

J. B. B.

KING'S COLLEGE, CAMBRIDGE
May 1958

Preface to the 1967 edition

This book was first published in 1960 but I finished writing it in 1958 so I was not able to take advantage of Mrs Isabel MacCaffrey's "*Paradise Lost*" *as* "*Myth*" (Cambridge, Mass., 1959). I am sorry that she allowed, as she says, her speculations to be curbed; but her work, especially Chapter 5 on Milton's imagery, opened up some of the themes and sub-myths that operate behind the main action of *Paradise Lost* and which have been of increasing interest to readers since about 1950.

Milton's God by Empson (1961) is a model of how practical and urgent the learned discussion of highly artificial literature may be. For me, however, though not behind in criticising Christianity, it uses the poem too polemically. On pp. 290–92 I discussed what I take to be Empson's thesis, that *Paradise Lost* is a conscious critique of the theology it postulates; but I still do not think it can be taken that way except by special reading.

The Muse's Method: An Introduction to "*Paradise Lost*" by Joseph Summers (1962) is the most complete of the studies I shall mention. It treats the poem on its own terms—that is, it takes Milton's puritanism-straight—and provides solid professional help of various kinds; the effect is to reveal themes which we can accept as food for thought and as pleasurable details of craft. Summers' comment on the worship of Ashtoreth in Book I in relation to the love of Adam and Eve in Book IV, for example, is exactly the sort of annotation we most profit from: it points to facts, to structure and to words.

In *Milton's Grand Style* (1963) Christopher Ricks includes a review of recent criticism (except for Summers) to that date, especially the Milton-Eliot-Leavis controversy; but it is his references to 18th- and 19th-century comment on Milton which are most interesting. They declare our need for a new kind of history of criticism—a history of practical criticism. It might take off from Empson's essay on Milton and Bentley. *Milton's Grand Style* is the most thorough study —really, the only detailed one we have—of the language, syntax and imagery of *Paradise Lost.* Ricks does not treat style as R. M. Adams did in his brief dense chapters at the end of *Ikon* (1955), as ultimately a symptom of personality and way-of-living; but he brilliantly displays how lines and figures of speech and individual words in the poem "go". For example, the way *deck't* refers to both flowers and smells, and then to Eve, at V. 379:

> So to the Silvan Lodge
> They came, that like *Pomona's* Arbour smil'd
> With flourets deck't and fragrant smells; but *Eve*
> Undeckt . . .

There are times when this kind of analysis seems to relish technique for its own sake; yet the operation of such a word as *deck't* implies a precision, and an awareness of the relations between things, and a sometimes equivocal evaluating force, which Milton has often been blamed for lacking. Ricks is in any case awake to the moral implications of language. Of Milton's latinisms for instance he asks: "Is Milton reaching back to an earlier purity—which we are to contrast with what has happened to the word, and the world, since? Or is he simply being forgetful? The answer is likely to depend on one's general estimate of Milton" (p. 111). Of course, that general estimate is in its turn likely to depend on how far you press your judgement of technical detail. If, as I often do, you treat it as a judgement of symbolic behaviour, you are bound to raise questions which have a priggish and enigmatic air. However efficient in the poem a technique may be (you will say), what kind of living is represented by a habit of purifying etymological diction? or by the oscillating precision of *deck't* in conjunction with flowers and nakedness? Such questions will always baffle because they come from shifting about between "art" and "life"; but even if you stay in one universe of discourse they will probably go on baffling because sometimes you will answer them absolutely and sometimes relatively. You may in the absolute condemn a style of writing, or of behaving, and yet become increasingly aware of the excuses for it; you may at times admire it as the solution to an intolerable dilemma. I say "at times" because—another cause for bafflement—our responses alter with our experience and moods. We can hope only to indicate what sort of factors interest us; they will remain fairly stable.

PREFACE

So I could not alter the substance of this book, except by expansion, and that has already been done for some of the factors I was trying to attend to. There has been an historical change of attention. From the rise of academic criticism in the late 19th century until about 1950, discussion of *Paradise Lost* centred on simple oppositions of opinion about large general issues: Satan is a hero, a fool; Milton wrote in the grand style and that is good, bad; Milton mismanages the myth—Milton's talent is for architectonics. These are the "antithetical exam questions of the Raleigh type" which I swiped at on p. 292 because they put students off Milton—their terms are so obviously blunted. Milton can be used as a talisman by either party in an argument. Many of the arguments about him are really shadows of other arguments—I suggested what some of them may be in my last few pages; they mostly boil down to a conservative-radical opposition of a peculiarly English kind. The literary point is that it is characteristic of Milton's way of writing to drive one to controversy, to make one take sides. Of course we still consider what sides he presents—it is a major function of his writing to make us do so—but perhaps we look more at the subtler ones now: art and nature; innocence and experience; idolatry and religion; lust and love; mysticism and rationalism; body and soul. And we have begun to study the terms of those old disagreements more critically: who is Satan, historically speaking? how does the grand style actually work? what kind of existence can God be said to have in a poem? what is the myth of *Paradise Lost*? This closer attention has characterised, apart from the books I have mentioned, Empson's essay in *Some Versions of Pastoral* (1935) and some later publications of the 50s, especially Arnold Stein's *Answerable Style* (Minneapolis, 1953), and the essays on syntax by Donald Davie, and on "Adam unparadised" by the editor, in Frank Kermode's collection, *The Living Milton* (1960). J. M. Evans is preparing a study of recensions of the Fall myth which should be valuable; and C. A. Patrides is collecting a volume of essays on *Paradise Lost*.

I am aware that my own arguments are sometimes difficult to follow. Again, I could not make them much easier except by expansion, for some of the compression was forced on me by the economics of publishing. But usually it represents my struggling with questions which I came to ask only as I wrote; so the book is a discourse, not a thesis. I have tried since to state more formally some of the questions and propositions I was groping for, but most of them seem to make less sense outside the tangle of my essay than in it. I think this may be because they are the sort of issues that arise typically from reading the poem, rather intensely but with one eye looking out of the window at things which are not poems. Anyway I shall not try to summarise myself, but make three points a little in extension of what I wrote.

The first and major point is this: *Paradise Lost* is a highly artificial poem by genre and style; it is forbiddingly learned, and virtuous; its materials are deeply traditional. These characteristics can initiate all sorts of intriguing comment—how did a religious epic like this come to be published in 1667? is Milton a Stoic? in what way have attitudes to the Fall changed in history? what is the significance of this classical allusion, these precious stones, this reference to Arabia, the spices in Paradise? So people writing about Milton tend to indulge in footnotes. The remarkable thing is that they also tangle themselves, as I have indicated, in a great variety of moral or behavioral discussions: what is innocence? how can the imagination of Belial be evil? why does Milton associate technology with hell? what sort of ideal of human life is suggested by his teleology? is chaos as undesirable as he makes out? Adam and Eve are theological figures yet they also enact a domestic comedy—marriage, separation, temptation, remorse, contentment: is this valid in itself, or in relation to the divine comedy? The point I am making is that for all its artificial and scholarly characteristics, *Paradise Lost* invites us to *think* about the concepts it so coolly embodies. This is most unusual. The poetry, and the criticism, of the last 150 years have encouraged us to rely on the excitements and perceptions they provide to feel and think for us; Milton leaves it to us. Here is a tiny example: at the end of the Flood, Milton points out that to Adam it is "The end of all thy Ofspring, end so sad,/Depopulation" (XI.751). There are times when I still regard this as at best a clumsiness, the crushing of the simple *end* and *sad* by the abstract *depopulation*; at worst, a move in an insensitive language game, a deliberate recession from feeling into pomposity. But more often than not I find myself being invited by the dull ringing of *depopulation* to consider what it means—not, I admit, locally, in terms of Adam and the Flood, but for myself: to consider the unpeopling of a world as a possible event, and also as a way of reconsidering what it means to have people in the first place. This is the sort of thing, on a very small scale, that I mean by the hospitality of *Paradise Lost*. But it is a conceptual hospitality: the invitation comes usually through abstract words, or through the orthodox presentation of opposing states of being or alternative actions; or, if through the imitation of physical things, very simple ones like Eve's tears and hands.

Secondly, and in spite of that, I remain aware in all Milton's work, of a division, a polarisation such as I described in my last chapter. It is easy to simplify a writer's characteristics into pairs, but there does seem to me to be a clash or tension (it varies in effect) between, as I would now put it, authority and eccentricity. Authority is represented by Milton's respect for literary ancestors, for traditional genres and forms, for etymological language, ultimately I suppose by his respect for God; eccentricity by his habit of testing authority to destruction. He overfulfills each genre and form and convention, he not only matches the classical and Italian epics but outdoes them and sometimes consigns them to hell, he writes his own kind of English verse. In fact, he is extraordinary, within a rigid framework. But I no longer feel quite so surprised or disturbed at any of this, as I did.

No doubt there is a psychological explanation for this conflict, or for my assertion of it, but I won't go into it because many readers objected to the hints I threw off in that direction initially. I can only repeat—and this is my third point—what I said on p. 71, that it really isn't respectable any longer for students of literature to apply words of aesthetic and moral value without any attempt at psychological description. Of course our attempts will often be shoddy because our materials are more difficult to control than those put together in the laboratory. In the case of *Paradise Lost* we are bound to talk about the Freudo-Jungian myth (and that is how I usually refer to it) because it covers a good deal of the same ground as the poem's myths; for that reason we cannot ignore it except by deliberately stopping our ears. Naturally it is embarrassing to encounter in a classic poem issues which the very act of reading it may be intended to allay; but if that is so, we should avoid reading poems about our first parents. Not that anyone reads *Paradise Lost* as a psychological allegory all through, but these issues do crop up—sometimes explicitly, as in the birth of Sin and Eve's dream. I wanted to emphasise that by virtue merely of its subject this poem contains much that is interesting to reflect upon which, having nothing to do with either poetry or theology, sometimes gets left out of discussion.

Since I wrote the 1960 preface I have had increasing reason to be grateful for support and stimulus from the members of King's College; and I am also grateful to the University of Chicago for giving me the opportunity in the summer of 1965 to discuss Milton with a class of most helpful graduate students.

J.B.B.

King's College, Cambridge
1966

Corrigenda

Technical considerations preclude corrections being made in the text, so I list here those which might cause confusion.

page	line	
21	2	*for* disparable *read* disparate
45	4	*for* 1664 *read* 1654
69	15	*for* demi-urge *read* demiurge
73	10	*of quotation, for* behalf *read* half
	14	*of quotation, for* fading *read* faded
143	14	*for* ἐρος *read* ἔρως
174	22	*for* argentes *read* argentea
184	34	*for* α᾽ιγδώς *read* α᾽ιδώς
	39	*for* classical *read* classically
185	23	*for* difficult *read* difficulty
190	37	*for* as *read* a
197	29	*for* anachronistic *read* anachronism
216	29	*for* a stoical *read* Stoicism
220	26	*for* immortality *read* immorality
	29	*for* heroics balanced *read* heroics are balanced
254	33	*for* Part *read* Chapter
276	18	*for* Conconiandi *read* Concionandi
278	12	*for* not *read* now
292	1	*for* in the form, by saying *read* in another form, as

Contents

CONTENTS

Illustrations

I

INTRODUCTION

1. *The Demand for Divine Epic*

> Literature is to man in some sort what autobiography is to the individual; it is his Life and Remains. Moreover, he is this sentient, intelligent, creative, and operative being, quite independent of any extraordinary aid from Heaven, or any definite religious belief; and *as such*, as he is in himself, does Literature represent him; it is the Life and Remains of the *natural* man . . . or man *in pura natura*.[1]

TO an English reader of the early 17th Century, with a Puritan religion and a Humanistic sense of antiquity's glory, it must have been even more apparent than it was to Newman that the literature of the centuries of grace had not been very Christian; and much more shocking, because as a Protestant he would not make quite Newman's distinctions between natural and supernatural, and as a Renaissance patriot he would believe that literature ought to celebrate the culture of Christendom. But with the exception of Dante's *Paradiso*, important literature had so far been secular, even pagan. Sometimes the content had been Christian, as in Vida's *Christiad*, written at the command of Pope Leo X (a Medici who had ridden to his coronation on a Turkish charger on which he had fought at Ravenna, in a procession adorned with effigies of the Greek pantheon); and as in religious lyrics and drama up to the 16th Century. Sometimes the attitude had been at least superficially Christian, as in Petrarch's Latin *Africa* and the subsequent vernacular epics and romances of the 15th and 16th Centuries which celebrated the victory of Catholic Europe over Islamic Asia or Catholic Arthur against pagan barbarism—Malory, Boiardo, Ariosto, Camoens, Tasso, Spenser (though in some of these, notably Camoens, the real theme was commercial imperialism). But there had been little concatenation of content and treatment in a fully Christian literature of large scale. This separation was particularly evident in England in the 16th Century. The lyric was secularised on

[1] *Idea of a University*, Discourse IX (ed. Harrold, 1947), p. 201.

Italian models. Drama was deprived of religious content by law in the first year of Elizabeth's reign. Much of the divinity of the Middle Ages was turned to translating the Bible.[1] Homiletic energy was directed to composing the Prayer Book,[2] and preaching. Donne and Lancelot Andrewes follow a Latimer who began preaching in 1525. The sermon was the dominant form of religious literature throughout the century. But, like its private counterpart the devotional lyric, it could not be permanent and comprehensive; unless it were "metaphysical" it could not incorporate secular learning (and Metaphysical sermons were distasteful to the Puritans precisely because they did this); nor, however splendid or logical its rhetoric, could the sermon, especially the later, Puritan brand, satisfy the poetic urge of either writer or reader.

Yet by 1600 there was a reading public wider than the courtly, determined to reap in literature, as well as in political and economic fields, the harvest of Renaissance and Reformation. The Renaissance had promoted the "idea" of literature, as a token of civilisation, and an expression of the culture of large communities; and whether national or European, Protestant or Catholic, the most comprehensive myth for such a literature was Christianity. The Reformation, though felt by many[3] to be incomplete because of continuing episcopacy, had irrevertibly made it possible and necessary for each man to minister to his own spiritual needs. Yet it was the Reformation and its accompanying social changes which had made the literary expression of the earlier Renaisssance obsolescent even when it was not quasi-pagan: the serious purpose of fashioning a gentleman with moral virtues, for instance, was better served by Henry Peacham's *Compleat Gentleman* than *Arcadia* or the *Faerie Queene*, which could be more than a pleasantly versified *Bevis of Southampton* only to readers with a medieval sense of allegory and an Elizabethan sense of court.

Some "renaissance" literature was "reformed". The Counter-Reformation forced Tasso to explain the "allegory" of *Gerusalemme Liberata* :

[1] Tyndale *c.* 1520, Coverdale 1535, Rogers 1537, Rogers-Coverdale 1539, Taverner 1539, Geneva 1560, Bishops' under Parker 1568, Douai 1609, AV 1611.

[2] Chiefly Cranmer, 1549, 1552.

[3] Such as Bacon: i.e. not only fanatical Puritans.

> The *Flowers*, the *Fountains*, the *Rivers*, the *Musical Instruments*, the *Nymphs*, are the deceitful Inticements, which do here set down before us the Pleasures and Delights of the Sense, under the shew of *Good*.[1]

Ovid, having contributed largely to Tasso and the romantic narrative poets of the 16th Century, was *moralisé* by Golding in the middle of the 16th-Century, and bowdlerised by Sandys in 1626. But English readers wanted some original expression of Christian myth in its Protestant version—revelation of the glory of God to each individual in the glorious facts of Nature; wholesome devotional nourishment; and a progressive, pragmatic view of history in which the Catholic scheme of salvation centred on the supernal drama of Incarnation, Passion and Resurrection, should be replaced by the Protestant scheme centred on the individual and more naturalistic drama of human depravity, effectual calling and imputed righteousness—involving a shift of emphasis from the crucified and risen Christ to the fallen and regenerate Adam.

This demand explains the huge success of Du Bartas' *La Sepmaine, ou Creation* (1578) and his *Seconde Semaine* (1584), a sequel on the Fall and subsequent history of man. Du Bartas was a noble French Huguenot. His work, as translated serially from 1592 to 1599 by Joshua Sylvester (a wool-merchant) into *The Divine Weeks and Works*, was so popular outside France that he was received in Scotland by James VI, who published his own translation, and in England by Queen Elizabeth, and Sidney, who also made his own version. Praised by Spenser and Drayton, he was the childhood reading of Milton, Cowley and Dryden. Du Bartas' achievement was to run into easy verse—made even more homely by Sylvester—the central Protestant drama; and to bulk the story out into a magazine of information and morality for the middle class. Du Bartas had reason for being respectable. The press had begun to be used for commercial pornography. This was being bitterly complained of by 1600, and in 1640 the Root and Branch petition asked for obscene publications to be censored. But Du Bartas' respectability was so much more ingrained than deliberate that it gave out the text for all literary prudery of the next three hundred years:

[1] Pref. Trans. Fairfax 1600, repr. H. Morley 1890.

> Therefore, for my part I haue vow'd to heau'n
> Such wit and learning as my God hath giu'n;
> To write, to th'honour of my Maker dread,
> Verse that a Virgine without blush may read.[1]

As a result he is competent at the domestic level, in a James Thomsonian way, but helpless in sublimity. Constantly drawing on Cicero's *De Natura Deorum* for assurance that all things are as they should be, and tying every phenomenon of the universe down to daily affairs, his work has more the effect of a vast insurance policy than an epic.

Du Bartas' material was a Plinian mixture of fable and science. He drew most of his elaborations of the Bible story from the Dark Age hexemerons.[2] Like many of the apocryphal books written either side of the birth of Christ, these commentaries were the product of Hellenistic speculation about Hebrew myth; so affinities with the Reformation-Renaissance a thousand years later were inherent in them. They were not yet "Catholic"; they were interested in the Fall rather than Incarnation; their concern with the Creation was scientific, encyclopaedic; and their impulse was literary and philosophical as much as devotional. One of the earliest was Philo's attempt to reconcile the *Account of the World's Creation Given by Moses* with the teaching of Plato; Philo himself was a non-Christian Jew living in Alexandria. The seminal work for western literature and especially Du Bartas was the 4th-century hexemeron of St Basil the Great, concentrated on Paradise and the Fall. This was the source for the theological treatises of the Latin Fathers, notably Ambrose and Augustine. During the Middle Ages[3] the earlier hexemeral

[1] I. ii (1621 ed.).

[2] I rely mainly on Maury Thibaut de Maisières, *Les Poèmes inspirés du Début de la Genèse à l'Epoque de la Renaissance* (Louvain, 1931) and Watson Kirkconnell, *The Celestial Cycle: The Theme of "P.L." in World Literature, with Translations of the Major Analogues*, (Toronto, 1952); see also F. E. Robbins, *The Hexaemeral Tradition* (Chicago, 1912); Grant McColley, "*Paradise Lost*", *Harvard Theological Rev.* XXXIII (1939) and "*P.L.*"*: an Account of its Growth and Major Origins, with a Discussion of Milton's Use of Sources and Literary Patterns* (Chicago, 1940); Arnold Williams, Milton and the Renaissance Commentaries on Genesis", *MP*, XXXVII (1940) and *The Common Expositor* (Chapel Hill, 1948).

[3] The Cædmonian paraphrases of *Genesis* and *Exodus* (which Junius published in 1655) and *Daniel* were part of the primitive movement to assimilate Christianity, in the second generation after the 650 conversion, into the existing Germanic culture. Balance of heroic with mystical in

material was little read in the West: much of it was lost; Greek was forgotten; and the emphasis of theology became more "Catholic", the Fall being regarded less as the outrageous beginning of human depravity and ignorance than as the unfortunate loss of the superhuman gifts which had been a deified Adam's in Eden. But the Reformation revived interest all over Europe in the Fall, while the Renaissance stimulated Hellenistic speculation and the publication of Greek manuscripts, including the surviving hexemerons. Ambrose's Latin treatise, after a preliminary issue in 1490, was printed in 1527, and Basil's Greek hexemeron in 1532, both with a preface by Erasmus. The literary and rationalistic bias of the material was confirmed now, for Erasmus read Ambrose as a master of Latin prose, and regarded Basil as a classical author, one of the Ancients. New non-literary material was produced. Some of it, such as the Bible commentaries of Calvin and Luther, owed most to Augustine, giving detailed Puritan attention to the Fall and treating the Creation with a cautious, unscientific Humanism. Some was devotional—Lancelot Andrewes delivered a course of lectures at St Paul's on the first four chapters of *Genesis*, text by text. Some was secular: every world history of the time began with an extensive and often interpretative account of *Genesis*. These days we are more familiar with the graphic use of hexemeral material. It followed the same historical pattern. There were local treatments of hexemeral themes in the Middle Ages, such as the Creation of Eve, Noah's ark and the sacrifice of Isaac plaited into the *Genesis* initial of the Winchester Bible (12th-century), and of course the mystery cycles; but major medieval art concentrated on the incarnation and crucifixion, and on hagiography. Then from the 15th Century, in Italy, interest focussed more and more on the potentially Humanistic—philosophical, heroic, dramatic—material of Creation, War of Angels and Fall, with its huge vertical division of creation into heaven, world and hell, and horizontal division of time into prelapsarian, temporal and eternal. This was the tradition that culminated in Raphael's loggia frescoes of the Old and New Testaments, and

religious literature, as Christianity becomes dominant, may be seen in *The Dream of the Rood* (c. 740), continued in the 9th-century work of Cynewulf (*Juliana*, *Christ*, etc.) and his school. Subsequently, in medieval drama and lyric, the motive ceases to be heroic. The Renaissance made another effort similar to Cædmon's necessary.

Michelangelo's Sistine Chapel fresco. But it was never manifest in England. That is one reason why *Paradise Lost* was written, and is read, with such effort. Most of the literary monuments of the tradition had already been forgotten by the 17th Century, or were not known in England because written in Continental vernaculars. But they ran from Antonio Cornozano's *Discorso in Versi della Creazione del Mondo sine alla Ventua di Gesu Cristo* (1472) through Antonio Alfani's *Battaglia Celeste tra Michele e Lucifero* to Erasmo di Valvasone's *Angelida*, a three-canto epic in ottava rima published in 1590 which ends with a sonnet in honour of its hero, Michael, and has some parallels in *Paradise Lost*. Until Du Bartas, they were all Italian and Catholic; his importance lay in being a Huguenot, and Sylvester kept him uncompromisingly Protestant. His translation was also a more impressive accomplishment than the paraphrases of *Jonah*, *Esther*, *Job*, *Samson*, *Jeremiah* and the *Song of Solomon* turned out in the 1620's by the episcopal Quarles, or the Puritan Sandys' *Job* (1638); and it was more contemporary and bourgeois in spirit than the religio-metaphysical work of Sir John Davies (*Nosce Te Ipsum*, 1599), John Davies of Hereford and Sir Thomas Browne. But it was an encyclopaedic impressiveness, and an unheroic spirit. There had been attempts at heroic Christian poetry in England. Giles Fletcher, addressing the readers of *Christ's Victory and Triumph*, defended the ideal of Christian poetry and cited the hexemeral commentators and poets, including Basil, Prudentius, Sannazaro, Du Bartas and Spenser. But like Milton's early religious poems, *Christ's Victory* did not elaborate the essentially Protestant myth and was not really epical in construction: Fletcher was an avowed anti-papist—"oh hellish scorne!"—but so rhetorical and allegorical, so Spenserian in style, that the atmosphere of his poems is medieval.

In a different way the great devotional poetry of the early 17th Century was unsatisfying. It was small in quantity, limited in scope and not readily available. Donne's poems, open to his circle of patrons and friends as soon as written, perhaps, were not published until 1633 and Herbert's in the same year—when they had to compete with the glibness of Quarles' and Wither's *Emblems* (both 1635) and Cowley's *Blossoms* (1633). The Catholic spirit of "La Corona", "The Litanie", and especially the dedication "To the Lady Magdalen Herbert: of St Mary Magdalen" would have been offensive; the fusion in Donne's mind of disparable elements was not easy to appreciate under Laud's persecution. Furthermore, although we find in Donne and the other Metaphysicals this ability to interfuse divine and secular, the poets themselves were aware of a distinction. Donne, Vaughan, Herbert, Crashaw, as well as Herrick, divided their poems into profane and holy, and lamented the expense of their talents on the former:

> O Might those sighes and teares returne againe
> Into my breast and eyes, which I have spent,
> That I might in this holy discontent
> Mourne with some fruit, as I have mourn'd in vaine;[1]

Vaughan separated *Silex Scintillans, Or Sacred Poems* from his "Idle Verse":

> Go, go, queint folies, sugred sin;
> Shadow no more my door;[2]

Herbert either did not write any profane poetry in English, or destroyed it. When as an undergraduate, about 1610, he dedicated himself to religious poetry, secular inspiration was dominant:

> My God, where is that ancient heat towards thee,
> Wherewith whole showls of *Martyrs* once did burn,
> Besides their other flames? Doth Poetry
> Wear *Venus* Livery? only serve her turn?
> Why are not *Sonnets* made of thee? and layes
> Upon thine Altar burnt? Cannot thy love
> Heighten a spirit to sound thy praise
> As well as any she? Cannot thy *Dove*
> Out-strip their *Cupid* easily in flight?

The literary realism sought by Metaphysical poets was close to the religious sincerity demanded of poetry by Protestants:

> Why should I *Womens eyes* for Chrystal take?
> Such poor invention burns in their low mind
> Whose fire is wild, and doth not upward go
> To praise, and on thee, Lord, some *Ink* bestow.[3]

[1] *Poetical Works* ed. Grierson (1929).
[2] *Works* ed. L. C. Martin (2nd ed. Oxford, 1958).
[3] Sonnet to his mother. *Works* ed. Hutchinson (Oxford, 1941).

In the preface to the second edition of Crashaw's *Steps to the Temple, Sacred Poems* (with a separate title-page for the secular *Delights of the Muses*) we are told:

> Here's *Herbert's* second, but equall, who hath retriv'd Poetry of late, and return'd it up to its Primitive use; Let it bound back to heaven gates, whence it came. Thinke yee, St *Augustine* would have steyned his graver Learning with a booke of Poetry, had he fancied its dearest end to be the vanity of Love-Sennets, and Epithalamiums? No, no, he thought with this our Poet, that every foot in a high-borne verse, might helpe to measure the soule into that better world. *Divine Poetry* . . . is the Quintessence of Phantasie and discourse centr'd in Heaven; 'tis the very Out-goings of the soule . . .[1]

The connection between Metaphysical and religious verse is explicit. The preface goes on to arraign contemporary poetasters "whose onely businesse in verse, is to rime a poore six-penny soule a Suburb sinner into hell", using the same terms as Milton in *The Reason of Church Government.* Then the Reformation spirit joins the Renaissance in declaring:

> with what a triumphant brow shall our divine Poet sit above, and looke downe upon poore *Homer, Virgil, Horace, Claudian?* &c. who had amongst them the ill lucke to talke out a great part of their gallant Genius, upon Bees, Dung, froggs, and Gnats, *&c.* and not as himself here, upon Scriptures, divine Graces, Martyrs and Angels.

At the same time, though, Crashaw had "under locke and key in readinesse, the richest treasures of the best Greek and Latine Poets". This preface has a note which explains why it was so difficult for 17th-century England to rival Continental religious verse. Crashaw is praised for having "made his skill in Poetry, Musick, Drawing, Limming, Graving . . . to be but his subservient recreations for vacant houres, not the grand businesse of his soule": yet until a man with Crashaw's learning and a great deal more than Crashaw's literary talent would make divine poetry the grand business of his soul, neither Reformation nor Renaissance aspirations could be fulfilled.

Because they were part-time poets the Metaphysicals wrote perfect momentaneous poetry; but they could not write narrative or dramatic poems. Crashaw's inadequacy is apparent in "Musicks Duell" where he describes the lutemaster playing:

[1] Ed. A. R. Waller (Cambridge, 1904), p. 67.

His nimble hands instinct then taught each string
A capring cheerefulnesse; and made them sing
To their owne dance; now negligently rash
He throwes his Arme, and with a long drawne dash
Blends all together; then distinctly tripps
From this to that; then quick returning skipps
And snatches this again, and pauses there.

The gay breathlessness is attractive and appropriate here, but it is a talent for language and rhythm which could not be used without bathos in a serious large construct:

He lookd and saw a spacious Plaine, whereon
Were Tents of various hue; by some were herds
Of Cattel grazing: others, whence the sound
Of Instruments that made melodious chime
Was heard, of Harp and Organ; and who moovd
Thir stops and chords was seen: his volant touch
Instinct through all proportions low and high
Fled and pursu'd transverse the various fugue.
(*P.L.* XI. 552)

This is architectonic. The natural tendency of both Metaphysical poetry and Protestantism towards ecclesiastical and therefore literary individualism, antipathetic to epic, is summed up in Herbert's "Decay":

Sweet were the dayes, when thou didst lodge with Lot,
Struggle with Jacob, sit with Gideon,
Advise with Abraham, when thy power could not
Encounter Moses strong complaints and mone;
Thy words were then, *Let me alone.*

One might have sought and found thee presently
At some fair oak, or bush, or cave, or well:
Is my God this way? No, they would reply:
He is to Sinai gone, as we heard tell:
List, ye may heare great Aarons bell.

But now thou dost thy self immure and close
In some one corner of a feeble heart:
Where yet both Sinne and Satan, thy old foes,
Do pinch and straiten thee, and use much art
To gain thy thirds and little part.

For Herbert, the scale of spiritual drama is microcosmic, so that even when he celebrates the might of God, magniloquence is brought low:

> Of what supreme almightie power
> Is thy great arm, which spans the east and west,
> And tacks the centre to the sphere!
>
> (*Prayer ii*)

The refinement of feeling and intensity of experience in these Metaphysical poems is superior to all subsequent religious verse; but it could not survive the coarser needs of the 17th Century. Marvell wrote its epitaph:

> *Humility* alone designs
> Those short but admirable Lines,
> By which, ungirt and unconstrain'd,
> Things greater are in less contain'd.
> Let others vainly strive t'immure
> The *Circle* in the *Quadrature!*
> These *holy Mathematicks* can
> In ev'ry Figure equal Man.[1]

2. *Milton's Epic Motives*

Milton grew up towards 1630.[2] The Fletchers were exhausted, the influence of Donne and Herbert not yet spread, little religious poetry of any value being written (except Drummond's *Flowers of Sion*, 1623, 1630, whose quality Milton recognised); yet the desire for divine literature intense. Now Milton, in his late teens, picked out the notes of Christian epic, in Latin. Writing to his old tutor, Thomas Young, beleaguered

[1] "Appleton House", *Poems and Letters* ed. Margoliouth (2nd ed. 2 vols. Oxford, 1952).

[2] For Milton's life I rely mainly on Masson, with some details and adjustment of dates from Hanford, "The Chronology of Milton's Private Studies", *PMLA*, XXXVI (1921) and "The Youth of Milton: An Interpretation of His Early Literary Development", *Studies in Shakespeare, Milton and Donne*, being *Univ. of Michigan Publications, Language and Literature*, I (1925); M. Y. Hughes's ed. (2 vols. New York, 1935); and Arthur Sewell, *A Study in Milton's Christian Doctrine* (1939: the best spiritual biography). On the importance of personal experience, especially marriage, in Milton's literary development, I find Saurat, *Milton: Man and Thinker* (1944) more sympathetic and convincing than Hanford.

in Hamburg, he turned into Latin the military heroics of *II Kings* vii and xix:

> the loud trumpet broke the empty air, the horny hoof beat the dusty plain, the driven chariot shook the sandy earth, when the whinnying of horses plunging into battle was heard, the clash of steel and the shouting of men.[1]

In the elegy on Lancelot Andrewes he presented an Ovidian paradise:

> Streams of silver washed the green fields, their sands gleaming richer gold than in Iberian Tagus. Through the rich fragrance stole the light air of Faunus, breathed dewy from beneath uncounted roses.

The epyllion on the Gunpowder Plot exercised epic mechanics —chronographia, voyage, speech, plot—on a Protestant theme, and descended into hell, "a place wrapped eternally in the darkness of night". But his main urge was towards cosmic vision. In the elegy on the Bishop of Ely Milton is

> borne aloft to the stars on high like the aged prophet of old caught up to heaven in a chariot of fire. The wain of bright Boötes, clogged with cold, made me not afraid, nor the claws of the frightful Scorpion, nor thy sword, Orion. Beyond the sphere of the glittering sun I flew and far beneath my feet saw the triform goddess checking her dragon-yoke with reins of gold. Through the ranks of the planets, through the Milky Way I was carried, marvelling at my fantastic speed, until to the portals of Olympus I came, the palace of crystal and the jasper-paved courts.

It happens to him again in the elegy on spring:

> At once my soul is caught up into the limpid heights of the sky and, free of the body, I pass through the drifting clouds. Through glooms, through caves, secret places of the poets, I am borne, and the inner shrines of the gods lie open to me. My soul perceives all that goes on on Olympus and the dark secrets of Tartarus escape not my gaze. What is it that my spirit's open mouth so loudly utters?

[1] "Elegy IV", 111. My renderings of Milton's Latin are based on the trans. in Hughes' ed. and W. MacKellar's *Latin Poems* (*Cornell Studies in English*, XV), 1930.

This is what he said in the "Vacation Exercise" of 1628 that he wanted to do in English:

> Yet I had rather if I were to chuse,
> Thy service in some graver subject use,
>
> . . .
>
> Such where the deep transported mind may soare
> Above the wheeling poles, and at Heav'ns dore
> Look in, and see each blissful Deitie
> How he before the thunderous throne doth lie
>
> . . .
>
> Then passing through the Spherse of watchful fire,
> And mistie Regions of wide air next under,
> And hills of Snow and lofts of piled Thunder,
> May tell at length how green-ey'd *Neptune* raves,
> In Heav'ns defiance mustering all his waves;
> Then sing of secret things that came to pass
> When Beldam Nature in her cradle was;
> And last of Kings and Queens and *Hero's* old,
> Such as the wise *Demodocus* once told . . .

In all these, the flight is more kinesthetic, the vision more concrete than in their classical and medieval analogues. There is a fierce desire to seek out the secrets of the universe, to control the world by linguistic comprehension. Upper, middle and nether regions, gods and men, science and history must all be visited. It was a usual ambition of the 17th Century: Lord Herbert of Cherbury seeking the unified sanction of natural religion to control an atomising world; Hobbes drawing out leviathan with a hook; Raleigh writing his last testament in the form of world-history; Burton mustering all knowledge to his mind's defence; Donne making one little room an everywhere; Bacon preaching an object lesson on the dismemberment of Orpheus, that, since science cannot preserve bodies from dissolution, philosophy must integrate and civilise society.[1] And for Milton, having rejected academic life, or a tutorship, or the Inns of Court, there was not much else to do with his learning.[2]

[1] *The Wisedome of the Ancients*, xi. Trans. Sir A. Gorges, 1620.

[2] As usual, there was little scope for the direct employment of what had been learned at the university. Milton was not offered a fellowship and if he had been it would have involved him in college domesticity, teaching a syllabus he disapproved of, uncongenial company, and holy orders in a

But as a graduate at Christ's, between 1629 and 1632 when he went to Horton, Milton made several attempts at religious verse in English which did not carry on the ambition of the Latin poems or the "Vacation Exercise", or even his juvenile paraphrases of the *Psalms*. They had been more heroic than devotional: the mountains skipping like rams and "Let us with a gladsome mind Praise the Lord, for he is kind", for "large-limb'd *Og* he did subdue, With all that overhardy crew". But "Upon the Circumcision" is by turns Ovidianly Elizabethan—"Through the soft silence of the list'ning night"; and fashionably manneristic—"Burn in your sighs and borrow Seas, wept from our deep sorrow"; as well as heroic—"Ye flaming Powers, and winged Warriors bright". But in the second half of the poem he writes consistently as the poet of thirty years later:

> O more exceeding love or law more just?
> Just law indeed, but more exceeding love!

The rhetorical figuring which in Spenser and the Fletchers had been fluent decoration of piety here solidifies a theological concept. The demonstrative pronoun in "that great Covenant which we still transgress" points to *Paradise Lost*. So in the induction to the "Nativity Ode": "That far-beaming blaze of Majesty". But the Ode's hymn is notoriously mixed:

church which he thought corrupt. The Inns of Court, a tutorship, politics, would have dissipated his talents. But these were the avenues for both scholars and poets. Fuller (born the same year as Milton) became a private chaplain. Jeremy Taylor (b. 1613) was a fellow of All Soul's, chaplain to Laud, rector of Uppingham, and after the Restoration a bishop. Crashaw (b. 1612) was a fellow of Peterhouse and later a Roman Catholic priest in Italy. Cowley (b. 1618) was a fellow of Trinity and a political agent for Charles I. Waller (b. 1606) was an M.P. at sixteen, rapidly became the widower of an heiress, was an indispensable courtier, and spent seven years abroad as an exile. Davenant (b. 1608 also) and Denham (b. 1615) were personal friends of Charles I. Marvell (b. 1621) was an M.P. and tutor to the Fairfax family. A few writers had trades or regular professions: Sir Thomas Browne and Vaughan country doctors, Izaak Walton an ironmonger, Bunyan a tinker. Of all these the only one to produce major work in quantity was Bunyan and he did it during twelve years of imprisonment. Herbert seems to have combined writing with proper attention to his parochial duties; but his writing did not require the sustained effort that Milton's did, and he was a parish priest for only the last three years of his life; before that he had had seventeen years as undergraduate, B.A. and fellow of Trinity. Milton took seventeen years of education before earning a living at all.

But he her fears to cease,
Sent down the meek-eyd Peace,
  She crown'd with Olive green, came softly sliding
Down through the turning sphear,
His ready Harbinger,
  With Turtle wing the amorous clouds dividing,
And waving wide her mirtle wand,
She strikes a universall Peace through Sea and Land.

No War, or Battails sound
Was heard the World around:
  The idle spear and shield were high up hung;
The hooked Chariot stood
Unstain'd with hostile blood,
  The Trumpet spake not to the armed throng,
And Kings sate still with awfull eye,
As if they surely knew their sovran Lord was by.

The first stanza is allegorical, its inspiration masque or painting; the second is actual, its inspiration *Isaiah*, its reference to England as well as to the Pollio and the Pax Romana.

The unfinished "Passion", in the same stanza as the hymn, is consistently mannered. The stanza itself is a mixture. It is based on rime royal, with heroic associations in *Troilus and Criseyde*, the *Mirror for Magistrates*, *Lucrece*; but Spenser had used rime royal for his platonising *Hymnes*, and Milton for the polymythical "Death of a Fair Infant". Now he added the final alexandrine of the *Faerie Queene* to it:

Out of the bosome of eternall blisse,
In which he reigned with his glorious syre,
He downe descended, like a most demisse
And abiect thrall, in fleshes fraile attyre,
That he for him might pay sinnes deadly hyre,
And him restore vnto that happie state,
In which he stood before his haplesse fate.
(*Hymne of Heavenly Love*)

That glorious Form, that Light unsufferable,
And that far-beaming blaze of Majesty,
Wherewith he wont at Heav'ns high Councel-Table,
To sit the midst of Trinal Unity,
He laid aside; and here with us to be,

Forsook the Courts of everlasting Day,
And chose with us a darksom House of mortal Clay.
(*Nativity Ode*)

He sov'ran Priest stooping his regall head
That dropt with odorous oil down his fair eyes,
Poor fleshly Tabernacle entered,
His starry front low-rooft beneath the skies;
O what a Mask was there, what a disguise!
Yet more; the stroke of death he must abide,
Then lies him meekly down fast by his Brethrens side.
(*Passion*)

Clearly the heroic mood of the Ode's induction, not the mannerism of "The Passion", was true to his talent. Yet he says:

These latter scenes confine my roving verse,
To this Horizon is my *Phoebus* bound,
His Godlike acts, and his temptations fierce,
And former sufferings other where are found;
Loud o're the rest *Cremonas* Trump doth sound;
Me softer airs befit, and softer strings
Of Lute, or Viol still, more apt for mournful things.

He admits the theme constricts his heroic urge—Milton could never have operated in Gethsemane and he did not finish this poem; then why did he deny affinity with Vida of the *Christiad*, and falsely claim that manneristic religiosity suited him? The confusion was due to his wanting to write religious poetry in a vacuum. There was no strong or suitable tradition for him to write it in; his desire to write it was not yet intense, or religious enough, for him to start a tradition of his own; yet he seems to have been anxious to justify his continuing a student at his father's expense, and, in the face of the revolutionary Thomas Young, at continuing a scholar at all in such times; and to have felt "th'shame of slow-endeavouring art" before the native genius of Shakespeare.[1] He tried to assuage these anxieties by a

[1] The chief documents are: English letter to Gill, his former headmaster at St Paul's, written in the year of the "Vacation Exercise", expressing disappointment with Cambridge and especially ordinands; long English letter to a friend, probably Thomas Young, including sonnet "How soon hath Time", in his first year at Horton (1633)—attempt of a Puritan idealist to explain himself to a pragmatic Calvinist, excusing himself from mere curiosity, dilettantism, etc., and for not going into the church; Latin elegy to his father, about the beginning of the Horton period, suggesting that his father thought more of scholarship than art.

sudden dedication of immature powers and unreal motives. But in all these poems the writer's relationship with God matters much less than the artifact he can construct out of Christian mythology. So the "Nativity Ode", technically as accomplished as anything in *Paradise Lost*, and one of the most thrilling works of literary music in English, fails to make even Christmas the vehicle of devotion: though it is itself a votive offering. The difficulty was still to be obvious in the epic, though by then—and this was his achievement—Milton had a more than literary relationship to God, to Christian mythology and the classics.

The tendency to agonising in "The Passion" was also a side-effect of eroticism. With Milton this did not translate into love of God, as with Donne and Hopkins for instance, but at first was sublimated into a Platonic idealism which prevented him for a time from realising in English the visionary solidity of his Latin verse. Milton had been aware of *objets d'amour* at eighteen when he was producing his first Latin heroics. He described for Diodati how he spent his time in London while rusticated from Cambridge:

> But I do not always confine myself indoors or even to the city, nor does the spring pass me in vain. I too resort to the favourite place outside the walls, the shade of a grove of close-ranked elms. Here you may often see troops of maidens passing by like stars that breathe caressing flames. Oh, how often I've been struck dumb by the marvellous grace of a figure that might resuscitate the old age of Jove himself! Oh, how often have I seen eyes brighter than jewels, brighter than every star that wheels round either pole; necks surpassing the shoulders of resurrected Pelops and the hue of the Galaxy's pure nectar-flow; the excelling beauty of a brow, and waving tresses that were golden snares set by deceitful Love; and alluring cheeks beside which hyacinth and the blush of your anemone, Adonis, pale.
>
> (*Elegy I*, 47)

Two years later his Ovidianism was as solid as his heroic exercises. He wrote *In adventum veris*:

> The reviving Earth throws off her loathed old age and craves to submit to thy embraces, Phoebus; worthy what she craves: for what more beautiful than she as voluptuously she bares her all-sustaining breasts, breathing the vintage of Arabia, pouring from her lovely lips sweet spices and the roses of Venus? . . . Thus the

> wanton Earth breathes her desires; her children troop to her example. . . . Girls throng to the glad pleasures of spring, their virgin breasts girdled with gold. . . . Lustful Faunus hunts some Oread to ravish and the Nymph looks with trembling knees to hide herself: and now she hides, yet in her hiding shows herself; flees and fleeing longs to be caught. . . .

About the same time (1627-8) Milton admitted, or pretended, to a first passion, in *Elegia septima, Anno aetatis undevigesimo*:

> Not yet, O fascinating Amathusia, had I learned thy laws and my heart was void of the Paphian fire. Often I mocked love's arrows as toys and made light especially of thy godhead, Cupid.

The elegy describes how Cupid had sworn vengeance for this contempt, and unexpectedly achieved it when Milton, innocently mingling with the temptations that crowded the city and the environs of country-houses, was smitten by the momentary sight of one girl supreme in beauty:

> Instantly, unwonted passions assailed my heart: the inward fire of love consumed me, I was all aflame. But she who alone could allay my suffering was borne away, never to return to my sight. Silent and grieving, confused, I yet went my way, often wondering whether to go back. I am torn asunder: part of me stays here, the other follows my desire, happy to weep for the joys so suddenly snatched away. . . . Wretched and stricken with grief, what shall I do? I can neither forget the love begun, nor yet pursue it. Oh, would that I might look on that beloved countenance once more, and tell my sorrows to her face. . . . Now, son of Venus, thy bow is my dread indeed, thine arrows are strong as fire. Henceforth thine altars shall smoke with my offerings and, for me, thou alone shalt be supreme among the gods. Take then my passion away—no, rather take it not: I know not why, love is such sweet pain.

There seems to be a genuine experience here, and there may be discoveries of Milton's own about the nature of love—"Raptaque tam subito gaudia flere juvat" and "Nescio cur, miser est suaviter omnis amans". Next year, his twenty-first, Milton seems to have reached that mood of idealism-tinged sensuousness which often results in an early marriage. Probably at the Diodatis' London house he had met an Italian girl called Emilia. She provoked five sonnets and a canzone written, at her request, in Italian as "lingua di cui si vanta Amore". They owe a good deal to Petrarch but are prefaced (in the 1645 edition and probably in time also) by the English sonnet to the nightingale. Milton was conscious that the moment for love had come:

> Now timely sing, ere the rude Bird of Hate
> Foretell my hopeless doom in some Grove ny:
> As thou from year to year hast sung too late
> For my relief; yet hadst no reason why,
> Whether the Muse, or Love call thee his mate,
> Both them I serve, and of their train am I.

There is no conflict between poetry and love—on the contrary, for this is not Cavalier jest or Ovidian exercise:

> It is not golden tresses or vermeil cheeks that so bedazzle me, but beauty peregrine, uniquely formed, filling the heart with joy: nobility and sanctitude of bearing, eyes serenely radiant with a lovely black, speech adorned with divers tongues, and singing such as might well lure the labouring moon from her course through middle heaven—but so strong a fire darts from her eyes that to seal my ears against it would do me little good.

Milton "ought" to have married this girl, and his last sonnet amounts to a proposal, for it offers her the self-commendations he had formerly reserved for his father and Diodati:

> Diffident youth and unsophisticated lover I, since I know not how to be but as I am, Lady, I will make you a humble gift of my heart. I have proved it faithful enough, brave, constant, and in disposition gracious, courteous and kind. When the great world roars and thunder crashes, it arms itself from within with compleat diamond, no less secure against fortune, envy and the hopes and fears of common clay than it is ambitious of genius, high valour, the sounding lyre and the Muses. You will find only one weak spot: where Love's arrow has immitigably pierced it.

But the incident closed. Perhaps it was only a passing flicker; more probably genuine but Milton too insecure financially and the lady too high-born for a match: she knew several languages and was engaged in foreign travel; in this sonnet Milton seems to excuse his social obscurity and defend himself from any taint of the *popol*. But he had become conscious of his inexperience—"giovane piano, semplicetto amante Poi che fuggir me stesso in dubio sono"—and of adult sexual need.

Probably a little later he wrote *Elegy VI* in reply to Diodati's excuse of a hangover for the badness of his own previous verse-letter:

> light Elegy is favoured by many of the gods, and she calls whom she will to her measures. Liber attends on Elegy, and Erato, Ceres, Venus, and stripling Cupid beside his peach-skinned mother. To such poets then large feasting is permitted, and the frequent quaffing of old wine. But he who tells of wars, and heaven under the maturity of Jove, of pious heroes and captain demi-gods, who sings now of the sacred counsels of the gods on high, now of that infernal kingdom where the fierce dog barks, he must live frugally, like the master of Samos, and his wholesome fare be herbs. Let him drink abstemious draughts from the pure spring and have at his side clear spring-water in a beechen bowl. Moreover, his youth must be chaste and innocent of vice, his conduct strict, his hands unstained: even as thou, O priest, arising in thy priesthood resplendent with sacred vestments and holy water to enter the presence of the incensed deities.

He goes on to describe the "Nativity Ode" he has just been writing. This passage has been read as a dedication to heroic poetry and the requisitely Nazarene way of life. It is more likely, I think, at this stage, to have been a decorated way of saying merely what he felt like just now. He had become aware of passion, and the difficulty, for a *giovane piano*, *semplicetto amante*, of satisfying it. So far it was only an intermittent distraction which ambition, ordinary idealism and retirement could overcome. But when he retired, almost completely, to Horton, just after the attempts at religious poetry, he must have found it harder, alone, to defend himself. His father was there too. We know little about Milton senior, but he must have been a strong personality to have defied his own father's Catholicism and made his way up to scrivener and the friend of Lawes. It seems likely that, powerful, widowed, son-ambitious, a jealous god, he had a "castrative" effect on Milton, especially at this crucial age when they were alone together in Horton for five years. It was for these reasons, I think, that Milton's poetry occasionally went hysterical just now; and that he formulated, against the grain of a quite unmystical mind and a fully sensual heart, the mystique of chastity adumbrated in the letter to Diodati and dramatised in *Comus*. In the *Apology for Smectymnuus* he was to tell it as literary history, how he passed from Ovid to Dante and Petrarch as poetic models. They encouraged him to write in the vernacular; but it was "abstracted sublimities" that he hoped to catch the ear of the public with when peace came. This was partly an apology for poetry before Puritan comrades and ecclesiastical enemies; but an apology that he had needed to make much earlier to himself and to Young. The statement is supported by a postscript to his Latin elegies added in the 1645 edition but probably of earlier date:

> These vain trophies of my profligacy I set up once out of a flippant mind and misguided zeal. I was led so far astray by delusive error, of course, and my untutored youth was a perverse teacher—until the groves of Academe supplied me with Socratic streams and freed me from the yoke I had submitted to. Then those flames were instantly extinguished, and from then on my heart has been frozen in thick-ribbed ice: the Boy fears its frost for his arrows and Venus herself is afraid of my Diomedean strength.[1]

His masques provided some relief, and social contact. Wotton's commendation of *Comus* and the popularity of it in manuscript show that Milton could now have entered the literary society of England. But he gave the edited version of the poem a motto from Virgil's second eclogue, a homosexual pastoral in which Corydon turns on himself and cries, "Alas! poor wretch, what I have tried to do? Madman, I have let in the sirocco on my flowers . . . my vine is but half-pruned on the leafy elm." In this context, I would account for *Comus* by saying it availed Milton's mythologising faculty, absorbed his lone impressions of country life, permitted him some English Ovidianism. A balance is just held between the Elder Brother's philosophising and Comus' naturalism on one hand, and on the other the Lady's defiant mysticism and Sabrina's compensatory feminine magic. Similar conclusions may be drawn from "Lycidas". But Milton was not being stayed by religion. He did not, like Herbert, really "know the wayes of Pleasure, the sweet strains, The lullings and the relishes of it"; nor could he say "Yet I love thee", dedicating his sinful wanting nature to God. He survived by rationalising into a pseudo-Platonic

[1] Phrases like "studioque supino" and "admissum dedocuitque" are in the idiom of the early anti-prelatical period.

doctrine of chastity what were really three aspects of the same complex, his shyness, his lust, and his cosmosophical ambition.

At the end of the Horton period, in 1637, he tried to revive his letter-borne friendship with Diodati at a startlingly Platonic level:

> I assure you that it is impossible for me not to love such men as yourself, for though I know not God's intent toward me in other respects, yet of this I am sure, that he has imbued me especially with a mighty passion for Beauty. Ceres never sought her daughter Proserpine (as the legend tells) with greater ardour than I do this Idea of Beauty, like some image of loveliness; ever pursuing it, by day and by night, in every shape and form ("for many forms there are of things divine") and following close in its footprints as it leads. And so, whensoever I find one who spurns the base opinions of common men, and dares to be, in thought and word and deed, that which the wisest minds throughout the ages have approved; whensoever, I say, I find such a man, to him I find myself impelled forthwith to cleave.
>
> (*Letter* 7)

Now he went to Italy, and while he was there Diodati died. After his return to England, Milton wrote *Epitaphium Damonis*. The elegy concludes with an apotheosis for Diodati that shall compensate for the maiden youth he wanted to think they had shared:

> Because the blush of shame, and youth without a stain, were dear to you, because you did not taste the delights of the marriage-bed, lo! the trophies of virginity are laid up for you. Your gloried head bound with the shining wreath and in your hands the joyful shade of branching palm, you shall celebrate eternally the nuptials of heaven, while song and the sounding lyre mingle in ecstacy with blessed dancing, and festal orgies rage under the thyrsus of Zion.

Critics disagree about the tone of this, and much depends on the conventions of pastoral elegy and of the use of apocalyptic imagery in classical contexts (but also on what one thinks the motives for those conventions might be). It seems hectic to me, the fantasy of a desperate virgin.

The emphasis no longer falls on chastity as either a positive principle or a means to an end for man or poet, but on the reward it must have. A year later Milton wrote in *Of Reformation*:

> Well knows every wise nation that their liberty consists in manly and honest labours, in sobriety and rigorous honour to the marriage bed, which in both sexes should be bred up from chaste hopes to loyal enjoyments.
>
> (ii. 401)

This exigent mood may partly explain the mixture of muddle and uncreative listing in the plans for a major work that, prompted by literary conversation in Italy, Milton sketched in the Cambridge Manuscript on return to England. Sometimes, allied to Tasso, he moved towards his narrative fulfilment. Writing to his Italian host Manso, he congratulated Tasso on having also been patronised by him:

> I would that fate might bestow such a friend, capable of honouring the disciples of Phoebus, on me, if ever I should summon up in song our native kings, and Arthur waging war beneath the very earth, or if I should tell of that loyal band, the great-hearted knights of the invincible Table, and—if only the spirit prompt! —shatter the Saxon phalanxes under the onset of the Britons.
>
> (*Mansus*, 78)

In the same year he had said in the elegy on Diodati :

> As for me—I know not (it being now eleven nights and a day) what high utterance my pipe was sounding—perhaps I had put my lips to new pipes, but their bindings burst, they fell apart and could carry the solemn notes no further. I hesitate, lest I seem conceited—yet I will tell. Wood-notes, give way.
>
> Go home unfed, my lambs, your master cannot tend you.
>
> I then, I would tell of Trojan sails along the coast of Kent, and the ancient kingdom of Imogen, daughter of Pandrasus, and of the chieftains Brennus, Arviragus and old Belinus, and those who settled at last under British law in Gaul; then I would tell of the fateful deception of Igraine, pregnant with Arthur by Gorlois whose face and armour Merlin's cunning had made counterfeit.

But excepting a note that "A Heroical Poem may be founded somewhere in Alfred's reign, especially at his issuing out of Edelingsey on the Danes", all the subjects listed in the Cambridge Manuscript are for tragedy; Arthur is not included, and only four topics are British, the rest Saxon. I conclude that the ambition to write an Arthuriad was the result of patriotic envy of Italian culture, settled in continuity with Rome, and of Tasso whose epic task had been performed at a simpler level than Milton was really content to write on. In any case, Arthur was now a political figure, as closely associated through the Stuarts with the Royalist cause as he had been, through Henry Richmond, with the Tudors, and Milton was planning a Puritan work: several of the themes have notes like that on Edward the Confessor's "slackness to redress the corrupt clergy, and superstitious pretence of chastity".

Paradise Lost, even in the form sketched at this time, does not stem from nationalistic Christianism; it is far more the manifesto of an individual mind. I think Milton was sent back from Tassonic errancy after "some king or knight before the Conquest", to the Fall, by his uncomfortable idealism, and kept there by his subsequent political career, and marriage. Most of the Biblical subjects listed in the Cambridge Manuscript are historical, but the details Milton added to a few of them suggest no genuine narrative or tragic impulse towards Bible story. They would have issued in Euripidean and Jeremiac spectacle as a sort of anti-*Comus*, assaulting lust more than it celebrated chastity. Apart from the sketches on Adam the two most detailed notes are on the sacrifice of Isaac, and the destruction of Sodom. "Abraham from Morea, or Isaac Redeemed" shares the dying youth theme with "Lycidas" and the sketch for a "Baptistes". Sodom, which Milton added to when he came back to the manuscript to make the final draft on Adam, was to be treated under the titles "Cupid's Funeral Pile" or "Sodom Burning". Like "Baptistes" it would have satirised the lasciviousness of contemporary society:

> The first Chorus, beginning, may relate the course of the city—each evening everyone with mistress, or Ganymede, glittering along the streets, or solacing on the banks of Jordan, or down the stream. At the priest's inviting the Angels to the solemnity [at the temple of Venus Urania or Peor], the Angels, pitying their beauty, may dispute of love, and how it differs from lust, seeking to win them.

No doubt the notorious courtezanry of Rome had enflamed Milton as much as the lubricity of London. In the last scene, when Sodom has suffered its frightful retribution, an angel arrayed in the flames of true love is to explain to the King of Sodom (burning in real fire), the justice of his fate.

But the Adam theme would have brought a more positive treatment to this sort of thing, even in dramatic form. In the first three drafts there is a character called Heavenly Love, and then in the second and third Hesperus, the Evening Star, as well. But in the fourth and most elaborate draft Heavenly Love and Hesperus have both been dropped, and what in the third draft was a whole act devoted to a choric marriage song and description of Paradise has become a relation, more integrated with plot, of what Gabriel "knew of Man, as the creation of Eve, with their love and marriage". The action has become less allegorical and more realistic. The fall of Lucifer is now separated from that of man in an act of its own, with the episode of his meeting with the angels in Paradise and a narrative of the war in heaven. But even the fourth draft agrees with the first three in certain non-epical particulars. No person of the Trinity is included (impossible on stage). The first two acts lyrically present the creation of the world and ideal love in a Paradise which would probably have been like Spenser's Isle of Friendship. A chorus closes each of the five acts, and though the general structure is Greek it tends toward elaborate mystery play, on the model of the Italian *sacre rapprezentazione*—an ethical rather than religious tendency.

The first three drafts of an Adamic tragedy head the list of Old Testament subjects only because the list is in Biblical order; but the command of structure and detail in the fourth draft is much firmer than in the comparably lengthy elaborations of Isaac and Sodom. The question is how Milton emerged from muddle? He was not attracted to the Fall pessimistically—his mood though tense was buoyant. It seems likely that, as well as distracting him to an Arthuriad for a while, the visit to Italy had set him in the European tradition of large-scale Christian poetry, which was based on the Fall, as sketched above. The tradition had begun in Italy and received its fullest treatment there in a variety of forms. Milton probably saw an anonymous Latin oratorio on the Fall in Italy, and since Du Bartas the productions had increased. Tasso's *Le Sette Giornate del Mondo Creato*, a blank-verse redaction of Basil's *Hexaemeron* with borrowings from Du Bartas, had been published in 1607 as an act of the Counter-Reformation; Gasparo Murtola's *Della Creatione del Mondo* (1608) followed Tasso but in long-lined ottava rima;

Felice Passero's *L'Essamerone, overa l'Opera de Sei Giorni* (1609) was a straight imitation of Du Bartas. The best was Andreini's *Adamo* (1613), a multi-scenic lyrical drama emphasising the temptation, with a great deal of machinery and allegory (Cowper wrote a verse translation of it). By the time Milton went to Italy this Counter-Reformation school was declining, but the motive was reaching other parts of Europe. On his way to Italy he had been the guest in Paris of "that most learned man, Hugo Grotius, then ambassador from the Queen of Sweden to the French king, whom I was desirous to visit" (*2nd. Def.* i. 255). In 1601 Grotius had published *Adamus Exsul*, a Latin tragedy on the classical model, with sure parallels in *Paradise Lost*. This contact may have assumed even more importance to Milton by the publication in 1640, when perhaps he was busy on the Cambridge Manuscript, of a translation by Sandys of Grotius' later *Christus Patiens*. There were to be later Dutch contributions, *Lucifer* (1654) and *Adam im Ballingschap* by Vondel, under political circumstances similar to Milton's in the forties; there had been versions by German and Spanish poets (e.g. Taubmann's *Bellum Angelicum*, 1604, Azevedo's *Creacion del Mundo* in 1615); and of course Milton may have glanced at the Sistine Chapel fresco.

The casting of his Adamic schemes into dramatic form, I take to be due to the success of his masques, a desire to reach the public directly, imitation of Andreini (greatest of the Italian Fall-poets) and Grotius, as well as a still unsettled impulse toward the mannered lyricism of his own early religious poetry. For two and a half years after his return from Italy Milton did not find a wife. For this reason, I think, his inspiration would at this stage still have issued in the "abstracted sublimities" of lyrical drama as suggested in the *Apology* (quoted above). *Paradise Lost* as it came to be written was geared down from this impulse by political and domestic experience.

In this condition Milton entered the controversy over whether the Church of England should remain episcopal. At first he refused to admit the political implications—"No bishop, no king"—and his pamphlets were quite ineffectual. But they projected his idealistic verve on to a solid object. From the first paragraph of *Of Reformation* Milton's other-worldliness leaps out—his conception of rebellion against the bishops as some

Platonic drama in which the soul of the Church is to be freed of the clogs that "draw down all the divine intercourse betwixt God and the soul . . . into an exterior and bodily form." The pamphlet ends with an apocalyptic vision in which the damnation of the obstructors of reformation is a mere corollary to the apotheosis of the saints, who

> shall receive, above the inferior orders of the blessed, the regal addition of Principalities, Legions and Thrones into their glorious titles, and in supereminence of beatific vision progressing the dateless and irrevoluble circle of eternity shall clasp inseparable hands with joy and bliss in over-measure for ever.
>
> But they contrary . . . shall be thrown down eternally into the darkest and deepest gulf of Hell . . .

The projection of his Horton idealism on to the public cause involved the projection of his literary ambition into theocratic patriotism:

> Then amidst the hymns and hallelujahs of saints someone may perhaps be heard offering at high strains in new and lofty measures to sing and celebrate thy divine mercies and marvellous judgments in this land throughout all ages;

The pressure of his talents and learning was becoming intolerable. At the beginning of the second book of the *Reason of Church Government* (contemporaneous with the Cambridge Manuscript drafts) he made a statement which corresponds with our interpretation of the "Vacation Exercise" written nearly fifteen years earlier:

> How happy it were for this frail and . . . mortal life of man (since all earthly things which have the name of good and convenient . . . are withal so cumbersome and full of trouble) if knowledge, yet which is the best and lightsomest possession of the mind, were as the common saying is, no burden; and that what it wanted of being a load to any part of the body, it did not with a heavy advantage overlay upon the spirit. For, not to speak of that knowledge that rests in the contemplation of natural causes and dimensions, which must needs be a lower wisdom as the object is low, certain it is that he who hath obtained in more than the scantest measure to know anything distinctly of God, and of his true worship, and what is infallibly good and happy in the state

> of man's life, what in itself evil and miserable (though vulgarly not so esteemed)—he that hath obtained to know this, the only high valuable wisdom indeed, remembering also that God even to a strictness requires the improvement of these his entrusted gifts, cannot but sustain a sorer burden of mind, and more pressing than any supportable toil or weight which the body can labour under: how and in what manner he shall dispose and employ those sums of knowledge and illumination which God hath sent him into the world to trade with.
>
> (ii. 472-3)

Milton is speaking of the historical and theological knowledge that he wanted to use in the battle for ecclesiastical freedom; but this is the knowledge he had been accumulating for some great poem. The digression on his literary ambitions in the *Reason of Church Government* confirms that Milton had entered the Reformation controversy as arena for his poetic genius, and entertained hope of an earthly Kingdom of Heaven as this idealism's consummation. The historical situation offered the social and national status he needed as a prospectively cosmic poet. So he explains that, having received confirmation into the republic of letters at the hands of the Italians,

> I began thus far to assent both to them and divers of my friends here at home, and not less to an inward prompting which now grew daily upon me, that by labour and intent study (which I take to be my portion in this life), joined with the strong propensity of nature, I might perhaps leave something so written to aftertimes as they should not willingly let it die. These thoughts at once possessed me, and these other: that if I were certain to write as men buy leases, for three lives and downward, there ought no regard be sooner had than to God's glory by the honour and instruction of my country. For which cause . . . I applied myself . . . to fix all the industry and art I could unite to the adorning of my native tongue . . . to be an interpreter and relater of the best and sagest things among mine own citizens throughout this island in the mother dialect; that what the greatest and choicest wits of Athens, Rome, or modern Italy, and those Hebrews of old, did for their country, I in my proportion, with this over and above of being a Christian, might do for mine.
>
> (ii. 477-8)

The "inward prompting" of the Spirit turns his poetry into prayer; the "labour and intent study" gives it Calvinistic strenuousness; his "portion in life" predestinates him to poetry; so "the strong propensity of nature" can be dedicated at last, and justified in public action.

Although by the time he wrote *Reason of Church Government* he had probably sketched his dramatic plans in the Cambridge Manuscript, he remained publicly vague, anxious to vindicate only the forms and function of literature by Biblical analogy. His survey of epic, tragedy and ode follows a conventional hierarchy of genres; and the point of his references to *Job* as a brief epic, the *Song of Solomon* as a pastoral drama, *Revelation* as a tragedy and of "those frequent songs throughout the law and prophets" as parallels to Pindar and Callimachus, is religious rather than literary. He was chiefly concerned to defend, in Sidneian manner but with more immediate application, the ethical function of poetic genius:

> These abilities . . . are of power, beside the office of a pulpit, to imbreed and cherish in a great people the seeds of virtue and public civility, to allay the perturbations of the mind, and set the affections in right tune; to celebrate in glorious and lofty hymns the throne and equipage of God's almightiness, and what he works, and what he suffers to be wrought with high providence in his Church: to sing the victorious agonies of martyrs and saints, the deeds and triumphs of just and pious nations doing valiantly through faith against the enemies of Christ, to deplore the general relapses of kingdoms and states from justice and God's true worship.

Some of his historical subjects might have been used in this way—the second and third books of his *History of Britain* open with exemplary sermons; but what he really wanted to do was write poetry of his own:

> Lastly, whatsoever in religion is holy and sublime, in virtue amiable or grave, whatsoever hath passion or admiration, in all the changes of that which is called fortune from without or the wily subtleties and refluxes of man's thought from within, all these things with a solid and treatable smoothness to paint out and describe; teaching over the whole book of sanctity and virtue through all the instances of example with such delight to those especially of soft and delicious temper who will not so much as look upon Truth herself unless they see her elegantly dressed; that whereas the paths of honesty and good life appear now

> rugged and difficult, though they may be indeed easy and pleasant, they would then appear to all men both easy and pleasant though they be rugged and difficult indeed.

He goes on to ask for the reformative institution of "the learned and affable meeting of frequent academies and the procurement of wise and artful recitations sweetened with eloquent and graceful enticements to the love and practice of justice, temperance and fortitude". His early Ovidianism had been Platonically chastened but he had recovered now the urge to celebrate whatever is sublime, amiable, passionate, admirable, and to give these things solidity, outline, colour and polish.

It was at this stage, in the bliss of reformation dawn, determined to be a poet anyway, and with at least fourteen lines of "Adam Unparadised" written down, that Milton got married. Milton's father had lent £500 to Richard Powell, the squire of Forest Hill, a village to the east of Oxford neighbouring Stanton St John where the Miltons originated. Powell had been of the gentry for some generations, but he fell into debt to several other people and his manor was mortgaged. In 1627 he admitted his debt of £500 in writing, and promised to pay it to the scrivener, or his son, either in full at an unspecified date or commuted to £312 on demand on or before 12 December 1627. In May 1642 our Milton left the house in London where he was working and tutoring and went into the country. A month later he came back married to Mary Powell, the third of the Powell's eleven children, then aged sixteen and four months. We don't know whether Milton went there to collect his debt, though this seems likely—if the troubles went against the Royalists, the Powells would lose all their money (as they did); if things went the other way, Milton would have even greater need of his £500; in any case he had now been living on his father for twelve adult years. We don't know whether he went, after the loss of Diodati and with only a housekeeper to look after his houseful of pupils, to find a wife. However it happened, though, the marriage was not the realisation of any ideal; but an expedient, whether social, economic, domestic, or simply sexual. Milton's choice may have been, at these levels, rational; but on the personal level it was ill-considered, and disastrous. His house was filled with Mary's uncongenial relatives, celebrating a marriage which was either not consummated, or consummated without spiritual coition. Milton, chained to a carcase,[1] was gripped with horrified despair. Mary moped about the little academy, finding it too "philosophical" an existence for her liking, and probably suffering from shocked frigidity. Two months later she went back to her parents, promising to return in another two months. She did not return, and her family spurned Milton's messages of recall. He wrote his treatises on divorce, and gave some practical thought to polygamy (the theory being worked out in his Commonplace Book and *De Doctrina Christiana*) and concubinage. He is said to have made some moves towards a bigamous marriage with the "handsome and witty" daughter of a London doctor, but she was "averse". Three years after the marriage, the Powells were ruined by sequestration of their property. It was engineered that Mary should be found unexpectedly by Milton in the house of one of his friends, beg his pardon on her knees and offer humble repentance. They were reunited, and the whole Powell family came to stay in his larger Barbican house. A year later their first child, a girl, was born crippled.

The emotional product to be expected of this kind of misfortune includes many of those elements in Milton's poetry and prose which are sometimes attributed to "Puritanism" or "the dissociation of sensibility"—aggressiveness, coarseness, misogyny, materialism, angelophily, Stoicism. Similarly, a good deal has been made of the effect on Milton of the Civil War—how it forced him to use his left hand while his right stiffened. But as a matter of fact Milton had two separate periods of pamphleteering: a very short ecclesiastical one before his marriage, 1641-2, when he produced *Of Reformation*, *Of Prelatical Episcopacy*, *Ammadversions*, *The Reason of Church Government* and the *Apology for Smectymnuus*, only the third and the last being actually controversial, the others primarily expressions of idealism; and the longer but less concentrated political period, 1649-55, of his defence of regicide, the war over then and the years of comparative peace and political satisfaction having set in. Certainly, during the forties he was not writing poetry (neither were many other people); but his activities then are more likely to have

[1] See *Div.* iii. 249. Milton seems to have thought about divorce before his marriage, but the repeated references to "brutish congress" in the pamphlet are not theoretical.

stemmed from the shock of marriage than any political or religious trauma. He used drudgery to cicatrise his wounds: concentration on teaching (hence the move to a larger house) and the publication of *On Education* in 1664, with work on a Latin dictionary and grammar and a textbook of logic; editing of his early poems (1645); compilation of the *History of Britain* and *De Doctrina Christiana* (both begun *c.* 1645); paraphrasing the *Psalms* (1648); his Latin secretaryship (1649). At the same time, bursts of self-respecting defiance and self-forgetting idealism escaped in his divorce tracts (five of them, counting both editions of the first, running from 1643 to 1645), and *Areopagitica* (1644). These remedial exercises were performed in a household which at one time included his father, his brother Christopher and family, his wife and child, his father- and mother-in-law, his nephews Edward and John Philips, and his ordinary pupils. He was going blind, to lose his sight completely in 1652. In that year Mary Powell died. Four years later he married again; in the second year of that marriage his wife had a daughter and both of them died shortly after the birth. It was about this time that his nephew John Philips, whom Milton had educated, published *A Satyre against Hypocrites* mocking the rule of saints, and edited a collection of obscene and nonce-verses called *Sportive Wit or the Muses' Merriment*, for which he was fined by Order in Council—six members of the Council being friends of Milton's whom he admiringly named in the *Defensio Secunda*.

These last five years of misfortune, 1649-54, crushing his idealism, measured Milton to epic. At the beginning of them the King was executed and Milton appointed Latin Secretary to the Commonwealth government. His position was not exalted, he initiated no policy; but having avoided fighting and been refused office in the two wars, he was now at the elbow of great affairs: a scrivener's son addressing impeccable diplomatic Latin in the name of England to the sovereign states of Europe. He was also commissioned to write pamphlets. Because Milton's personal feelings were less involved and he was writing for public duty, *The Tenure of Kings and Magistrates* and especially *Eikonoklastes* are sane and confident compared with his early pamphlets, the prose of less doubtful hue. His two defences of the English "people", though more directly polemical against the regicidal accusations of Salmasius and More, allowed him to exploit fully his talent for Latin and his knowledge of history. Without having had to follow an uncongenial and distracting career through the Inns of Court and a tutorship, or a fellowship and the Church, he found himself suddenly able to deploy all his faculties in the service of man and God. These defences were his Arthuriad, realising his *Reason of Church Government* ambition to celebrate God's election of England:

> Which things, if I should so much as hope by any diligence or ability of mine, such as it is, to discourse of as I ought to do, and to commit them so to writing, as that perhaps all nations and all ages may read them, it would be a very vain thing in me.
>
> (*1st Def.* i. 4)

It was just what his vanity needed, and there can be no doubt of his answer to the question that ensues:

> For what style can be august and magnificent enough, what man has ability sufficient to undertake so great a task?

So he can "invoke the great and holy God" to inspire him even in "the cool element of prose". In the prelude to *Defensio Secunda* he looks back lovingly on this work, able to excuse himself with it for not having been at the hot gates nor fought in the warm rain:

> For since my youth I was devoted to the pursuits of literature, and my mind has always been stronger than my body, I did not court the labours of the camp, in which any common person would have been of more service than myself, but resorted to that employment in which my exertions were likely to be of most avail.
>
> (i. 219)

The *Defensio Secunda* ends with an explicit statement of the fulfilment of his ambition to be a patriotic poet:

> I have delivered my testimony, I would almost say, have erected a monument, that will not readily be destroyed, to the reality of those singular and mighty achievements which were above all praise. As the epic poet, who adheres to all the rules of that species of composition, does not profess to describe the whole life of the hero whom he celebrates, but only some particular action of his life, as the resentment of Achilles at Troy, the return of Ulysses, or the coming of Aeneas into Italy; so it will be sufficient, either for

> my justification or apology, that I have heroically celebrated at least one exploit of my countrymen; I pass by the rest, for who could recite the achievements of a whole people?
>
> (i. 299)

He was released from an Arthuriad, given a function in society, and he had, to his conscious satisfaction at least, performed that single act of manly assertion which intellectuals of his type need for their peace of mind.

3. *Decay of the Heroic and Divine*

Ten years before, Milton had shown Edward Philips some lines of Satan's address to the sun now at *Paradise Lost*, IV. 32, and during those ten years he may have written other bits—dramatic relics are scattered all over the poem.[1] The change to narrative form may not have occurred until the Restoration; but it was now, in the fifties, that Milton was able to start serious work on what was to be his epic. Yet it was at just this time that the possibility of divine epic seemed to be slipping away from the culture he was trying to write it for. When Crashaw died, a Roman Catholic, in 1649, Cowley wrote an elegy less apostolic than Carew's on Donne, and less confident of successful Christian poetry:

> Still the old *Heathen Gods* in *Numbers* dwell,
> The Heav'enliest thing on Earth still keeps up *Hell.*
> Nor have we yet quite purg'd the *Christian Land*;
> Still *Idols* here, like *Calves* at *Bethel* stand.
> And though *Pans Death* long since all *Oracles* broke,
> Yet still in Rhyme the *Fiend Apollo* spoke:[2]

Cowley's own attempt to solve the problem in *Davideis* was gallant, and in many ways similar to Milton's; but his self-consciousness is a sign that the moment for a poem which might be genuinely Christian and heroic had passed. In his preface (*Poems*, 1656) he made an impassioned plea for Biblical poetry, "in the wise managing and illustrating whereof the *Glory* of *God Almighty* might be joyned with the singular utility and

[1] See C. S. Lewis, *A Preface to P.L.*" (Oxford, 1942), notes on pp. 134-5; and my pp. 170, 200, 248, 265 below.
[2] *English Writings* ed. A. Waller (2 vols. Cambridge, 1905-06).

noblest delight of *Mankinde*". Classical fictions were worn out, and in any case

> Does not the passage of *Moses* and the *Israelites* into the *Holy Land* yield incomparably more Poetical variety then the voyages of *Ulysses* or *Aeneas*? Are the obsolete threadbare tales of *Thebes* and *Troy* half so stored with great, heroical, and supernatural actions (since *Verse* will needs *find* or *make* such) as the wars of *Joshua*, of the *Judges*, of *David*, and divers others?[1]

It was in this field of invention, of great, heroical and supernatural *actions*, that neither the Metaphysicals nor the Spenserians had accomplished anything: "for though some in other languages have attempted to write a *Divine Poem*; yet none, that I know of, has in *English*" (note to *Dav*. i. 28). The Metaphysicals had not been concerned with heroic action; and the Biblical paraphrasers had not written poems:

> For if any man design to compose a *Sacred Poem* by onely turning a story of the *Scripture*, like Mr *Quarles's*, or some other godly matter, like Mr *Heywood of Angels*, into *Rhyme*, He is so far from elevating of *Poesie* that he onely abases *Divinity*. . . . The same fertility of *Invention*, the same wisdom of *Disposition*, the same *Judgement* in observance of *Decencies*, the same lustre and vigor of *Elocution*, the same modesty and majestie of *Number*

are required in a sacred as in a secular poem; but if they are not present the result will be even worse. So, given the divine theme, Cowley's first business in *Davideis* was to write a heroic poem. He used a formal book-structure, heroic couplets interspersed with Pindaric (i.e. heroic) odes, and centred his action on "the Troubles of David":

> Too long the *Muses-Land* have *Heathen* bin:
> Their *Gods* too long were *Dev'ils*, and *Vertues Sin*;
> But *Thou*, *Eternal Word*, hast call'd forth *Me*
> Th' *Apostle*, to convert that *World* to *Thee*;
> T' unbind the charms that in slight *Fables* lie,
> And teach that *Truth* is truest *Poesie*.
>
> (i. 37)

Yet the poem quite failed to do what he wanted. The reason is

[1] Spingarn, ed. *Critical Essays of the 17th Century* (3 vols. Oxford, 1908-09). ii. 89.

that Cowley's own religious attitude was not heroic. In this he belonged to his time. Already, in 1656, when he and Milton had, in different degrees, the talent and maturity to write a Christian epic, and when the "warlike, various and . . . tragical age" that both complained of had gentled into temporary peace, other conditions had changed so much as to make the performance impracticable. It was partly that the desire for realism shared by Metaphysicals and Protestants was being sharpened by empirical science so that fiction was distrusted not merely if it were pagan but because it was silly; partly that the language was rapidly cooling down into the level correctness of the early 18th Century; partly that the concept of the heroic was altering; and, perhaps most importantly of all, the Metaphysical and Protestant interest in the drama of the soul was being replaced by the unenthusiastic and, though unsectarian, more typically "Catholic" humanism of the Augustans. So that by the time Milton was ready to outdo Du Bartas the circumstances which had made Du Bartas admirable were nearly past.

Basil Willey has set out the changed attitudes to fiction and language in his chapter on "The Heroic Poem in a Scientific Age". The suspicion of fiction was counterpart to the failure to invent. The Metaphysical desire for literary and the Protestant for religious realism join in Herbert's "*Jordan*":

> Who sayes that fictions onely and false hair
> Become a verse? Is there no truth in beautie?
> Is all good structure in a winding stair?
> May no lines passe, except they do their dutie
>   Not to a true, but painted chair?
>
> Is it no verse, except enchanted groves
> And sudden arbours shadow coarse-spunne lines?
> Must purling streams refresh a lovers loves?
> Must all be vail'd, while he that reades, divines,
>   Catching the sense at two removes?
>
> Shepherds are honest people; let them sing:
> Riddle who list, for me, and pull for Prime:
> I envie no mans nightingale or spring;
> Nor let them punish me with losse of rhyme,
>   Who plainly say, *My God, My King*.

Dislike of sapless classical allusion, pastorality, and amorose conceits, is not peculiar to any age. Herbert is mainly attacking what were 17th-century faults resulting from the very effort to write Christian poetry in secular mood: preciosity; excessive typologising (perhaps of the degree Vaughan was to take it to); and illicit allegorising, such as Bacon's in *The Wisdom of the Ancients* and Tasso's of his own epic. The cabbalistical Henry Reynolds's forming of scientific interpretations and Christian analogues out of classical myth, in *Mythomystes* (c. 1633), is a good example of the desperate efforts that had to be made to redeem the undeniably poetic fictions of the ancients. Davenant, in his preface to *Gondibert* (1651), objected to esoteric methods of the kind Reynolds had recommended and especially to Tasso, whose "Councell assembled in Heaven, his Witches Expeditions through the Air, and enchanted Woods Such as are inhabited with Ghosts" are symptoms of a primitive and undemocratic religion.[1] So by the mid-century an Augustan dislike of the Gothic was added to the other suspicions of literature. Classical mythology was falling together with medieval magic into anthropology, and the supernatural elements of Christianity itself were in danger. That they persisted at all, as they did in dilution, was due to the failure of poets until the Romantics to create a humanistic myth; and to the success of Milton in holding them together just at their moment of dissolution.

Davenant presented himself as "a Christian Poet, whose Religion little needs the aids of Invention"; yet he refused to be cut off from "probable fictions, because austere Historians have enter'd into bond to truth". In practice he sidestepped the religious problem: *Gondibert* is a non-supernatural and dully "probable" poem. This is what Waller praised it for:

> *Mars* nor *Bellona* are not named here;
> But such a *Gondibert* as both might fear.
> *Venus* had here, and *Hebe* been out-shin'd
> By thy bright *Birtha*, and thy *Rhodalind*.
> Such is thy happy skill, and such the odds
> Betwixt thy *Worthies* and the *Grecian Gods*.
> Whose Deities in vain had here come down,
> Where Mortal Beautie wears the Sovereign Crown;[2]

[1] Spingarn, ii. 5.
[2] "To Davenant", 33. *Poems* ed. G. T. Drury (2 vols. 1905).

So did Cowley:

> Methinks Heroick Poesie 'till now,
> Like some fantastick Fairy-land did show,
> Gods, Devils, Nymphs, Witches, and Giants race,
> And all but Man, in Man's chief work had place.

But Cowley's fragment, though much better poetry than Davenant's, is inconsistent. His David is human and dull; his heaven and hell, though, are fantastic Fletcherian fairylands; his Satan is an ogre; his God neither "probable" nor divine, but merely David's ally and Saul's enemy like any minor diety in Homer. It is almost as though Cowley and Davenant came to feel the difficulties of Christian epic that each admitted in his preface were insuperable and even unworthy of solution.

Perhaps we should not put too much down to the requirements of natual philosophy as declared in Sprat's *History of the Royal Society*, which came out in the same year as *Paradise Lost*. For although like Puritan preachers the scientists abjured the Elizabethan rhetoricians' *enargia*, and Metaphysical wit, the spread of scientific discussion through the reading public had brought a number of technical words and phrases into common currency, so that what in Donne would seem esoteric and peculiarly "Metaphysical" seems in Milton to be, if anything, rather commonplace—though most of his scientific terms (e.g. "optic tube") were recent coinages (cf. p. 238). It would be an advantage to a classically trained poet with a cosmic imagination that the terms of astronomy, mathematics and so on were not inkhorn any longer. Natural science probably had less effect than mental philosophy. Even before Locke's *Essay Concerning Human Understanding* (1690), Bacon, Descartes and Hobbes had given special attention to the nature of knowing, with a gradual effect on educated thought similar to that of 19th-20th-century analytical philosophy: an effect of nervousness, even timorousness, in handling words, which were now seen to be much more dangerous things than they had previously appeared to be. Even more influential, I think, though I can produce little evidence, must have been the increased writing of prose by the middle classes for non-literary purposes—notably for published sermons, and in the pamphlet war, but also for private, commercial and legal purposes. This would make a heightened diction essential, but unpopular: as more and more people become competent to write, it becomes more and more difficult to read or write anything but what is simply competent. Long before Sprat wrote his *History* his hopes came true in Cowley's verse. Sprat was anxious lest scientific work should be "eaten out by the luxury and redundancy of speech". These are precisely the qualities that Cowley avoids. His vocabulary feels small, his words do not spill over into fields of association. Waller, twin model with Denham for Augustan diction, completed the change in his *Divine Poems* of 1685. His six cantos "Of Divine Love" are a trial-run for Pope's *Essay on Man*, the emphasis being clear in this sentence from the argument: "How necessary this love is to reform mankind, and how excellent in itself." Waller was aware of the attractions of the Creation as a theme:

> But on so vast a subject who can find
> Words that may reach the ideas of his mind?
> Our language fails; or, if it could supply,
> What mortal thought can raise itself so high?
> Despairing here, we might abandon art,
> And only hope to have it in our heart.
> But though we find this sacred task too hard,
> Yet the design, the endeavour, brings reward.
>
> (iv. 13)

Marlowe would not have felt his tongue inadequate in this way, and Milton's invocation to his native language, though it admitted the difficulty, did not expect the language to fail him. (When the time came, though, he had to use not so much a heightened version of ordinary speech or of the prevailing poetic diction, as a language so idiosyncratic and yet so authoritatively derived from Latin, Italian, Elizabethan poetic diction, philosophy and modern science that it would trample on Cowley, Waller and Denham. It was to defend his great argument against them on one hand, and the mannerism of his early religious poems on the other, that he built his Chinese wall.)

The late 17th-century attitude to heroism was paradoxical: as the sense for actual heroism weakened, demand for the heroic in literature strengthened into a rule. In 1711 Alexander argued against the multiplex improbabilities of reality as Gothic, in favour of one ideal Augustan hero:

> the Poet, soaring above the Course of Nature . . . may liberally furnish his imaginary Man with all the Qualities requisite for the accomplishing of a perfect Creature . . .[1]

Dryden was complaining at the same time that *Paradise Lost* had no hero. The demand was for one personage on what they assumed to be the classical model, refined into a gentleman capable of heroics. While inherent heroism was no longer a social or political or religious ideal, the heroic became a literary device. So it was just as amusing to be mock-heroic: hence *MacFlecknoe*, *The Battle of the Books*, *The Dunciad*. These works were not just political satires like *Hudibras* or, like Cotton's *Scarronides* (a burlesque on the *Aeneid*), the product of cheap wit weary of its own education. They are instances of tremendous creative and celebratory energy thwarted of its natural objects, disconcerted by restriction, so turning to destroy and denigrate. In Pope at least the satire is based on a positive concern for order and decency; but the positive is nearly always given negative expression. "*Let Spades be Trumps!* she said, and Trumps they were" takes its effect from a reverence for creativity which the sterile and sexless Belinda has not got; but that is the only way in which Pope does celebrate creation.

Yet as "Mans chief work" epic was still regarded as a cultural palladium. Plenty were written in the 1690s (mostly by Sir Richard Blackmore); but as creative talent turned more to mock-heroic, and translation of classical epic, the critical attitude hardened against Christian epic in particular. Opinion was divided, but it tended to the view that a deliberately Christian epic was not merely impracticable but even indecorous, and in a way irrelevant: what would the ancients have cared? So Sheffield asked, in his *Essay upon Poetry* (1682):

> But what, alas, avails it poor Mankind
> To see this promised Land, yet stay behind?
> The way is shewn, but who has strength to go?
> Who can all Sciences exactly know?
> Whose fancy flyes beyond weak reason's sight,
> And yet has Judgement to direct it right?
> Whose nice distinction, Virgil-like, is such,
> Never to say too little nor too much?

[1] *Anacrisis*, Spingarn, i. 186. Cf. Blackmore's preface to his epic on Arthur.

> Let such a man begin without delay;
> But he must do much more than I can say,
> Must above *Cowley*, nay, and *Milton* too prevail,
> Succeed where great *Torquato*, and our greater *Spencer* fail.[1]

The way had been shown by Bossu, the French apostle of neo-classicism, rather than by the more moral *Discorsi sulla Poema Eroico* of Tasso. Lumping together Cowley, Milton, Tasso and Spenser, Mulgrave is preoccupied with genre. This secularised attitude to epic was part of the Battle of the Books, in which the critical case between classical and modern literature was fought, not on such religious grounds as are implied in Elizabethan criticism, but at a gentlemanly aesthetic level, as if the advantage "over and above of being a Christian", which Milton had claimed (*R.C.G.* ii. 478), was not fair play. Thus in 1690, when *Paradise Lost* had already gone through four editions, Sir William Temple could think of "none of the Moderns that have made any Atchievments in *Heroick* Poetry worth recording"; and where Cowley had admitted the relative difficulty of Christian epic, Temple asserts its utter impracticability:

> The Religion of the Gentiles had been woven into the Contexture of all the antient Poetry with a very agreable mixture, which made the Moderns affect to give that of Christianity a place also in their poems. But the true Religion was not found to become a Fiction so well as a false had done, and all their Attempts of this kind seem rather to debase Religion than to heighten Poetry.[2]

The most interesting critical remarks in this line, though, are Voltaire's, for he seems to combine the more modern secular attitude with the earlier, 17th-century concern for religion; and is therefore more sympathetic to Milton. In his essay on the European epic[3] (1727) he objected to Camoens' bad taste in the *Lusiads* (1572) in having Vasco da Gama pray to Christ and be answered by Venus. Tasso too "is guilty of indulging the inacurate Custom of calling the evil Spirits by the Names of *Pluto*, *Alecto*, and of mingling often Pagan Ideas with Christian Mythology" (p. 122). He agreed with Temple about the funda-

[1] Spingarn, ii. 296.

[2] *Essay on Ancient and Modern Learning*, Spingarn, iii. 99. On the Battle of the Books generally see Highet, *The Classical Tradition* (Oxford, 1949).

[3] *An Essay . . . upon the Epick Poetry of the European Nations. From Homer down to Milton*, repr. by Florence D. White as *Voltaire's Essay on Epic Poetry: A Study and an Edition* (Albany, N.Y., 1915).

mental intractability of Christian mythology, yet he argues from reverence rather than aesthetics:

> 'Tis strange that none of our modern Poets are free from that fault [of Tasso's]. It seems that our Devils and our Christian Hell have something in them low and mean, and must be rais'd by the Hell of the *Pagans*, which owes its Dignity to its Antiquity. Certain it is that the Hell of the Gospel is not so fitted for Poetry as that of *Homer* and *Virgil.*

At the same time Voltaire makes no allowances for religious enthusiasm for at heart he found Christian material *a priori* uncongenial to poetry. In condemning Andreini's *Adamo* he speaks of "That Topick, so improper for a Drama, but so suitable to the absurd Genius of the *Italian* stage (as it was at that Time)," being "handled in a manner intirely comformable to the Extravagance of the Design". Therefore when he praises *Paradise Lost* it is because he finds in it qualities of historicity, rationality and common sense not to be expected in the literary treatment of such a theme:

> *Milton* pierc'd through the Absurdity of that Performance to the hidden Majesty of the Subject, which being altogether unfit for the Stage, yet might be (for the Genius of *Milton*, and for his only) the Foundation of an Epick Poem.

So Milton's genius was irrevocably bent on a divine epic which the public no longer wanted, when even the private circumstances which had made him need to write it no longer mattered. In some ways the poem that he wrote ran with the time: in structure, in Virgilian tone, and particularly in depth of pious and learned allusion, *Paradise Lost* is neo-classical, much more up to date than the lyrical drama and romantic history he had been thinking of in 1640. But the poem was most reactionary in *matériel.* The epic treatment of the Fall of Man had been a 16th-century ideal, part Humanistic, part Protestant, consummated in a way, as we have seen, by Du Bartas. But any similar work, however superior aesthetically, could only be an anachronism now. Thus Primaudaye's *French Academy* was intended as a popular encyclopaedia, so written in the vernacular and translated into English in 1618. It offered a Bartasian view of the universe, corresponding to the unspecialised condition of 16th-century learning: Book II comprehends psychology, pneumatology, ethics, physiology and anatomy as a single subject; Book III descends via geography from astronomy to horticulture. But by 1667 this was impossible (e.g. the Galilean astronomy of *Paradise Lost* was already out of date). Its impossibility accounts for Pope's more generalised and distant handling of encyclopaedic materials. Primaudaye's method also required a peculiarly Humanistic and Protestant stance. The main positions, all explicit, were dualism of body and soul (Chapter III), a Platonic condition of which post-Restoration writers came to be much less acutely conscious; the ideal of self-knowledge (preface to Book II), in a more physiological sense than the social-minded Augustans were to take it; a defiantly non-clerical, secular approach to natural history—this anti-scholastic issue was dead for literature by the end of the century; and generally a reverent anthropocentrism (preface to Book I): this typically Humanist attitude had lost the distinction of a literary tone and become simply correct posture by the time of the essay *on* Man. Pope's firmest common ground with Du Bartas, Primaudaye and Humanism is his reliance on a prudential hedonism that stretches back to More's *Utopia*. There questions of virtue, though "perteyning to religion, yet they thincke it mete that they shoulde be beleved and graunted by proses of reason". The steady movement, under Reformation, Humanist Renaissance and Enlightenment, towards a rationalised religion, secularly-sanctioned morality and constituted institutions, bore Milton towards his poem and simultaneously carried away the value of its traditional materials. Ideographically then *Paradise Lost* was the last integration of a world-view that had already disintegrated and was being put together again in slightly different shape. In the history of European literature it appears as the last of all significant redactions of the celestial cycle.

The cycle consists of the Fall of the Angels, the Creation of the World, and the Fall of Man. We have already considered some of the ways in which Du Bartas had satisfied a Protestant demand; we can also guess at some secular attractions of the celestial cycle as a literary theme. The enhanced prestige of Satan (relative to the Middle Ages) looks like a mirror reflex of Renaissance and Reformation ambitions. The Church which had previously stood between men and spiritual wickedness in high places, allowing them to make a joke of the devil, had gone. Men were left to face the adversary who was themselves alone. To a history-conscious people the Fall of the Angels was most obviously a supernatural counterpart to the Wars of the Roses—an object lesson in the danger and wickedness of political rebellion, and the reverential necessity for immutable law and absolute monarchy; it also afforded the only military action in the Bible that can compare in grandeur with the siege of Troy. The Creation afforded an opportunity to write cosmic panegyric *in extenso*—it could be a celebration of the glories of the universe as evidence of divine providence, and also of human ingenuity in understanding them. It was as Creator, and Governor of the cosmic plot of which Satan is villain and man pawn, that the religion of Humanism regarded God—"L'Imitazione del Padre"—in contrast to the humbler, Christ-centred religion of the later Middle Ages. But of the three, the Fall offered most scope for Humanist interests. It could be used, as it perpetually had been in sermons, emblems and books of devotion, as a warning against the illimitable perils of a presumptious scepticism, whether scientific or philosophic; and also against both domestic and political disobedience. Paradise gave opportunity for the celebration of ideal love, and for primitivism of the kind excited by geographical discovery. There could also be satire on the casuistical rhetoric of the actual temptation; and it was usual to complete the cycle, as Milton does in Books XI-XII, with a comfortably pessimistic survey of world history.

Now nearly all these opportunities are for the satisfaction of demands that are typically Humanistic, arising—reviving, rather: cf. Books XI-XX of *De Civitate Dei*—so far as England is concerned in the 16th Century and losing much of their urgency in the 17th. By the time Milton came to satisfy them, the public temper had altered, politically, philosophically and in religion. Politically, quite apart from theory, a rebellion had in fact succeeded, and not only against one bad king but against individual sovereignty as a principle. In natural philosophy many of the glories of the universe were being opened to physical or instrumental perception, measurement and classification, and hence to intellectual apprehension, in a way that made metaphorical apprehension and poetic marvelling redundant. In mental philosophy, the very grounds of knowing were being questioned. "Religion" has to be put in inverted commas after about 1650, or at least used to cover a variety of quite different attitudes: the deism of Lord Herbert of Cherbury, for instance, who by 1624[1] had reduced all religion to five propositions; and the quietism of the Cambridge Platonists who even earlier had contracted into themselves so far that the religion which had previously been the multiform body of Christ became a canopy to shield the candle of the Lord.

These changes affect all three parts of the celestial cycle, but evidence for a shifting attitude to the Fall of Man is apparent in the best-known poetry of the 17th Century and may be used to typify the others. The Fall was central to Protestant theology. It was partly a matter of personalities: Paul and Augustine, temperamentally obsessed with sin, appealed to the Renaissance and Protestant mind; Aquinas, much less interested in sin, appealed less and was rejected, by empiricists and Protestants alike, as the representative of scholastic casuistry and Catholic error. This appeal and rejection were not accidental: it is because they were concerned about sin that Paul and Augustine are great literary figures while Aquinas is just a theologian. The theology of Paul and Augustine—and Calvin and Milton—is autobiographical. It satisfied the Renaissance craving for realism, and the Reformation craving for a direct man-God relationship. Another reason for the interest is perhaps that at this time people began to inquire more closely than before into origins, whereas during the Middle Ages they had been concerned more with ends and means. *Genesis* was taken as seriously by the 17th Century as *The Origin of Species* was by the 19th. Behind this again there may be social factors: the aristocratic and the lowest classes take their origins for granted; the bourgeois trace their pedigrees.

Perhaps the most important historical consideration is that concern with the Fall reflects a strong sense of the importance of man, and of individual men. The Fall explains why we seem unworthy of our potentialities, and why the world seems unworthy of us. This concern may issue, under the pressure of

[1] Date of Paris ed. of *De Veritate*. The propositions are: there is a supreme power; he should be worshipped; the best worship is ethical behaviour; vices and crimes can and should be expiated and repented of; there will be rewards and punishments after death.

psychological derangement and historical determinations, in a ridiculous obsession with the total depravity of all men. But Milton was a humanist, not a Calvinist, on this point, and all the hexemeral poems are celebrations of man and the God-created world, rather than jeremiads. Milton shows little sign of any personal sense of guilt, certainly when compared with Baxter or Bunyan or even Donne and Shakespeare.

In fact this was a weakness in his position. The sense of general sin and degradation which the Middle Ages had expressed in the sad demeanour and tortured postures of Gothic art became, either side of 1600, literary motive; therefore more individualistic. This personal sense of sin issues more naturally in autobiography than myth: the straightforward autobiography of Augustine's *Confessions* and *De Civitate Dei* or Baxter's *Life of Faith*; the gloomy survey of Godfrey Goodman's *Fall of Man*; a fictionalised testament of conversion such as *Pilgrim's Progress*; sublimation into theology as by Luther and Calvin, or preaching as by Donne and Andrewes; or the poem of personal introspection or devotion as practised by Shakespeare in Sonnet cxlvi and in dramatic soliloquies, and by the Metaphysicals in their divine poems. In all these, a temperamental concern with man as a fallen being is hithered past the actual myth into the present actualities of individual life—is made existential. So in "A Hymne to God the Father" Donne starts by confessing original sin—

> Wilt thou forgive that sinne where I begunne,
> Which was my sin, though it were done before?

—but he does not go on at all Biblically or theologically. On the other hand, when he does use the Fall thematically it is not in reference to his own sin but, in the "Anniversaries" for instance, to historical change: he is concerned with the gradual decay of the universe. Herbert typically reduces the epic struggle between good and evil to the microcosmic scale of personal sin. In "Sion" he describes Solomon's temple and says,

> Yet all this glorie, all this pomp and state
> Did not affect thee much, was not thy aim;
> Something there was, that sow'd debate:
> Wherefore thou quitt'st thy ancient claim:
> And now thy Architecture meets with sinne;
> For all thy frame and fabrick is within.

There thou art struggling with a peevish heart,
Which sometimes crosseth thee, thou sometimes it:
  The fight is hard on either part.
  Great God doth fight, he doth submit.
All Solomons sea of brasse and world of stone
Is not so deare as one good grone.

Nearly all Metaphysical and Cambridge Platonist references to Milton's materials—Adam and Eve, the Creation, the Garden of Eden, Hell, the Tower of Babel—are slight, even metaphorical. So the problem of the religious epic was even more acute than it appeared when discussed above: *Genesis* did not give Milton all he wanted, but in a way it gave him too much. As soon as you begin to elaborate the myth of the Fall and make it temporal and concrete you lose the sense of sin which first arouses interest in it.

The interest itself had declined far by the time Milton came to write *Paradise Lost*. The Fall could be a serious metaphor to devout Metaphysicals; for Cavalier poets it was a conceit. Herrick uses the Fall with a frivolity distinct from the catholic familiarity of Donne and Herbert:

JVLIA was carelesse, and withall,
She rather took, then got a fall:
The wanton *Ambler* chanc'd to see
Part of her leggs sinceritie:
And ravish'd thus, It came to passe,
The Nagge (like to the *Prophets Asse*)
Began to speak, and would have been
A telling what rare sights h'ad seen:[1]

Waller is deliberately irreverent:

THE FALL

See! how the willing earth gave way,
To take the impression where she lay.
See! how the mould, as loth to leave
So sweet a burden, still doth cleave
Close to the nymph's stained gardment.

. . .

'Twas such a chance as this, made all
The world into this order fall;
Thus the first lovers on the clay,
Of which they were composed, lay;

[1] *Poetical Works* ed. L. C. Martin (Oxford, 1956).

So in their prime, with equal grace,
Met the first patterns of our race.
Then blush not, fair! or on him frown,
Or wonder how you both came down . . .

This sort of thing led rapidly into the denigrating blasphemy of Dryden:

From dusty shops neglected authors come,
Martyrs of pies, and relics of the bum.

Sinking he left his drugget robe behind,
Borne upwards by a subterranean wind.
The mantle fell to the young prophet's part
With double portion of his father's art.[1]

Mock-heroic, anyway as practised by Dryden, is a literary manifestation of a primary religious irreverence; so that the lines, "The sire then shook the honours of his head, And from his brows damps of oblivion shed Full on the filial dulness" (134) is first a satire on God—implying that the Trinity is absurd—subsequently a satire on Homer and Milton, and only trivially a satire on Shadwell. The decline specifically of the Fall as either metaphor or plot is complete in Dryden's verses "On the Death of a Very Young Gentleman":

Thus then he disappear'd, was rarified;
For 'tis improper speech to say he died:
He was exhal'd; his great Creator drew
His spirit, as the sun the morning dew.
'Tis sin produces death; and he had none,
But the taint Adam left on ev'ry son.
He added not, he was so pure, so good,
'Twas but th'original forfeit of his blood;
And that so little, that the river ran
More clear than the corrupted fount began.
Nothing remain'd of the first, muddy clay;
The length of course had wash'd it in the way:
So deep, and yet so clear, we might behold
The gravel bottom, and that bottom gold.

The second line echoes Donne's "For that word [death] wrongs her"; but the calm, unbelieving management of the

[1] *MacFlecknoe*, 100, 214. *Poetical Works* ed. G. R. Noyes (2nd ed. Cambridge, Mass., 1950).

dead youth's sinlessness is quite different from the overt hyperbole of Metaphysical elegy, as we have it, in, say, the "First Anniversarie". In Dryden's works generally the division between religious and satirical poems is much wider than the division in Donne's between religious and erotic.

Pope follows the orthodox Augustinian attribution of the Fall to pride; but the pride he is thinking of is philosophic and social vanity rather than passionate ὕβρις:

> In Pride, in reas'ning Pride, our error lies;
> All quit their sphere, and rush into the skies.
> Pride still is aiming at the blest abodes,
> Men would be Angels, Angels would be Gods.
> Aspiring to be Gods, if Angels fell,
> Aspiring to be Angels, Men rebel:
> And who but wishes to invert the laws
> Of ORDER, sins against th'Eternal Cause.[1]

He has a lot more to say about degree, but it is a museum exhibit, with neither the passionate seriousness attached to it by Ulysses nor the dynamic beauty with which Raphael describes it:

> See, through this air, this ocean, and this earth,
> All matter quick, and bursting into birth.
> Above, how high, progressive life may go!
> Around, how wide, how deep extend below!
> Vast Chain of Being! which from God began,
> Natures ethereal, human, angel, man,
> Beast, bird, fish, insect, what no eye can see,
> No glass can reach; from infinite to thee,
> From thee to Nothing . . .

This is closer to Erasmus Darwin and H. G. Wells than it is to Hooker, Shakespeare and Milton, who had to fight for their visions of an ordered cosmos. Similarly Pope's utilitarianism is more Victorian than Renaissance in tone: he describes how "Two Principles in human nature reign; Self-love, to urge, and Reason, to restrain" (ii. 2)—but both are directed at pleasure as an end, and he is suspiciously vehement in crying "Fools! who from hence into the notion fall, That Vice or Virtue there is none at all" (212). So in his description of man's ascent from creation the Fall has no place.

[1] *Essay on Man*, I. iv (125). *Works* ed. Warton *et al.* (9 vols. 1797).

The fate of epic ambition in the 17th Century is recorded in Pope's projected plan for an epic. Its hero, Brutus, was to have "benevolence" as ruling passion, so that when on the way from Troy to Britain he and his crew reach an uninhabited Lotos-land (not a paradise), Brutus rejects the plea of his crew to stay there,

> as incompatible with his generous plan of extending benevolence, by instructing and polishing uncultivated minds. He despises the mean thought of providing for the happiness of themselves alone, and sets the great promises of Heaven before them.[1]

Pope solved here, in theory, all the problems of religious epic that Milton faced, but at some loss. There were to be no miracles: an angel explains to Brutus the geophysics of a volcanic eruption that the natives had taken for the working of evil spirits. Love is restricted to one Didoesque episode. The direction of the project is summed up when

> Brutus gives it as his opinion, not to conquer and destroy the natives of the new-discovered land, but to polish and refine them, by introducing true religion, void of superstition and all false notions of the Deity, which only leads to vice and misery, among people who are uncorrupted in their manners, and only want the introduction of useful arts, under the sanction of a good government, to establish and ensure their felicity.

Because it was relatively easy for Pope to achieve a *Weltanschauung* and Brutus to ensure a Utilitarian felicity, the philosophical and religious effort needed actually to write an epic was no longer itself heroic, as it was for Milton when he began; and though in public the literary ambition was strong, the personal urge, especially as letters became a profession, slackened.

These currents and ebbings Milton opposed by grim wilful perseverance of rhythm and language. Marvell saw it happening. He starts his poem "On Mr *Milton's* Paradise Lost" by admitting that

> the Argument
> Held me a while misdoubting his Intent,
> That he would ruine (for I saw him strong)
> The sacred Truths to Fable and old Song . . .

[1] *Ed. cit.* iv. 363.

Then, reconciled to the epic treatment of divine material, he wondered

> Through that wide Field how he his way should find
> O're which lame Faith leads Understanding blind;
> Lest he perplext the things he would explain,
> And what was easie he should render vain.

Then Marvell is worried, like Voltaire, lest "some less skilful hand"—such as Dryden's—

> Might hence presume the whole Creations day
> To change in Scenes, and show it in a Play.

His retraction of these doubts is not quite wholehearted, and his statement of the excellencies of *Paradise Lost* continues to hint at the difficulties we have been discussing:

> That Majesty which through thy Work doth Reign
> Draws the Devout, deterring the Profane.
> And things divine thou treatst of in such state
> As them preserves, and Thee inviolate.
> At once delight and horrour on us seize,
> Thou singst with so much gravity and ease;
> And above humane flight dost soar aloft,
> With Plume so strong, so equal, and so soft.
> The *Bird* nam'd from that *Paradise* you sing
> So never Flags, but alwaies keeps on Wing.
> Where couldst thou Words of such a compass find?
> Whence furnish such a vast expense of Mind?

"Majesty" and "state" raise the whole problem of the hero and divine monarchy in a Commonwealth epic; "preserves inviolate" may suggest that, as most later readers have felt, Milton's neo-classical decorum in presenting Heaven and God is taken to the point of dulness. Perhaps it is reading into Marvell too much of subsequent criticism to say that the "delight and horror" which seized him when reading *Paradise Lost* were critical—that he saw the dangers of Milton's strength of prosodic pinion and vast expense of vocabulary just as clearly as he must have seen the more topical danger of his soaring so far "above humane flight". At face-value these lines describe the fulfilment of precisely those ambitions which Milton had listed in the "Vacation Exercise". The fulfilment came "an age too late" to be plenary; yet its inadequacies are not merely regrettable failures of technique, but symptoms—often concealed by technical splendour—of distortions that occurred within Milton himself, between him and his environment, and in the Christian tradition.

2

HELL

1. *Invocation*

OUR first disobedience is to our mother. It is later in the Freudo-Jungian myth that, stirred up with envy and revenge, we try to usurp our father's place and are exiled into the unfamiliar world. The 20th-century reader must face this discrepancy between his own domestic mythology and Milton's cosmic one because *Paradise Lost* is at once more personal than any other epic, yet its characters more elementally related to one another, its scenes more archetypal.

Milton's first invocation settles the discrepancies we feel by settling those he was conscious of. All his invocations lift the poet and reader out of the phantastic and philosophical perils of the narrative flux into stable moments of real devotion. More lyrical than the environing verse yet partaking of the same form, they sanctify it. They have to do this because the epic poet is responsible for the content of his work, even the sayings of his characters, in a way that the dramatist is not. In primitive and classical and even Renaissance epic the poet could answer his premonitory *Hwaet*! assured that his present—perhaps physically present—audience shared the ancestor-worship or patriotism or Catholicism that his epic was to celebrate: so Virgil could confer Roman citizenship on a Bronze Age Trojan. But Milton's myth had extraordinary religious valency. The schism between this on one hand, and on the other its literary interest as story, and the ethical values intimated by characters within it, was severer than in any comparable work. Most earlier treatments of the War in Heaven, the Creation and the Fall had been written as Humanistic exercises in the classical expression of Christian mythology; few had anything like the personal pressure and devotional valency of *Paradise Lost*—they were at the level of Milton's poems on the Circumcision and the Passion. The best epics had been secular anyway, appealing like Virgil to political rather than religious piety:

INVOCATION

> Cease *man of* TROY, and cease thou *Sage of* GREECE,
> To boast the *Navigations* great *ye* made;
> Let the high Fame of ALEXANDER cease,
> And TRAIAN's Banners in the EAST display'd . . .
> A brighter *Valour* rises in the *West.*[1]

Milton was more acutely harassed by all those worries of the 17th Century, about the Battle of the Books, truth and fiction, the decorum of religious emotion, inner light and public order, that we have been discussing. Shortly before Milton began *Paradise Lost*, Davenant had remarked that to invoke the Holy Ghost savoured of "saucy familiarity with a true God",[2] and Hobbes agreed:

> But Why a Christian should think it an ornament to his Poem, either to profane the true God or invoke a false one, I can imagine no cause but a reasonless imitation of Custom, of a foolish custom, by which a man, enabled to speak wisely from the principles of nature and his own meditation, loves rather to be thought to speak by inspiration, like a Bagpipe.[3]

Inspiration meant to them much what enthusiasm was to mean fifty years later; "the principles of nature" is an Augustan phrase. Because it was an age too late, as well as for personal reasons, Milton had to sanctify the poem with special effort.

[1] Camoens, *The Lusiad*[*s*], trans. Fanshawe (1655). Virgil says he is going to relate Aeneas' adventures to the point when he establishes a city and his gods in Latium, source of the Latin nation; from this will spring the city of Alba Longa, ancestral home of the patricians; then the Rome built by Romulus and Remus. Tasso appeals to the expansive energy of young Europe:

> For if the Christian Princes euer striue
> To win faire Greece out of the tyrants hands,
> And those vsurping Ismalites depriue
> Of wofull Thrace, which now captiued stands,
> You must from realmes and seas the Turkes forth driue,
> As *Godfrey* chased them from Iudais lands,
> And in this Legend, all that glorious deed
> Reade, whil'st you arme you; arme you, whil'st you reed.

Even the half-serious Ariosto says he will write about the heroic ancestors of his patron cardinal. The minor English attempts at epic, like the historical drama, were insular in their political appeal, loyal to sovereign and nation rather than Christendom.

[2] Pref. to *Gondibert*, Spingarn, ii. 25.

[3] *Answer to Davenant*, Spingarn, ii. 59.

His first paragraph does more than invoke divine inspiration: its allusions subvert classical myth and every previous epic, and single out a fit audience; its rhythms propel Milton's myth into an orbit beyond comparison and scepticism, and establish him in the rostrum of conductor. "Of Mans First Disobedience" recalls Homer's "Tell me, O Muse, of that man", Virgil's "arma virumque", Ariosto's "Le donne, i cavalier, l'arme, gli armori" and so on, only to spurn them all as fruits of that forbidden tree now to be sung, their heroes' virtues forced upon them by our impudent crimes. The delayed impulse of "*Sing* Heav'nly Muse" swings us up from secular considerations, claiming what John Smith counted world-highest, the inspiration both divine and literary which dictated the Pentateuch and Ten Commandments to Moses on Sinai; then that which on Mount Zion taught the psalms to David, and made the prophets oracular in Shiloh. Even further Milton presumes, to associate himself with the creative power of God: his muse is not Urania but Knowledge, the daughter of God, who with her sister Wisdom is to help God create the world in Book VII.[1] The two offices, of masculine prophetic poetry and feminine copiousness, unite in the final appeal to the Holy Spirit, itself impregnator and hatcher of the cosmic egg. The Spirit prefers "Before all Temples th'upright heart and pure". This is the only, and typically Protestant way for Milton to reach an audience: the liturgical rhythm invokes ordination of himself as priest, and consecration of his poem as church, for a scattered minority parish—as the prophets preached in Babylonian captivity. He exacts a precise though dual culture from his congregation. They are supposed to know already the whole Christian scheme of Creation, Fall and Chosen People "till one greater Man Restore us" (the verb is theological); to be intimate enough with the Bible to recognise "That Shepherd" as Moses, and trained in doctrine sufficiently to appreciate the typology adumbrated in that phrase, and

[1] This is elaborated in Rabbinical allegory. Milton's direct knowledge of Rabbinical writings is suspect now, and he attacked them in his prose (iii. 58, 131, and *2nd Def. passim*), but Wisdom and Knowledge are sistered in the Bible. See Hughes's note to *P.L.* VII. 9. The standard source is *Prov.* viii. 30, where Wisdom plays before Yahweh; but *Wisdom of Solomon* vii. 15-22 is a more humanistic invocation of Wisdom as, especially, a cosmographical muse. A nymph seeming to be Wisdom or Knowledge rides with God on his creative expeditions in the Sistine Chapel fresco.

the economy with which the trans-Testamental power and grace of the Holy Spirit are affirmed by the lines which identify the *ruach 'Elohim* of *Genesis* i. 1 with the baptismal Dove of the Gospels. At the same time the subversion of secular material demands secular learning. The well of Aganippe by the altar of Zeus on the Aonian Mount—Mount Helicon—which was the haunt of the Muses and inspired anyone who drank from it, is replaced by the Pool of Siloam flowing past the temple in Jerusalem, where the man blind from birth washed away the clay that Jesus had spread on his eyes, and saw for the first time (*John* ix). This is the supra-mythological ground of Milton's beseeching, "What in me is dark Illumine". Shining out of the humble monosyllables and line-ending pause of "What in me is dark", the imperative enacts the miracle it invokes. Milton is the demi-urge of his own poem. So his cadences, having knelt before the Spirit and hovered with it over the abyss, come to a halt on the iambic plateau of the invocation's last two lines. The whole story is to be related from the eyrie of eternal Providence. Trained to close reading, we often trespass on this vast aesthetic distance; but it insulates Milton's priestly office from his office as narrator.

It gives him now the literary advantage of plunging us shockingly as Satan plunged from Heaven into Hell and *in medias res*. The verse takes a deep breath; it shakes with question and answer as if on the edge of a precipice; and with the Homeric and Virgilian "Say first" formula it commits itself so frankly to the conventions of secular epic that devout gravity, and doctrine, decorously give way to histrionics:

> and with ambitious aim
> Against the Throne and Monarchie of God
> Rais'd impious War in Heav'n and Battel proud
> With vain attempt.

The Marlovian rhythm is like an up-rearing of spears and banners which the typically Miltonic half-line of derision, "With *vain* attempt", hurls down again. Milton, acting God, remains secure as Satan ruins from his stroke. The tenses shift imperceptibly into an immediate Hell. Down to line 53 the tense is past: "he with his horrid crew Lay vanquisht"; but "now the thought Both of lost happiness and lasting pain Torments him" and "round he throws his baleful eyes That witness'd huge affliction and dismay".

From the level of these tense-shifts and such neat transitions between description and speech as "Know ye not mee?" (IV. 827), to the attitudinal device of presenting the action as a series of seen and heard *events*, Milton's narrative craft is cinematic, as Eisenstein has remarked.[1] Here we have, what can only be done by film and orchestra, an overture, opening crash, and, through the sparkling eyes of the chief character, a focus into expanding areas of the dismal situation which is the first act's scene. Another instance of tense-shifting serves to introduce Satan as a topic: Beelzebub delivers him a speech and "He scarce had ceas't when the superior Fiend Was moving towards the shore". It is a montage effect that heightens the air of fantasy, as of dumb Moore-stone figures stalking a surrealist landscape.

2. *Satan*

> The character of Satan engenders in the mind a pernicious casuistry which leads us to weigh his faults with his wrongs, and to excuse the former because the latter exceed all measure. In the minds of those who consider that magnificent fiction with a religious feeling it engenders something worse.
>
> SHELLEY

Satan's mobility, his articulacy, and muscularity ("Forthwith upright he rears from off the Pool His mighty stature") make him the most vital character in *Paradise Lost*. So far as we value vitality, and so far as the characters symbolise ideal states of existence, we must then accept Blake's inversion of the values the myth assigns to them. Satan's response to environment is more progressive than the aristocratic theorising of the Father, the phantastic omnipotence of the Son and the passivity of Adam. This is not a Nietzchean perversity but so much a matter of common experience that Blake could properly call his aphorisms "proverbs" of Hell: "The tygers of wrath are wiser than the horses of instruction", "Damn braces. Bless relaxes", "Exuberance is beauty". But it is perverse to read so ethico-symbolically, as if all literature were directly propagandist, and the characters in *Paradise Lost* as flatly symbolic as the figures in

[1] In *The Film Sense*, trans. J. Leyda (new ed. 1948).

Blake's etchings and prophetic books; or as if all that were "life-enhancing" were absolutely good.

Hell and Satan in it are Milton's vision of human powers corrupted by ὕβρις. In this they simply extend the invocation's subversion of all that had previously been regarded as sublime. We should be happier if the powers which are corrupted in Satan were to be found pure in some opponent of his. But Satan succeeds as a symbol of human corruption because, like us, his own best self is foil to his worst. This duality has worried critics: is Satan hero or fool? The question may be argued in psychological terms[1] but the literary symptoms are obvious enough. Books I and II are full of paradoxical expressions—antithesis, antimetabole, oxymoron, etc.—of which "darkness visible" is only the most familar. These are facets of the total paradox: Satan is an angel in Hell and as such an exaggerated version of fallen man: "infinite in faculties! in form and moving, how express and admirable! in action, how like an angel! in apprehension, how like a god! the beauty of the world! the paragon of animals! . . . quintessence of dust".[2] So his feats of energy derive from a power not his own: his elevation from "Prone on the Flood" like a whale through the stages of reared upright, "incumbent on the dusky Air", moving towards the shore and standing like a tower, to enthronement at the beginning of Book II, is mechanical, seen by the reader to be done rather than done by Satan as a living person. This frankensteinian quality is most apparent when Satan returns to his throne after the Fall, incognito, and without volition, dubiously,

> as from a Cloud his fulgent head
> And shape Starr-bright appeer'd, or brighter, clad
> With what permissive glory since his fall
> Was left him, or false glitter:
>
> (X. 449)

[1] See Ernest Jones, *On the Nightmare* (1931), and J. C. Flugel, *Man, Morals and Society* (1945), Chap. XVII. The reaction against psychology as an element in literary criticism has reached the stage of dishonesty, as if a late 19th-century clergyman had pretended Darwin was a lunatic and the Higher Criticism an undergraduate joke, so as to preserve his own universe of discourse inviolate.

[2] *Complete Works of Shakespeare* ed. Alexander (1951).

Milton's frank casuistry about the permissive existence of evil (I. 211) is supported by Satan's poetic nature. Even at the beginning, before his angelic accoutrements drop off as he persists in unheroic behaviour, Satan's glory is derivative, inhering in the ikons that clutter him as much as in personality. Sun, moon, star, cloud, storm, vulture, wolf lend him vitality and virility, but any admiration we have for Satan on their account must rely more on our own symbolic valuation of them than Milton's. When Satan strides to the edge of the lake to call his legions,

> his ponderous shield
> Ethereal temper, massy, large and round,
> Behind him cast; the broad circumference
> Hung on his shoulders like the Moon, whose Orb
> Through Optic Glass the *Tuscan* Artist views
> At Ev'ning from the top of *Fesole*,
> Or in *Valdarno*, to descry new Lands,
> Rivers or Mountains in her spotty Globe.
> His Spear, to equal which the tallest Pine
> Hewn on *Norwegian* hills, to be the Mast
> Of some great Ammiral, were but a wand,
> He walkt with to support uneasie steps
> Over the burning Marle, not like those steps
> On Heavens Azure, and the torrid Clime
> Smote on him sore besides, vaulted with Fire;
> Nathless he so endur'd . . .
>
> (I. 284)

With the shield, Satan outdoes Goliath and Achilles as epic hero. But while he is left king of that castle, the verse drifts into an area where Galileo represents a culture quite different from, and implicitly superior to, the military heroism and phallicism of the moon's blank orb and the flagship's mast, fixing the gaze of 17th-century rationality on the heroic shield. We are brought back to Hell by the sudden change of scale—"were but a wand"—and the realistic description of Satan's gait; just as in the earlier volcanic simile we are brought back by "Such resting found the sole of unblest feet". These physical details are strong, but not enough to withstand the evacuating force of the great similes. Thus again, when the devils parade before Satan,

> he above the rest
> In shape and gesture proudly eminent
> Stood like a Towr; his form had yet not lost
> All her Original brightness, nor appear'd
> Less then Arch Angel ruind, and th' excess
> Of Glory obscur'd: As when the Sun new ris'n
> Looks through the Horizontal misty Air
> Shorn of his Beams, or from behind the Moon
> In dim Eclips disastrous twilight sheds
> On behalf the Nations, and with fear of change
> Perplexes Monarchs. Dark'n'd so, yet shon
> Above them all th'Arch Angel: but his face
> Deep scars of Thunder had intrencht, and care
> Sat on his fading cheek, but under Browes
> Of dauntless courage, and considerate Pride
> Waiting revenge:
>
> (I. 589)

The tower is left merely towering; the sun, rising with the rhythm, is unexpectedly strained through fog, its strength lost like Samson's. So each chink of spendour is shuttered, each surge of vitality arrested before reaching the fulness traditionally endowing an epic hero—a fulness seen as uninhibited lustre in the poem's Son. Yet the repression is not external: it is a natural change of state in the phenomenal ikons.

Of course Satan is much more "real" than the hellish ogres of earlier epics and contemporary romances. He is related to Virgil's Cyclops, and other primitives such as the club-wielding giant Ascapard in *Bevis of Southampton*,[1] but only as distantly as his wand is related to "trunca manu pinus regit et vestigia firmat" (*Aen.* III. 659). The physiognomy of Tasso's Pluto, who had eyes like beacons, "feltred locks, that on his bosom fell" and whose yawning mouth "fomed clotted blood", "Gapte like a whirle-poole wide in Stygian flood" and "as mount Etna vomits sulphur out" (iv. 7-8), is reserved to the landscape of Milton's Hell.

Satan's prototype is not the villain but the epic hero. But because he starts where Tamburlaine ends, raging against fate, he is fitfully more human, tragical, than he would have been if presented first in the flush of heroic success. On these occasions

[1] One of the most popular romances in 16th and 17th Centuries. See Wright, *Middle-Class Culture in Elizabethan England* (1934).

his role is reversed, he appears as a tragic hero[1] caught in an epic plot. Thus the last-quoted description of him as epic hero *manqué* is followed by one of his most dramatic moments—he weeps: "Thrice he assayd, and thrice in spite of scorn, Tears such as Angels weep, burst forth". All these suppler moments, as when he is rendered stupidly good by the beauty of Paradise and of Eve (IV. 373; IX. 469), are spontaneous acknowledgments of tragic weakness, the emotions negative—fear, doubt, misery. In each case he wilfully indures himself again with cries, much less convincing, of positive, epical determination—"evil be thou my good". So here it is the tears, not Satan, which govern their own "burst forth"; stored in his eyes before sin dried them, they transpire through his heroic shell of thunder-scarred responsibility like the other permissive glories, like the shuttered sun. But at once he draws them in, reverting in the peroration of his first public speech to extraordinary epical crudity—"Warr then, Warr/Open or understood must be resolv'd", as if he were the rebel general of some Middle Eastern state (ikons suggest that he is). The devils respond appropriately with brazen sound-effects: "Clashd on thir sounding shields the din of war". This fluctuation is a model of an historical shift in sensibility: as the Renaissance matured, to conscious guilt at its own temerity and rottenness, and as the revival of learning turned inwards to the learning soul, the heroic mood of *I Tamburlaine* altered to tragedy of the Jacobean sort with flat characters caught in a rigid plot, though shooting occasional gleams of still-alive despair and pride. The whole movement was adumbrated by Marlowe: Faustus cries, "ah my God, I woulde weepe, but the diuel drawes in my teares" (1386). Shakespeare enjoyed a middle phase between the extremes of saga and melodrama, *Ur-Hamlet* and the *Revenger's Tragedy*. He moved in *Hamlet* from the primitive epical "overcoming of external difficulties and

[1] Satan's dramatic character also derives partly from the mutation of avenging furies into the heroes of revenge tragedy. Othello cries, "Arise, black vengeance, from the hollow hell" (III. iii. 451), and Hieronimo:

> Hieronimo, 'tis time for thee to trudge:
> Down by the dale that flows with purple gore,
> Standeth a fiery tower; there sits a judge
> Upon a seat of steel and molten brass,
> And 'twixt his teeth he holds a fire-brand,
> That leads unto the lake where hell doth stand.
>
> (III. xii. 7)

dangers by a singlehearted hero" to "the fateful unrolling of the consequences that result from an internal conflict in the hero's soul",[1] without declining into the guilty cynicism of the Jacobeans. Milton, though not skilled at dramatic expression, was intuitive of dramatic feeling; sometimes Satan fluctuates through a Shakespearean humanity. But these moments are always described, not dramatised. So Satan's nihilistic determinations to be absolutely wicked in spite of his angelic self, supposed to motivate the poem, are unconvincing, as verse, in relation to the squirts of vitalised description they suppress:

> To do aught good never will be our task,
> But ever to do ill our sole delight. (I. 157)
>
> Evil be thou my Good; (IV. 108)
>
> Save what is in destroying, other joy
> To me is lost. (IX. 473)

The difficulty is really that we do not see Satan's nihilism arising in direct reciprocity between his will and God's, as we see Gloster's, for instance, arising from the conflict between him and society:

> . . .
> I, that have neither pity, love, nor fear.
> Indeed, 'tis true that Henry told me of;
> For I have often heard my mother say
> I came into the world with my legs forward.
> Had I not reason, think ye, to make haste,
> And seek their ruin that usurp'd our right?
> The midwife wonder'd; and the women cried
> "O, Jesus bless us, he is born with teeth!"
> And so I was, which plainly signified
> That I should snarl, and bite, and play the dog.
> Then, since the heavens have shap'd my body so,
> Let hell make crook'd my mind to answer it.
> I have no brother, I am like no brother;
> And this word "love", which greybeards call divine,
> Be resident in men like one another,
> And not in me! I am myself alone.
> (*III Henry VI*, V. vi. 68)

[1] Ernest Jones, "Hamlet" in his *Essays in Applied Psychoanalysis* (2 vols. 1951).

We are convinced not by the content of the speech so much as its air of familiar actuality—Gloster had a mother. His histrionic manifesto as villain, "I am myself alone", is reached through the quizzical smile, as good fellow, "And so I was".[1] It is noticeable, though, that the provocation of Satan's nihilism is always "human"—his troops' steadfastness, the sun's glory, Eve's beauty. In this way Satan is made essentially the enemy of man, yet shown to be essentially a demon: "The demoniacal becomes thoroughly evident only when it is touched by the good, which now comes to its confines from the outside. . . The demoniacal is dread of the good".[2] We can also see that Milton is dealing with a theological process, hardening of the heart, which has a special significance in *Paradise Lost*. Whatever the technical causes, Satan is presented as undergoing a series of reactions which progressively extinguish his own gleams of self-knowledge and other-pity and block the angelic impulses that might have saved him; so that by Book IV and Book IX he embodies irredeemable despair more than absolute evil. Hardening is an awkward doctrine. Milton's exposition of it in *De Doctrina*, that God's "hardening of the heart, therefore, is usually the last punishment inflicted on inveterate wickedness and unbelief in this life" (iv. 207), is supported by dozens of texts; but none of them turns out to refer to permanent hardening as a punishment, and editors refrain from citing them at their parallel in *Paradise Lost*:

> This my long sufferance and my day of grace
> They who neglect and scorn shall never taste;
> But hard be hard'nd, blind be blinded more,
> That they may stumble on, and deeper fall;
> And none but such from mercy I exclude.
>
> (III. 198)

[1] Such breeding of motive was unusual though, outside Shakespeare, especially for villains. D'Amville labours to explain his motives intellectually, as an atheist, but he comes and goes pat like a morality Vice all the same: "Let all men lose, so I increase my gain, I have no feeling of another's pain" (I. ii. Tourneur's *Plays* ed. Symonds [1948, no line numbers, Mermaid]). This is like Chaos at *P.L.* II. 1009. All the same, D'Amville sins actually for personal gain; Satan, for all his imperialistic ambitions, is sinner *tout court*.

[2] Kierkegaard, *The Concept of Dread*, trans. W. Lowrie (1944), pp. 106, 113, etc.

Yet the doctrine is entirely orthodox. *Faustus* is built on it: "My hearts so hardend I cannot repent"[1] he says, and plunges away from faith into scholastic dispute again—"Tell me, are there many heauens aboue the Moone?" Later, "I do repent, and yet I do dispaire" (1301)—negative repentance can do nothing without positive love of God. At the end the febrility of his intellect drags his heart away from Christ's saving blood in the firmament—Latin tags, the nature of time, quotations from the Bible, astrology, meteorology, metempsychosis, how many drops of water in the ocean. With Bunyan's man in the iron cage it is a simpler lack of saving faith. The cage symbolises the despair he is shut up in because he "left off to watch, and be sober; I laid the reins upon the neck of my lusts; I sinned against the light of the Word, and the goodness of God: I have grieved the Spirit, and he is gone; I tempted the Devil, and he is come to me; I have provoked God to anger, and he has left me: I have so hardened my heart, that I *cannot* repent."[2] When Christian is told that there is no hope at all for this man, he expostulates, "Why? The Son of the Blessed is very pitiful"; but the man lists the unforgivable spiritual sins he has committed, and says he cannot repent because "God hath denied me repentance; his Word gives me no encouragement to believe; yea, himself hath shut me up in this Iron Cage: nor can all the men in the world let me out". This allegory is immediately followed by the dream of Judgment Day; but it is implied in the weakness of character displayed by the man in the iron cage that hope and hardening are both reciprocal actions: the sinner's original hardening provokes a reaction from God which, if it does not soften him, hardens him still more; so that the state of despair grows like a stalactite-stalagmite formation. Satan's despair only seems to be inhuman because it is, properly, what Kierkegaard called demoniac. Kierkegaard distinguishes between the introvert's despair at his own weakness, and defiance. This—Satan's first and public mood—is

> despair by the aid of the eternal, the despairing abuse of the eternal in the self to the point of being despairingly determined to be oneself . . . one might call it Stoicism—yet without thinking only of this philosophic sect. . . . It acknowledges no power over it,

[1] Line 629. *Works* ed. Tucker Brooke (Oxford, 1910).
[2] *Pilgrim's Progress* ed. Wharey (Oxford, 1928), p. 37.

> hence in the last resort it lacks seriousness and is able only to conjure up a show of seriousness when the self bestows upon its experiments the utmost attention . . . the self in its despairing effort to will to be itself labors itself into the direct opposite, it becomes really no self. . . .

The final stage is demoniac despair, which

> with hatred of existence wills to be itself, to be itself in terms of its misery; it does not even in defiance or defiantly will to be itself, but to be itself in spite; it does not even will in defiance to tear itself free from the Power which posited it, it wills to obtrude upon this Power in spite, to hold on to it out of malice. And that is natural, a malignant objection must above all take care to hold on to that against which it is an objection. Revolting against the whole of existence, it thinks it has hold of a proof against it, against its goodness. This proof the despairer thinks he himself is, and that is what he wills to be, therefore he wills to be himself, himself with his torment, in order with this torment to protest against the whole of existence.[1]

Publicly, such despair is most apparent in the peculiarly epical situation of total warfare waged to unconditional defeat; and it is in this milieu that Satan holds office in Books I and II. Hell's totalitarianism is most obvious in the devils; but Satan, though in the created world he occasionally turns humane, in Hell is predominantly a *führer*. Hell is of his own ordering and he carries its essence about with him. The device is familiar; but what Satan cannot escape is self-domination. It is his reputation as avenging demagogue that in his lonely subsequent soliloquies inhibits finer, personal feeling—"Thoughts, whither have ye led me, with what sweet Compulsion thus transported to forget What hither brought us [the royal and schizophrenic "we"], hate, not love" (IX. 473). Satan's essential duality constitutes a grave satire on corruption of the condition Milton valued above all others, rational sovereignty of the soul. When sin

> Lets in defilement to the inward parts,
> The soul grows clotted by contagion,
> Imbodies, and imbrutes, till she quite loose
> The divine property of her first being.
>
> (*Com.* 466)

[1] *The Sickness unto Death* trans. Lowrie (1941), pp. 108ff.

This happens to Satan, body and soul. But also:

> he that hides a dark soul, and foul thoughts
> Benighted walks under the mid-day Sun;
> Himself is his own dungeon.
>
> (383)

It is when Satan addresses the sun that he first confesses, "Which way I flie is Hell; my self am Hell" (IV. 75). He cannot relent, though:

> *Disdain* forbids me, and my dread of shame
> Among the spirits beneath, whom I seduc'd
> With other promises and other vaunts
> Then to submit, boasting I could subdue
> Th' Omnipotent.

Typically, Milton leaves it at the remote public level; how intimately we apply it will depend on our experience. Satan is archetype of all those we know who will not "come to the place where the word 'insult' has no meaning", who fearfully barricade their souls against the possibility of having been wrong, whose heroism fathers unnatural vices, and who die in the hell of deluded self-respect. Milton himself was in danger of it; the problem of whose side he was on is more complicated than Blake thought.

It is finally through Satan's bondage to himself that Milton escapes the limitations of a merely physical Hell:

> To banish for ever into a local hell, whether in air or in the centre, or in that uttermost and bottomless gulf of chaos, deeper from holy bliss than the world's diameter multiplied; they [classical poets and philosophers] thought not a punishing so proper and proportionate for God to inflict, as to punish sin with sin.
>
> (*Div.* iii. 224)

And through the very dramatic inwardness of Satan Milton marks him as sinful:

> the wicked and profane . . . think that they were out of danger, if God would forbear a positive infliction; and that hell is only an incommodious place, that God by his power throws them into. This is the grand mistake. Hell is not only a positive infliction . . . the fewel of *Tophet* burning is the guiltiness of man's conscience,

> malignity, and a naughty disposition against goodness and holiness; and God's withdrawing because the person is incapable of His communication. Sin is an act of violence in itself: the sinner doth force himself, and stirs up strife within himself; and in a sinner there is that *within* which doth reluctate, and condemn him in the inward court of his own conscience.[1]

We may feel that Milton, being a Puritan, was foolishly antagonistic to the dramatic attitude to life. But the kind of dramatics he condemns in Satan is the romantic villain's autocentricity, or the possessed's despairing egoism, not the interchange of personality that fruits to action and sympathy. The characters of *Paradise Lost* do not soliloquise until they have fallen; unfallen speech and gesture are directed always to another person, on the supreme model of light inter-reflected by Father and Son.

3. *The Nature of Hell*

The concept of an inner hell, though traditional in theology and hexemeral literature, was particularly attractive to educated men of the 17th Century who on the one hand were beginning to find it hard to believe in a physical place of torment and on the other were acutely aware of the mobility and transforming power of the mind. Also, as we have seen from *Comus*, it fitted Platonic psychology, so John Smith could preach as if on a text from *Faustus*:

> Would wicked men dwell a little more at home, and descend into the bottome of their own Hearts, they should soon find *Hell* opening her mouth wide upon them, and those secret fires of inward fury and displeasure breaking out upon them which might fully inform them of the estate of true *Misery*, as being a short anticipation of it. But in this life wicked men for the most part *elude* their own Misery for a time, and seek to avoid the dreadfull sentence of their own Consciences, by a tergiversation and flying from themselves into a converse with other things.[2]

Burton, discussing the emotions that caused the ruin of Milton's

[1] Benjamin Whichcote, quoted in Powicke, *The Cambridge Platonists* (1926), pp. 75-6.

[2] From "A Christian's Conflicts and Conquests" collected in his *Select Discourses*; quoted by Mitchell, *English Pulpit Oratory* (1932), p. 291.

Satan—"Emulation, Hatred, Faction, Desire of Revenge"—as causes of melancholy, remarks:

> But being that we are so peevish and perverse, insolent and proud, so factious and expeditious, so malicious and envious, we do *invicem angariare*, maul and vex one another, torture, disquiet, and precipitate ourselves into that gulf of woes and cares, aggravate our misery and melancholy, heap upon us hell and eternal damnation.[1]

And Browne sums up:

> MEN commonly set forth the torments of Hell by fire, and the extremity of corporal afflictions, and describe Hell in the same method as Mahomet doth Heaven . . . men speak too popularly who place it in those flaming mountains, which to grosser apprehensions represent Hell. The heart of man is the place Devils dwell in: I feel sometimes a Hell within myself; Lucifer keeps his Court in my breast, Legion is revived in me.[2]

Milton's was the last major exploration of a devils' hell; after him, although mental chaos was occasionally projected on to the denizens of a human underworld,[3] as in the *Dunciad*, the hatches were battened down for a century and more. Before Milton of course the tragedians had not hesitated to open an inner hell. It had been useful to them since the stage hell-mouth went out of fashion, because it was ubiquitous. We can follow its progress up to the soliloquies of Lear and Macbeth, and the tormented frenzies of Webster's characters, from the simple exposition given by Marlowe's Mephistophilis:

> *Fau.* First will I question with thee about hell,
> Tell me, where is the place that men call hell?
> *Me.* Vnder the heauens.
> *Fau.* I, but where about?
> *Me.* Within the bowels of these elements,
> Where we are tortur'd and remain for euer.
> Hell hath no limits, nor is circumscrib'd
> In one selfe place, for where we are is hell,
> And where hell is, must we euer be.
> *Fau.* How comes it then that thou art out of hel?

[1] *Anatomy of Melancholy*, I. ii. 3. VIII. Ed. Shilleto (3 vols. 1893).
[2] *Religio Medici*, i. 51. *Works* ed. Keynes, (6 vols. 1928-31). Cf. *Leviathan*, Chap. XXXVIII.
[3] Adumbrated in Dekker's *Newes from Hell*. Cf. note p. 263 below.

Me. Why this is hel, nor am I out of it;
Thinkst thou that I who saw the face of God,
And tasted the eternal ioyes of heauen,
Am not tormented with ten thousand hels,
In being depriv'd of euerlasting blisse?[1]

Thus Satan's opening words to Beezlebub ,"into what Pit thou seest From what highth fall'n" (84), might be footnoted by Bosola's dying sigh—

Oh this gloomy world,
In what a shadow, or deepe pit of darknesse,
Doth (womanish and feareful) mankind live! [2]

—as well as by Isaiah's "How art thou fallen from heaven, O Lucifer, son of the morning!" (xiv. 12), and Aeneas' vision of the broken Hector, "quantum mutatus ab illo Hectore" (II. 274).

The difficulty, as with the character of Satan, is to reconcile the subjective, dramatic hell with the concrete hell of epic.[3] Satan's first glance reveals

Regions of sorrow, doleful shades, where peace
And rest can never dwell, hope never comes
That comes to all; but torture without end
Still urges, and a fiery Deluge, fed
With ever-burning Sulphur unconsum'd:

(I. 65)

The way the stiff, harsh second half of this passage breaks in on the comparatively supple verse of the first may symbolise agony interrupting despair; but symbolic reading is discouraged by the reference to Dante's motto for his inferno, "lasciate ogni speranza, voi ch'entrate" (ii. 9). On the whole, it is the concrete hell that we are most aware of. The depth, darkness and fire of Hell are complemented by abstractions—"deep despare", "dark designs", Satan's inflamed ambition—and in Pandemonium

[1] *Faustus*, 547, 311. Cf. Francesca in the *Inferno*, "'Nessum maggior dolore che ricordarsi del tempo felice nella miseria'" (v. 121). *La Divina Commedia* ed. and trans. J. D. Sinclair, 3 vols. rev. ed. 1948.

[2] *Duchess of Malfi*, V. v. 24. *Complete Works* ed. F. L. Lucas, 4 vols. 1927.

[3] Waldock objected that in trying to reconcile a "genuine" (i.e. punitive) hell with his own intense dramatic one, Milton failed, and produced merely a military regrouping area without any sense of guilt but only of defeat and revenge; no real pain, only wounds. ("*P.L.*" *and Its Critics*, Cambridge, 1947). The militarisation of spiritual power, and the assuaging of guilt by revenge, are some of the things Milton is getting at.

each speaker acknowledges the dual nature of "This deep world of darkness" (II. 262). But the mental pains are crude compared with Macbeth's, say—"on the torture of the mind to lie In restless ecstacy"; and although most of the hellish material goes into imagery, not actual topography, it is of overwhelming physical force. Thus the only feature of Hell itself to be described at this stage is the volcano:

> whose griesly top
> Belch'd fire and rowling smoak; the rest entire
> Shon with a glossie scurff, undoubted sign
> That in his womb was hid metallic Ore,
> The work of Sulphur.
>
> (670)

But it gets confused with the volcanic *image* for "the burning Marle" which

> appear'd in hue, as when the force
> Of subterranean wind transports a Hill
> Torn from *Pelorus*, or the shatter'd side
> Of thundring *Aetna*, whose combustible
> And fewel'd entrails thence conceiving Fire,
> Sublim'd with Mineral fury, aid the Winds,
> And leave a singed bottom all involv'd
> With stench and smoak:
>
> (230)

We are given the impression of a cosmic defecation: in his over-enthusiasm for the violent purgation of evil (I. 141), Milton surrenders himself to Jung, so that Satan and the forbidden apple collapse into symbols of onanism.[1] I don't think we need despair at this. The aesthetic distance protects us, as we read on, and Milton almost encourages looseness of response within his own mythologies, as if he couldn't take Hell too seriously himself. Irony flickers unexpectedly out of the verse like flames from the lava:

> But wherefore let we then our faithful friends,
> Th'associates and copartners of our loss
> Lye thus astonisht on th'oblivious Pool,
> And call them not to share with us their part
> In this unhappy Mansion . . .?
>
> (264)

[1] *Psychology of the Unconscious*, trans. B. M. Hinkle (1919), pp. 103, 116.

At that point Satan *is* absurd and we are recalled to the general air of fantasy. The details of the volcanic image are drawn from Aeneas' description of Etna, under which Enceladus the giant had been buried by Zeus as punishment for rebellion. Taken along with all the other references to the Titanomachia, to Etna, and to the classical castration myths—"Though all our Glory extinct, and happy state Here *swallow'd up* in endless misery" (141)—the effect is not simply to outdo the classics, but by sheer encompassment to hold within the poem's frame of reference both their myths and Jung's. Such materials as this have also a structural function. Where in previous epics frightful natural phenomena such as the volcano, Orion's storm, the eclipse, a flood, a shooting star and the numerous lesser catastrophies of whirlwind, hail, cataract, had been used as isolated awe-inspirers, or as local allegory, anywhere in the poem, in *Paradise Lost* they are confined to Hell and its satellites, and used mostly not as events but images. Milton's diction treats these phenomena as outrageous—however marvellous to the ignorant and interesting to the scientific observer, they are models of bad behaviour in fallen nature generally, and for the chaos wrought on earth by sin: "Thus began Outrage from liveless things" (X. 706). The devils, like fallen men, are caught in a recalcitrant and dangerous world, of their own making: having tried to burst Heaven, they find themselves domiciled in a volcano. Although Milton's apocalyptic tit-for-tats are curiously relevant now, at the public level, as literature they seem to us to swamp their subject. Milton's audience would have been quicker to translate them into soul terms, and their point becomes clearer when we meet their obverse in the commodious arrangements of Paradise and the vast calm of Heaven. The dead rivers of Book II contrast with the living waters of Heaven and the fresh springs cascading through Paradise, the burning marle with the golden pavement and couch of flowers. In Paradise life springs from the sun in natural profusion, and the manifestations of it are imaged in art (enamelled flowers and so on). In Hell such life as there is lives in the imagery, for the landscape itself is dead, though violent. These ikons—the "frozen loyns" of the North (I. 352), the bowels of earth (687), the volcano's scurf, womb, entrails, belching, and so on—recall Milton's prose, where religious formalism is consistently imaged in disease, eruptions, vomit, scabs.[1] This corruption of the natural in Hell is elaborated in Book II,

> Where all life dies, death lives, and nature breeds,
> Perverse, all monstrous, all prodigious things,
>
> (624)

and in the monstrous fecundity of sin revealed in the devils.

4. *The Devils*

The treatment of the mass of devils in Book I is a crowded small-scale model of the treatment of Satan over the whole poem. At first they lie stunned on the lake; then, rising, they are inflated to terrific physical and spiritual dimensions; and in Pandemonium reduced to absurdity and impotence. The process begins when Satan sees them,

> His Legions, Angel Forms, who lay intrans't
> Thick as Autumnal Leaves that strow the Brooks
> In *Vallambrosa*, where th'*Etrurian* shades
> High overarch't imbowr; or scatterd sedge
> Afloat, when with fierce Winds *Orion* arm'd
> Hath vext the Red-Sea Coast, whose waves orethrew
> *Busiris* and his *Memphian* Chivalrie,
> While with perfidious hatred they pursu'd
> The Sojourners of *Goshen*, who beheld
> From the safe shore thir floating Carkases
> And broken Chariot Wheels, so thick bestrown
> Abject and lost lay these, covering the Flood,
> Under amazement of their hideous change.
>
> (301)

[1] Especially in *Of Ref.*, e.g.: "backslide one way into the Jewish beggary of old cast rudiments, and stumble forward another way into the new-vomited paganism of sensual idolatry" (ii. 165); proponents of episcopacy "like a seething pot set to cool, sensibly exhale and reak out the greatest part of that zeal and those gifts which were formerly in them, settling in a skinny congealment of ease and sloth at the top . . . their devotion most commonly comes to that queazy temper of lukewarmness, that gives a vomit to God himself" (372-3); "an universal rottenness and gangrene in the whole function" of episcopacy (373); "belching the sour crudities of yesterday's popery" (374); Rome "the womb and centre of apostasy" (377); "a universal tetter of impurity" in the Church (379). NT epistles are in the background but the eruptions are his own really, a squeezed boil of pent energy. He found the proper receptacle in Hell, where it is more controlled.

The similes refer explicitly to the number and huddled compactness of the devils—"Thick as . . . so thick bestrown"—and to their horizontal position—"who lay . . . strow . . . bestrown . . . lay these". But the reader is himself "intrans't" away from the vertical power of Satan and the horizontal grandeur of the "Angel Forms" by the verse closing up to autumnal leaves and scattered sedge (though the apparent idyll is kept in the valley of the shadow by the literal meaning of Vallombrosa and by the correspondence between "th'*Etrurian* shades high overarch't" and Hell's vault of fire). Then the view sidles up to realistic scale and the devils become the hosts of Pharaoh overwhelmed by the Red Sea in their pursuit of the children of God. The last three lines toss their carcases in contempt upon the waves; they are dismissed with impersonal flatness—"Abject and lost lay these, covering the Flood"; and we are brought back to the action by Satan's voice echoing, "He call'd so loud", from "he stood and call'd" at the beginning of the vision.

Once risen, the devils are characteristically active. They spring up, fly, hover, alight on the burning shore. The peers hasten to a preliminary council with Satan (357), the pioneer devils hasten to mine the ore for Pandemonium (675), "The hasty multitude" enters Pandemonium (730) and in its public hall they troop, throng, swarm. Their permissive freedom of movement is incongruous even when intended "to bring forth Infinite goodness" for man and on the devils "Treble confusion, wrath and vengeance pour'd" (217). Those ends are not to be demonstrated in the poem and it needs much subtler argument to escape the Duke's admission in *Measure for Measure* that "we bid this be done, When evil deeds have their permissive pass, And not the punishment". Even Jeremy Taylor, after stating the problem—

> Whose reason can give an account why, or understand it to be reasonable, that God should permit evil for good ends, when he hates that evil, and can produce that good without evil?[1]

—can only answer that so "we are taught by our Religion" and hasten into kindly obfuscation. But Milton is using the devils

[1] *Ductor Dubitantium* (1660), quoted in L.P. Smith, ed. *The Golden Grove* (Oxford, 1930), pp. 235-6. Taylor takes a similar view of the malignancy of Satan.

mainly for satire on the underside of tyranny. Their busyness betokens faithless ambition:

> Thus while the simple honest worshipper
> Of a fantastic providence groans under
> The burthen of a neglected misery,
> My real wisdom has raised up a state
> That shall eternise my posterity.
>
> (V. i)

says D'Amville. In the poem it contrasts with the effortless gliding of unfallen angels, the deliberate movements and stances of Adam and Eve, and the immobility of God: for their service is not that of perfect freedom, but willed by Satan with unconscious consent from them as from puppets: "They heard, and were abasht, and up they sprung", like soldiers roused for watch, dutiful in sleep; when they fly it is to "warp" (the verb—a heaving, shifting flying in formation—depersonalises them) as if conjured into existence by "the potent Rod" of Moses (339). The devils of *Revelation* are locusts (ix. 3), and real locusts were an object of peculiar 17th-century horror. All the travellers to the East had described them with disgust, and they became material for ecclesiastical insult. Marvell refers to the heretical plotters against Cromwell as

> Accursed Locusts, whom your King does spit
> Out of the Center of th'unbottom'd Pit;[1]

Milton prays of the priests in *Of Reformation*:

> O let them not bring about their damned designs, that stand now at the entrance of the bottomless pit, expecting the watch-word to open and let out those dreadful locusts and scorpions, to reinvolve us in that pitchy cloud of infernal darkness, where we shall never more see the sun of thy truth again. . . .
>
> (ii. 417)

In the third simile of this series the devils "fill all the Plain" like a river of barbarians unconscious of their role in history, spreading "like a Deluge on the South" to destroy the civilisation of Rome. So the devils are characteristically numerous, barbarous, military; they are associated with oriental and Roman Catholic tyranny; and, as in the Vallombrosa simile, they sometimes shine with a trodden beauty.

[1] "First Anniversary", 311.

They have the same qualities in the catalogue. Here, apart from outdoing Homer's ships and generals, Milton proves his control over the devils by sophisticated anthropological manipulation, and invites us to stand back from them without necessity of belief (his writing is closer to Hobbes's brisk rationality in Chapter XXXVIII of *Leviathan* than to Browne's gentle sentiment in *Religio Medici*). The lines referring to the grove Solomon built for Moloch-worship in "The pleasant Valley of *Hinnom*, *Tophet* thence And black *Gehenna* call'd, the Type of Hell" (404), forge the link between devils and Papists. Gehenna (γέεννα) represents the Hebrew and Aramaic for "the valley of Hinnom", a gorge in Jerusalem which included the wadi of Tophet. It was once cultivated as gardens, but various kings established shrines for foreign gods there. It was used for the rites of Moloch in which children were encased in the iron idol and burnt alive. The pious King Josiah burnt all the equipment of Moloch-worship and ritually defiled the grove (*II Kings* xxiii). This defilement, with the memory of what had been done there, and the fires that smouldered as it became a rubbish dump, made Gehenna a symbol of evil, destruction and horror. In the New Testament it came to designate some place of future punishment, and is translated "hell". It is difficult to decide whether it suggested to those who used it what we mean by hell: in the Old Testament it certainly did not (neither did *Sheol*, also translated "hell" in the Authorised Version). But the physcial details of the Christian hell derive more from David's battle-songs and the prophets' anathemas: "Upon the wicked he shall rain snares, fire and brimstone, and an horrible tempest" (*Ps.* xi. 6); "As for the head of those that compass me about, let the mischief of their own lips cover them. Let burning coals fall upon them: let them be cast into the fire; into deep pits, that they may not rise up again" (*Ps.* cxl. 9-10). It is at a siege of Jerusalem that Jeremiah laments:

> How hath the Lord covered the daughter of Zion with a cloud in his anger, and cast down from heaven unto the earth the beauty of Israel, and remembered not his footstool in the day of his anger! The Lord hath swallowed up all the habitations of Jacob, and hath not pitied: he hath thrown down in his wrath the strong holds of the daughter of Judah; he hath brought them down to the ground: he hath polluted the kingdom and the

> princes thereof. He hath cut off in his fierce anger all the horn of Israel: he hath drawn back his right hand from before the enemy, and he burned against Jacob like a flaming fire, which devoureth round about. (ii. 1-3)

Milton incorporated all these phrases in his Hell. Wielding the Bible is not an error that deserves to be immortalised. Our own historical sense will recognise Milton's blind identification of himself with the Hebrew prophets as one symptom of the Reformation, almost inevitably occurring along with worthier ones. But if we feel that liberal indifference is a better weapon than persecution against an absurd polytheism, we are being a-historical too. Josiah's and Milton's aggressive Puritanism was liberal in the more positive sense of being, as they felt, a fight for freedom. To Milton and his audience, Israel had fought for the western world a battle against obscene and multiplex superstition that must not be lost again. Thus he sees the abuses of the English church in the direct line of bestial idolatry:

> By falsities and lies the greatest part
> Of Mankind they corrupted to forsake
> God thir Creator, and th' invisible
> Glory of him, that made them, to transform
> Oft to the Image of a Brute, adorn'd
> With gay Religions full of Pomp and Gold, (367)

This is Milton the pamphleteer, horrified that the Church should

> backslide one way into the Jewish beggary of old cast rudiments, and stumble forward another way into the new-vomited paganism of sensual idolatry, attributing purity or impurity to things indifferent, that they might bring the inward acts of the spirit to the outward and customary eye-service of the body, as if they could make God earthly and fleshly . . . palls and mitres, gold and gewgaws . . . and all the inward acts of worship, issuing from the native strength of the soul, run out lavishly to the upper skin, and there harden into a crust of formality.
> (*Of Ref.* ii. 365; cf. 402)

The pamphleteer's indignation is not despicable—he is quoting *Paul*[1]—but in the poem it is restrained to hints such as the

[1] E.g. *Col.* ii., *Rom.* and *Cor.* *passim.* It is curious that the only great English writers to have been disciples of Paul's doctrines of spirit and flesh, ἀγάπη and ἔρος, and to show it verbally in their work, are Milton and Lawrence.

idolaters who "often plac'd Within his Sanctuary itself thir Shrines, Abominations", and "the Sons of *Belial*, flown with insolence and wine", wandering the streets of Sodom. Milton's radical polemic was not just an expression of lonely Puritanism. Apart from Paul tussling with Judaism and lascivious mystery-religious, gentle Herbert, as well as agonised Donne, wrote of the Roman Church in the conventional Protestant terms of whoredom and painted shrines.[1] Both sides in the pamphlet war had called each other by the names of devils, especially Belial, and Giles Fletcher had explicitly equated the Pope and his priests, as conspirators of the Gunpowder Plot, with Satan and his devils in *Christ's Victory in Heaven*. Milton's reversal of the convention gave his Hell topical interest; but as well as claiming cosmic justification for his own opinions it offers a personal attitude of more lasting value. These lines join with those in "Lycidas" and *The Doctrine and Discipline of Divorce* and the invocation of Book VII—"the rout that made the hideous roar", "the brood of Belial . . . will laugh abroad" (iii. 173), "the barbarous dissonance of *Bacchus* and his Revellers"—to express, beyond all connotations of epic devilry and ecclesiastical dispute, his constant and most civilised distaste for boisterous philistinism. It is one of the less-remarked themes of *Samson Agonistes* that he is the persecuted protagonist of a culture more civilised at all levels of society than its Asian aggressors, "Impetuous, insolent, unquenchable" (1422). Edwin Muir translates it to the present:

> Shut in his darkness, these [*sc.* the Bosch-like fiends]
> he could not see,
> But heard the steely clamour known too well
> On Saturday night in every street in Hell.[2]

Some of the catalogue carries over a gentler tone from the pre-war "Nativity Ode", which in places reads like a Swin-

[1] "The British Church"; "Satyre iii" and "Show me, dear Christ, thy spouse". It does not invalidate educated Puritan feeling of the 17th Century that anti-Catholic passions should have remained at the same level, for some Nonconformists, long after the actual danger of political Catholicism had passed. The sexuality of the imagery indicates that anti-Catholicism is often a substitute passion, of course; though it derives from OT phrases about whoring after strange gods and apocalyptic references to the Whore of Babylon which precisely suggest the attractiveness of Roman Catholicism to those who are inclined to promiscuous piety.

[2] "Milton", *One Foot in Eden* (1956).

burnian lament for the nymphs—"Vicisti, Galilaee". In *Eikonoklastes* Milton has used Thammuz-worship as an insult:

> let them who now mourn for him as for Thammuz, them who howl in their pulpits, and by their howling declare themselves right wolves, remember and consider in the midst of their hideous faces, when they do only not cut their flesh for him like those rueful priests whom Elijah mocked . . .
>
> (i. 330)

But in the catalogue:

> *Thammuz* came next behind,
> Whose annual wound in *Lebanon* allur'd
> The *Syrian* Damsels to lament his fate
> In amorous dittyes all a Summers day,
> While smooth *Adonis* from his native Rock
> Ran purple to the Sea,
>
> (446)

This is tonally similar—"all a Summers day"—to the Mulciber passage (I. 740); it is related to the militarism of Hell, especially the chivalric references, via the Celtic context of

> sweet as ditties highly penn'd,
> Sung by a fair queen in a summer's bow'r,
> With ravishing division, to her lute.
>
> (*I Henry IV*, III. i. 208)

and *Richard III*'s opening soliloquy; and it recurs in Book XI when the "sons of God" seduce the daughters of men:

> from the Tents behold
> A Beavie of fair Women, richly gay
> In Gems and wanton dress; to the Harp they sung
> Soft amorous Ditties, and in dance came on:
>
> (581)

Leavis regards the Mulciber passage as a smuggling-in of a beauty prohibited by the poem's overt ethic.[1] In *Milton's Royalism*[2] M. M. Ross sets out to prove "the conflict of symbol

[1] *Revaluation* (1936), pp. 62-4.

[2] Ithaca, N.Y., 1943. Quotes from the sub-title and p. 113. Like Patrick Cruttwell's *Shakespearean Moment* (1954), this is a cogent book. I react against them instinctively because I was brought up a Nonconformist and they seem to me versions of Chesterton-Belloc historiography revised in the light of *Scrutiny*, Tawney and Jung: salvation is Catholic, hierarchic, sacerdotal, so embracement, royalism, symbolism are good *per se* and any reservations about them in practice are likely to be symptoms of schizophrenia, if not actually sin.

and idea in his poetry", with special reference to such things as the chivalric images which he feels are "meant to conjure up positive visions of grandeur": there is a contradiction at the heart of the poem stemming from Milton's "insatiate desire for symbols of splendor and power" which "quite obliterated conscious intellectual distinctions". Now when these passages are read, one by one, as they come in the poem, they are fit: swift rhythm flashes the remote references across an already distant screen. We take them as transient aestheticisms like Wordsworth's Proteus with his wreathed horn, freshening us on the dark voyage. If we pause at the oases we find they are more: they are like Prufrock's mermaids and the glimmers of beauty in *The Waste Land*, ironic. Milton's yearning is not irrelevantly for the damsels and Mulciber and so on *per se*, but for their loss, the corruption of love into Syrian sexiness, the fall of human expertise into Hell's technological aggrandisement—the poignancy that promotes our sympathy for tragic heroes. Mulciber is Wolsey crying,

> Nay then, farewell!
> I have touch'd the highest point of all my greatness,
> And from that full meridian of my glory
> I haste now to my setting. I shall fall
> Like a bright exhalation in the evening,
> And no man see me more.
>
> (*Henry VIII*, III. ii. 222)

But Milton tramples on the victim:

> thus they relate,
> Erring; for he with his rebellious rout
> Fell long before; nor aught avail'd him now
> To have built in Heav'n high Towrs; nor did he scape
> By all his Engins, but was headlong sent
> With his industrious crew to build in hell.
>
> (746)

Landor was astonished: "My good Milton! Why in a passion?"[1]

[1] *Imaginary Conversations* (*Works* ed. C. G. Crump, 10 vols. 1891-3: iv. 205). Landor was an acute critic of inconsistencies in *P.L.* in the manner of Bentley and Waldock. He recognised the immense superiority of Shakespeare: "A rib of Shakespeare would have made a Milton"; but "the same portion of Milton, all poets born ever since" (i.e. when Shelley and Keats *fl.*). Thus, "After I have been reading the *Paradise Lost*, I can take up no other

The fault lies not in the beauty—Milton created it all (the Bible is not elegant about Thammuz-worship and Hephaestus' fall is a practical joke to Homer); or in the lament for its loss—that is the poem's theme; but that, having created it, Milton himself denies it wantonly. He contradicts Keats: here is beauty but it is untrue; here is ugliness, which is true. This is so alien that Milton's own conflicts spill into the poem. Hephaistos is related to Comus (he sent Hera a throne that bound her with invisible fetters). Some psychologists would regard lameness as a castration-symbol; and we remember the Nausicaa scene in *Ulysses*—"they were all green dewy stars falling with golden, O so lively! O so soft, sweet, soft!" (p. 350). So we re-read the fall of Mulciber as a symbolic detumescence, and its denial and correction a denial and "castration" of the libido that produced it. With more obviously pathological violence, the sexuality provoked by the Syrian maidens is castrated in Dagon:

> when the Captive Ark
> Maim'd his brute Image, head and hands lopt off
> In his own Temple, on the grunsel edge,
> Where he fell flat, and sham'd his Worshipers :

This is part of Milton's interest in Samson; his attack on "that uxorious King" Solomon who was "Beguil'd by fair Idolatresses" (I. 444), as if beauty and idolatry were cause-and-effect; and his hatred of Belial. It was probably fear of his own voluptuousness, and perhaps of a homosexual tendency caused by his too-devoted father, with mixed pride and shame in his own physical beauty and his role as man of letters rather than action, that impelled him to fondle every manifestation of Belialism, and then crush it with masculine hard rationality. The rippling softness of Eve is lovingly described, but she is forced to recognise "How beauty is excell'd by manly grace And wisdom, which alone is truly fair" (IV. 490). In *Paradise Regained* Belial is spat from Milton's lips as

poet with satisfaction". I find this particularly true of the 18th-century and Romantic poets myself; Landor almost included Shakespeare: "My ear, I confess it, is dissatisfied for days and weeks, after the harmony of *P.L.* Leaving this magnificent temple, I can hardly be pacified by the fairy-built chambers, the rich cupboards of embossed plate, and the omnigenous images of Shakespeare". The last phrase shows that he didn't respond just at the level of "style".

> the dissolutest Spirit that fell,
> The sensuallest, and after *Asmodai*
> The fleshliest Incubus,
>
> (II. 150)

He spreads the net of sexual allurement for Christ, but is opposed by Satan, whose scale of temptation-values is remarkably schoolboyish: "for Beauty stands in the admiration only of weak minds Led captive . . . Therefore with *manlier* objects we must try his constancy". We deduce that Milton's megalomaniac tendencies compensated for some central weakness, the introvert's impotent envy of love issuing in an aggressive horror of lasciviousness. At this level of biographical hypothesis, literary judgement evanesces: we suffer like passions with Milton, or others as bad, whatever terminology we use to describe them. But we are perhaps less deeply sunk than Milton in the common sexual error of orthodox Christendom, Catholic as well as Protestant. Discussing the Last Judgement sculptured on the tympanum of Bourges Cathedral, Watts writes:

> One must bear in mind, that, to a very considerable extent, the attainment of perfect sanctity was identified with a suppression of lust. However, this does not go along with a simple avoidance of or indifference to lust and its objects. It requires a positive and energetic opposition to so great a natural force, leading to a kind of fury, of divine wrath, against everything that incites to lust. Yet as this increases it *becomes* lust. The blessed delight in the punishment of the damned because the infliction of pain is the symbolic, "unconscious" substitution for sexual conquest. Thus the sculptor of Bourges can outwardly edify but secretly delight, because convention permits him to show the bodies of the damned naked. What is ostensibly a scene of the punishment of the lost by devils is *in fact* a portrayal of satyrs about to begin a sadistic orgy with a group of nymphs. By such a roundabout course a sculpture which might have adorned one of the more depraved Roman brothels turns up in the guise of ecclesiastical art.[1]

There is a similar inversion of values in the work of Bosch, and Victorian illustrations to the *Holy War*. These are symptoms of the dissociation of erotic life, dividing it into "two channels, the same two as are personified in art as heavenly and earthly (or

[1] *Myth and Ritual in Christianity* (1954), p. 225. Cf. Jung, *op. cit.* p. 227.

animal) love. Where such men love they have no desire and where they desire they cannot love."[1] Freud regards this pessimistically, as the price of civilisation and especially of the high ascetic value set on sex by Christianity in advance of the still animal constitution of man's genital equipment. Jung,[2] like Blake and Lawrence, more optimistically recommends that we cease to brutalise our natural impulses, and admit them; but it is easier to do this aesthetically—beatification of the genitalia and so on—than to live it.

Yet it was Milton who urged the claims of a total spiritual and physical love against law in the divorce pamphlets, and of fruitful marriage over coquetry in Book IV. Whatever the curious causes of his exaggerated expression, the issue is again a Puritanism clear-sighted within its limits and, in the end, positive. There were, too, historical causes. The feminine principles such as Love, Life[3] which we revere are no more absolute than the masculine Reason and Authority which Milton's patriarchal society trusted. It was an epoch when delinquent chaos was much closer and more usual, even at home and in the street, than it is for our middle classes; so that the strenuous rationality which Milton recommends, imposes on his material, and actually reins his verse with, had (whatever its psychological origins in him) a higher practical value than now.

The chivalric references accumulate in the devils' main episode when their army re-forms and marches past Satan. Classical as well as medieval armies are suggested, but the ideal is military heroism. There is the flag borne by Azazel, the "thronging Helms . . . and serried Shields in thick array" (547), the roll of crusading battle-honours with Arthur the doyen of chivalry himself overwhelming "th' Heroic Race . . . That fought at *Theb's* and *Ilium*"; the main hall of Pandemonium is like lists

[1] "Degradation in Erotic Life", *Collected Papers* trans. J. Riviere (5 vols. 1924-50), iv. 207. Cf. *Civilization and its Discontents.*

[2] *Op. cit.* p. 189.

[3] There is some continuity between the philosophic panpsychism of the Romantics (e.g. Coleridge in "Religious Musings": "There is one Mind, one Omnipresent Mind Omnific"), the moralism of Arnold (essay on Wordsworth: "let our minds rest upon that great and inexhaustible word *life*, until we learn to enter into its meaning") and of *Scrutiny* critics, the vitalism of Lawrence, and the aesthetic vitaminism of Berenson's notorious phrase "life-enhancing". What kind of life? is the question.

where Champions bold
Wont ride in arm'd, and at the Soldans chair
Defi'd the best of *Panim* chivalry
To mortal combat or career with Lance

(763)

And in Book II the devils organise military sports, as when

Armies rush
To Battel in the Clouds, before each Van
Pric forth the Aerie Knights, and couch thir spears

(534)

Ross finds this even more disturbing than the chivalric references in Heaven. In fact the chivalry in Heaven is entirely conventional, and slight compared with Phineas Fletcher's in *The Appolyonists*, where there are also pursuivants and feudal rank in hell (i. 8, 18). Milton makes chivalry almost peculiar to Hell, and to earth as Hell's satellite:

For in those dayes Might onely shall be admir'd,
And Valour and Heroic Vertu call'd;
To overcome in Battel, and subdue
Nations, and bring home spoils with infinite
Man-slaughter, shall be held the highest pitch
Of human Glorie, and for Glorie done
Of triumph, to be styl'd great Conquerours,
Patrons of Mankind, Gods, and Sons of Gods,
Destroyers rightlier call'd and Plagues of men.

(XI. 685)

In *Paradise Regained* Satan once more parades a host, alluding to

many Prowest Knights,
Both *Paynim*, and the Peers of *Charlemane*.
Such and so numerous was thir Chivalrie.

(III. 342)

Christ, echoing Milton's invocation of Book IX, sneers at this "cumbersome luggage of war" as "argument Of human weakness rather then of strength" and abjures it as

Much ostentation vain of fleshly arm,
And fragile arms, much instrument of war
Long in preparing, soon to nothing brought.

We may suspect that in both parading and condemning all that vainglory Milton was trying to have his cake and eat it. The reader who from the first line recognised *Paradise Lost* as an epic, but one bearing a peculiar relationship to all previous epics, would expect sooner or later a display of armed might simply as a *tour de force*, "a horrid Front of dreadful length and dazling Arms, in guise Of Warriers old with order'd Spear and Shield" (564). The vision is realistic, but it is the remotely distant reality of the classics, fading even further into "what resounds In Fable or *Romance* of *Uthers* Son". The subject of the passage is not so much the devils as Homer and Virgil, Tasso and Spenser: their work is taken up, outdone, and consigned to Hell. The consignment is not just literary self-betterment. These passages share their flickering remote beauty with Pandemonium, the *ignis fatuus* in which Satan glides to tempt Eve, the glister of the forbidden fruit itself. Milton's concern is with delusion: "in *guise* / Of Warriers old". Here we notice the checks on our response that Milton incorporates within the deluding visions. At the review's climax Satan numbers his troops

> And now his heart
> Distends with pride, and hardning in his strength
> Glories: (571)

At the moment of deepest involvement in the grandeur of the devils, the reader finds himself thrown by the enormous weight of that "Glories" into identity with a fascist Satan. The massed-bands hypnosis of the passage is broken a second time "When", under the momentum of the catalogue of battlefields, "Charlemagne with all his peerage *fell* / By Fontarabbia": the devils share in the fallen futility of the Crusaders. Thirdly, the devils change with the depressed mood and obscured aspect of Satan so that he sees them with

> Thir Glory witherd. As when Heavens Fire
> Hath scath'd the Forrest Oaks, or Mountain Pines,
> With singed top their stately growth though bare
> Stands on the blasted Heath.
>
> ((612)

Here the devils return to their ignoble automatism, and this is what Gabriel throws in Satan's face in Paradise (IV. 952).

They return also out of the legendary past into Hell, standing like Dante's suicides, withered and gnarled, sprouting poison twigs and tormented by harpies. One of them had cried, "Uomini fummo, e or siam fatti sterpi".[1]

A more subtle problem is whether Milton distinguishes between the devils' suicidal Stoicism, and Christian virtue? He recognised the problem, defining "stoical apathy" as an opposite of Christian patience in *De Doctrina* (v. 99). But he seems to have objected to an extreme and impracticable form of Stoicism, in which the response that a man ought to make to stimuli is evaded by becoming a skeleton, as sardonically recommended in the *Atheist's Tragedy*: "The penury of a prison is like a soft consumption. 'Twill humble the pride o' your mortality, and arm your soul in complete patience to endure the weight of affliction without feeling it" (III. iii). Milton also recognised the difference between patient courage and furious bravado. After the Fall Eve suggests suicide and Adam replies,

> *Eve*, thy contempt of life and pleasure seems
> To argue in thee somthing more sublime
> And excellent then what thy minde contemnes;
> But self-destruction therefore saught, refutes
> That excellence thought in thee, and implies,
> Not thy contempt, but anguish and regret
> For loss of life and pleasure overlov'd.
>
> (X. 1013)

But in the next book Adam declares that he will

> to the hand of Heav'n submit,
> However chast'ning, to the evil turne
> My obvious brest, arming to overcom
> By suffering,
>
> (XI. 373)

Later, horrified by the lazar-house vision, he seeks quick death, and Michael reproves, "Nor love thy Life, nor hate" (549). One distinction between this, and the devils' seeking by the study of "Passion and Apathie" to "arm th'obdured brest With stubborn patience", lies in the word "submit", which Adam constantly uses and Satan rejects. But a word is not enough,

[1] *Inf.* xiii. 37. Milton refers to this canto in his Commonplace Book (fol. 16) under the heading "Mors Spontanea".

and if it were submission could not adequately represent the faith which is Christianity's breastplate. In *Paradise Regained* Milton stated the difference between Godward faith and the self-sufficiency of philosophical Stoicism:

> The Stoic last in Philosophic pride,
> By him call'd vertue; and his vertuous man,
> Wise, perfect in himself, and all possessing
> Equal to God, oft shames not to prefer,
> As fearing God nor man, contemning all
> Wealth, pleasure, pain or torment, death and life,
> Which when he lists, he leaves, or boasts he can,
> For all his tedious talk is but vain boast,
> Or subtle shifts conviction to evade.
>
> (IV. 300)

But he could not dramatise it.[1] All the distinctions are double-crossed by words that work for both sides—contemn, arm, breast, patience; for Milton was really a stoic himself. The temperamental stoic is a man who confuses the weakness of his positive feelings—"passion"—with the strength of his negative-fear of "suffering" (the philosophy is riddled with word-play). His stoicism is a pretence that he is strong all through—strong in his passions, even stronger in his will to control them. So there is always a tendency for him to rehearse passion in imagination so as to achieve the satisfaction of crushing it. We have already seen this in Milton, and his temperamental inclination to it was allied with the philosophic Stoicism incorporated in orthodox Christianity.[2] Blake and Lawrence, revolting against the Stoic tendency to congeal love into duty, make Milton's work seem rigorified and his distinctions casuistical. Their writing charges us with surges of vitatily—as some of Milton's

[1] He had represented it as stupidity that Comus can see in the Lady of chastity only a disciple of "those budge doctors of the *Stoick* Furr" (707) when really she is spiritually minded in Paul's sense, faithful to a "sublime notion, and high mystery" as no Stoic could be. The Elder Brother is presented, I assume, with a healthy touch of mockery for his clumsy philosophising which cannot do anything against Comus' rhetoric; yet his conception of chastity as "compleat steel" (421), the bow of Diana (441) and even the Gorgon's head (447) seems serious and is in line with Milton's own feelings at the time: cf. the postscript to his Latin elegies quoted on p. 34 above.

[2] The "Ode to Duty" is a classic statement of Christian "stoicism" operant in the fallen world of *ichabod.*

early prose does, before suffering dammed up the spring. But these supercharges have only a temporary power: as it fades, there is either an overreaching into hysteria (a note heard in all three writers) as spontaneity meets its inevitable frustration; or a withdrawal to the mechanical power of interim ethics, as with Wordsworth. Milton's real excuse for making Adam as well as the devils vaguely stoical is that in them he exaggerates fallen life's reality. He was aware of the possibilities of joy:

> so every true Christian in a higher order of priesthood, is a person dedicated to joy and peace, offering himself a lively sacrifice of praise and thanksgiving, and there is no Christian duty that is not to be seasoned and set off with cheerishness; which in a thousand outward and intermitting crosses may yet be done well, as in this vale of tears. . . .
>
> (*Div.* iii. 197)

But in this poem their expression is restricted to a few lyrical contexts—the dancing of angels, Adam and Eve's hymns, and Milton's own invocations.

The orientalism is scattered—Pharaoh, "that fiery Couch" (I. 377), Babylon and Cairo (717), Satan as "their great Sultan" (348), the "dark Divan" of Hell (X. 457), and so on. To us these suggest an exotic splendour because we have not, imaginatively, quite recovered from the 19th-century fad for things oriental—*Vathek*, *Eothen*, Omar Khayam, Whistler's prints, Chinese ceramics. The 17th Century was also aware of the glamour of the East—"Dusk faces with white silken Turbants wreath'd" (*P.R.* IV. 76)—but less naïve about the values of oriental civilisation. The Ottoman Turks[1] had only just been kept out of western Europe at the siege of Vienna in 1529; there was an historical prejudice in favour of the Roman boundaries of peace; and the Middle Eastern powers were seen as the ancestral enemies of Christendom because they had persecuted the Israelites. Thus in his *First Defence* Milton, following classical

[1] In the *Purple Isle* G. Fletcher had described the Turk as Milton describes Satan at the end of Books II and III:

> And that black Vulture, which the dreadfull wing
> O're-shadows halfe the earth, whose dismall sight
> Frighted the Muses from their native spring,
> Already stoops, and flagges with weary flight.

(*Poetical Works* of G. and P.F. ed. Boas, 2 vols. Cambridge, 1908-09).

precedent, cites the Orient in general to exemplify tyranny, slavery and barbarism (i. 32-7). These attitudes to the oriental join with Milton's attitude to the technological in the building of Pandemonium:

> Anon out of the earth a Fabrick huge
> Rose like an Exhalation, with the sound
> Of Dulcet Symphonies and voices sweet,
> Built like a Temple, where *Pilasters* round
> Were set, and Doric pillars overlaid
> With Golden Architrave; nor did there want
> Cornice or Freeze, with bossy Sculptures grav'n,
> The Roof was fretted Gold. Not *Babilon*,
> Nor great *Alcairo* such magnificence
> Equal'd in all thir glories, to inshrine
> *Belus* or *Serapis* thir Gods, or seat
> Thir Kings, when *Ægypt* with *Assyria* strove
> In wealth and luxurie.

Milton may have had in mind as a model for his Hell the Forum Vulcani outside Naples.[1] There stand the ruins of an amphitheatre, described by Sandys, who says it "doe[s] yet affirme that prodigalities and luxury are no new crimes, and that we but re-do old vices".[2] Sandys, who struggled to write the Puritan poetry Milton achieved, had travelled widely in the Middle East and everywhere found symptoms like this. He joined Milton in regarding the pyramids as "barbarous monuments of prodigality and vain-glory", seeing in them the oriental equivalent of Europe's "gay Religions full of Pomp and Gold". Having lost these feelings we may miss the derision that under-runs Pandemonium's magnificence. The palace rises like the machinery of a masque—artificial, temporary, illusory.[3] "Exhalation", often use in this connection as well as to describe meteors and volcanic eruptions,[4] suggests the insubstantial, elusive, mystifying, the

[1] See Marjorie Nicolson, "Milton's Hell and the Phlegraean Fields", *UTQ*, VII (1938).

[2] *Relation of a Iournie* . . ., 1621 ed., p. 362.

[3] Miss Welsford notes this point in her *Court Masque* (Cambridge, 1927), Chap. XI. Verity notes masque-like effects also at V. 285 (Raphael's flight), XI. 203 (Michael's cohort) and XI. 576 (rites of Hymen), and elsewhere (ed. *P.L.*, 2nd ed. Cambridge, 1921).

[4] Cf. Vaughan's "Disorder and frailty": his "weak fire" aspires to the sun "like some sleeping Exhalation" waked by the heat, but falters and expires —"Poor, falling Star!"

edifice a façade for the ugly discomforts of Hell. The oriental similes place the building as a citadel of barbaric despotism. Milton's method is similar to Eliot's in the description of the neurotic woman's boudoir in *The Waste Land*, itself a parody of the genuine love-luxury of Cleopatra, and Eve ("the sylvan scene"). The devils, guided by Mammon, seek to escape Hell into a Heaven of like superficiality—from "the burnt soyle" to "the smooth and level pavement", from confinement to "ample spaces"; the arched roof is not "vaulted with fire" but hung with lamps that yield light "As from a sky"—an irony again clinched with Milton's sentence-ending half-line.

Voltaire recognised the ironical bent of Milton's fantasy as it runs over Hell, but found it indecorous:

> That Seat built for the Parliament of the Devils, seems very preposterous. . . . The Poet seems to delight in building his *Pandaemonium* in Doric Order with Freeze and Cornice, and a Roof of Gold. Such a contrivance savours more of the wild Fancy of our Father *le Moine* than of the serious spirit of *Milton.*[1]

Even as the writer of England's only Greek tragedy, Milton was much more classical than neo-classical, in his fusion of dignity with deeply affecting simplicity—"So much I feel my genial spirits droop, My hopes all flat"—and in his use of low diction: "avoided as a blab, The mark of fool set on his front."[2] In epic, Milton had left behind the gorgeous catholicity of the 16th Century, but he did not lurch into the dissociating decorum of the 18th: *Paradise Lost* includes the catastrophics of the *Dunciad*, the mockery of *The Rape of the Lock*, the elegiacs of Johnson, as

[1] *Ed. cit.* p. 137. The later French version is less interesting on this point.
[2] Yet occasionally relapsing into early Shakespeare:

> Hopeful of his Delivery, which now proves
> Abortive as the first-born bloom of spring
> Nipt with the lagging rear of winters frost. (1575)

Cf. the history-play Shakespeareanism in *P.R.*:

> For therein stands the office of a King,
> His Honour, Vertue, Merit and chief Praise,
> That for the Publick all this weight he bears. (II. 463)

Much of *Comus* might actually be the Shakespeare of *Midsummer Night's Dream*, and the *Tempest*. The point is not that these are occasional spurts of the true poet in Milton, but that he had to work very hard to escape the domination of Shakespeare's genius and write for himself. He is the only poet ever to have imitated Shakespeare naturally and seriously: the Romantics' attempts look like extravagant pastiche beside his.

well as the ethico-cosmic machinery of *The Essay on Man*. But Pandemonium belongs in the poem. It is a factitious parody of "how the Heav'ns and Earth Rose out of *Chaos*" and the satire on it leads to those "Palaces Where luxurie late reign'd" in Book XI, flooded to stable sea-monsters (750). It even reaches over into the sequel, where Christ rejects Satan's mirage of Rome—

> and there Mount *Palatine*
> The Imperial Palace, compass huge, and high
> The Structure, skill of noblest Architects,
> With gilded battlements, conspicuous far,
> Turrets and Terrases, and glittering Spires.
>
> (IV. 50)

The health of Milton's attitude is apparent in the way he preaches about the technological achievement of Pandemonium at just the right level of condescending weariness:

> Let none admire
> That riches grow in Hell; that soyle may best
> Deserve the pretious bane. And here let those
> Who boast in mortal things, and wondring tell
> Of *Babel*, and the works of *Memphian* Kings,
> Learn how thir greatest Monuments of Fame,
> And Strength and Art are easily outdone
> By Spirits reprobate,

One of the features of Paradise is to be the freedom of Adam and Eve from technology—"not nice Art . . . but Nature boon" provides all they need, a wall of shrubs, a floor of flower-mosiac as well as food. It is only after the Fall that Adam has to consider how he can apply the pure science of the sun's rays,

> how we his gather'd beams
> Reflected, may with matter sere foment
> Or by collision of two bodies grinde
> The Air attrite to Fire.
>
> (X. 1070)

Milton's position was quite ordinary, his materials conventional. He respected science but worried about its possibilities for abuse. His worrying has hints of the contemporary silliness, and is sometimes fed by personal motives: it is a peculiarly fierce literary convention that represents mining as incest perpetrated on Mother Earth; and Milton builds up Azazel (who is the angel of technology in *I Enoch*) into a figure of extraordinary phallicism.[1] It is more helpful though to recognise two less obtrusive devices: the social degradation the devils must suffer in a 17th-century epic by their manual skill, and the association of their skill with "suttle Magic" (727). Milton does not present science as black magic, but magic as false science. Long before the devils become pigmy-fairies they are hinted at as gnomes: "Here in the heart of Hell to work in Fire, Or do his Errands in the gloomy Deep" (151). They delude themselves with spells—"soft Pipes that charm'd Thir painful steps" (561) as Mercury's pipe lulled Argus; seeking in Book II "if there be cure or charm To respite or deceive, or slack the pain Of this ill Mansion" (460); and using philosophical disputation as "pleasing sorcerie" to "charm Pain for a while or anguish, and excite Fallacious hope" (II. 566). As in Books V and VIII, it is not Baconian empiricism but Scholastic theorising that is condemned (another Catholic-devil association). This was the common position, as in *Faustus*; D'Amville sums it up: "I will find out the efficient cause of a contented mind" (V. ii). The devils live in a world we know, of makeshift phantasy, expert self-hypnosis, the phatic communion of a lost intelligentsia.

There is a striking and pertinent originality in Milton's control over technical language. Earlier poets had written technically, at dull length or in occasional *tours de force*. Here is D'Amville the atheist exhibiting his control over nature:

> 'Tis a mere effect of Nature—an exhalation hot
> And dry involved within a watery vapour
> I' the middle region of the air; whose coldness,
> Congealing that thick moisture to a cloud,
> The angry exhalation, shut within
> A prison of contrary quality,
> Strives to be free and with the violent
> Eruption through the grossness of that cloud,
> Makes this noise we hear.
>
> (II. iv).

[1] Jung regards technological activity as a transfer for sexual energy. His argument is extravagantly etymological (p. 94, etc.), but there is a recognisable irony in the phallic mushroom cloud, ultimate symbol of technological expertise, being the instrument of sterility and mutation. This is precisely Milton's kind of irony about technology in *P.L.*

Borachio gummily agrees, "'Tis a fearful noise". Milton the theist really is in control: Satan, inventor of gunpowder, is pricked by Ithuriel's spear and starts up from the ear of Eve

> As when a spark
> Lights on a heap of nitrous Powder, laid
> Fit for the Tun som Magazin to store
> Against a rumord Warr, the smuttie graine
> With sudden blaze diffus'd, inflames the Aire:
>
> (IV. 814)

This is preparing for that verbal control over nature which the 18th Century exercised towards the Industrial Revolution. At the same time Milton dramatises his science more than a Thomson or an Erasmus Darwin: "Fit for the Tun som Magazin to store" reverberates like Hell. These passages are restricted to the hellish areas of the poem: the devils "scum'd the Bullion dross" to build Pandemonium, and Tubal Cain imitates them in Book XI (560). The point is not simply that derived power is being abused; the poetry's gritty jargon points to the wreckage of grace that ingenuity involves.

When "The hasty multitude Admiring enter'd" Pandemonium open-mouthed, they are finally degraded. They swarm numberless as bees, like Homer's councillors and the dead souls of Virgil and Dante. The simile is gentler than the locusts, almost pitying the devils' vain busyness. It slides into another comparison in which the devils become young politicians who in "The suburb of thir Straw-built Cittadel, New rub'd with Baum, expatiate and confer Thir State affairs" (773): Pandemonium is the Little Pig's house, a citadel built of straw in Hell like

> the painted battlements and gaudy rottenness of prelatry, which want but one puff of the king's to blow them down like a paste-board house built of court-cards.
>
> (*Of Ref.* ii. 397)

This leads on to their actual metamorphosis into pigmean or elvish shapes. Voltaire objected that the metamorphosis

> heightens the ridicule of the whole Contrivance to an unexpressible Degree. Methinks the true Criterion for discerning what is really ridiculous in an *Epick* Poem, is to examine if the same Thing

> would not fit exactly the Mock Heroick. Then I dare say that no-thing is so adapted to that ludicrous way of writing, as the Metamorphosis of the Devils into Dwarfs. (*loc. cit.*)

In fact this is another of Milton's mockeries of the falsely epical, all the more convincing than French and Augustan mockery for occurring in a genuine epic. His devils belong finally to the feigned world of romance and fairytale.[1] More importantly for the poem as a whole, the devils belong to the sublunary world of change over which the "Moon Sits Arbitress" (784). The noticeable fluency of verse here is reserved in *Paradise Lost* for metamorphoses, and the "belated Peasant" appears again as a mundane intensifier of the supernatural change when Satan alters in the face of Gabriel's troops (IV. 983) and at the final metamorphosis of Adam and Eve into inhabitants of the fallen world (XII. 631). Similarly, Satan's protean habit: assuming beyond his created nature the motives of vulture, wolf, cormorant, toad, he takes on their vesture too and in Book X becomes a snake without volition. All fluctuations of shape, changes of nature, here and in *Comus* and *Paradise Regained*, are presented as evil, symptoms of the Fall itself. On the other hand God never changes, his throne "fixt for ever firm and sure" (VII. 586), Milton's style is solid, hardwearing, on the side of the immutable. The poem is in a sense a celebration of permanence; a gigantic effort to reverse the decay of established order. Spenser had dealt with the problem in the Mutability cantos. It can be seen there how the acceptance of mutability involves naturalism, while salvation from it can only be supernatural:

> Then gin I thinke on that which Nature sayd,
> Of that same time when no more *Change* shall be,
> But stedfast rest of all things firmely stayd
> Vpon the pillours of Eternity,
> That is contrayr to *Mutabilitie:*
> For, all that moueth, doth in *Change* delight:
> But thence-forth all shall rest eternally
> With Him that is the God of Sabbaoth hight:
> O that great Sabbaoth God, graunt me that Sabbaoths sight.[2]

[1] More anti-Catholicism here; Hobbes associated fairies with Roman Catholics.

[2] *F.Q.* VII. viii. 2. *Poetical Works* ed. J. C. Smith and E. de Selincourt (1912).

This was not granted to him in narrative form, perhaps fortunately because the Mutability cantos make clear how difficult it is for poetry—the utterance of mortals—to be written in favour of the static; and how easily it flows when its values and its materials are mutable. As it is, Spenser's representative of constancy, Jove, is unable to pit anything but ethical imperatives against the description of the elements and the masque of the Seasons, Day and Night, the Hours and Life and Death that Mutability supports her case with (vii. 20-46); while the fact that Nature is empowered to arbitrate the case really suggests, not that the immutable law of God is mediated to man through the laws of nature, but that the laws of nature transcend both man and God. This was, in practice, the Deists' view of natural law, and even Hooker's.[1] In his time the dramatists had recognised the fact of decay, arraigned it, and eventually accepted it as ultimate. Shakespeare, though, suggested how it might be conquered in nature. The sonnets are about a mutability not really conquered by the conceits of immortality in verse. But it is conquered by the love that inspires the verse, and may be conquered by the "increase" recommended to that love:

> Then let not winter's ragged hand deface
> In thee thy summer ere thou be distill'd:
> Make sweet some vial; treasure thou some place
> With beauty's treasure ere it be self-kill'd. . . .

Similarly in the plays, there is a movement from fear of change—

> O, swear not by the moon, th' inconstant moon,
> That monthly changes

[1] Hooker didn't *want* to say God was fated by a Law superior to himself: the First Cause, "Being the first . . . can have no other than itself to be the author of that law which it willingly worketh by" (*Ecc. Pol.* I. ii. 3. Ed. R. Bayne [2 vols. n.d. 1907; Everyman]). I.e., God is autonomous. But, as such confusions as the use of the word "willingly" here show, the object of Hooker's theology was to control God, to bring him, analogically, on to the side of the Establishment in England. He was writing against revolutionaries; so was Salmasius; therefore, although Milton agreed with them in general, he, writing as a revolutionary, had to ease the bondage of a "naturally" legal monarchy over men by emphasising (*a*) God's ultimate *personal* super-eminence as the source of all power (Hooker's God is not a person); and (*b*) the utilitarian relativity of prescriptive, especially constitutional laws, in contrast to the (apparent) empirical absolutism of the descriptive "laws" of nature (e.g. *1st Def.* i. 70-71, 108-09).

—to a philosophical contemplation of it:

> And take upon's the mystery of things
> As if we were God's spies; and we'll wear out
> In a wall'd prison packs and sects of great ones
> That ebb and flow by th' moon.

Finally to a transcendence of it, even in death, not by supernatural agency but by a human love rooted in the clay but irrepressibly abundant. "Our terrene moon is now eclips'd", but of herself Cleopatra says: "I am marble-constant; now the fleeting moon No planet is of mine." The mortal moon hath her eclipse endured. Similarly in the last plays it is with natural symbols—sea, storm, plant-life, natural magic—that healing changes are effected: the fall is upwards. Milton was nervous of the dynamics of change, so he drained most of the incarnational essence out of his Christian doctrine, and in his poetry, though he could not deny change, he made it by implication always for the worse (except for the hypothetical change of man into spirit; but that is removal to another galaxy).

Milton descends into a deeper, darker and fierier Hell than any other epic poet, and keeps his eyes open. In Book II he will go even deeper; but he never descended as Shakespeare did and Eliot has to absolute depth, the dark night of the soul: he stayed in this twittering world, the obvious waste land. This is because he was not a dramatist or lyrical mystic, or a penitent, but a proud, Protestant epic narrator. The office has its limitations. But in reading this book one begins to see how wide they are, how Milton fulfilled the comprehensiveness of epic here, in a more than national or personal-scholarly way: he circumscribes Hell all round us, yet keeps it in the poem. The only hell comparable with it—and then lacking its dramatic personalities—is the top of Bosch's volet of Hell.[1] There, in red and black, are the desperate activity, the dark Satanic mills, the building and destruction, the hurrying to-and-fro, the flames reflected in a

[1] In his *Garden of Delights* triptych. Although Milton seems not to have been directly influenced by the plastic art he saw in Italy to the extent that, say, Yeats was, some comparisons are useful because so much Renaissance art depicted his materials. E.g. Gozzoli's *City of Babylon* illustrates the architectural promiscuity Milton had in mind for Pandemonium (repr. in Berenson).

carcassed lake of blood. The paint is laid on with gusto, your attention distracted by environing curiosities, but as you look it steadies, like Milton's vision, into a pattern that offers just enough scope for the recognition of your own devilry, and yet remains integral to the epic composition.

3

PANDEMONIUM AND CHAOS

1. *The Council*

BOOK II opens out wide and high from the pinpoint close of Book I:

> HIGH on a Throne of Royal State, which far
> Outshon the wealth of *Ormus* and of *Ind*,
> Or where the gorgeous East with richest hand
> Showrs on her Kings *Barbaric* Pearl & Gold,
> Satan exalted sat, by merit rais'd
> To that bad eminence;

This change of focus carries on the process of alternating inflation and deflation of the devils begun in Book I, and continued for Satan all through the poem—his furious "dilation" into the size of Teneriffe or Atlas (IV. 986) followed by his slinking into the darkness; his explosion from toad to proper shape at the touch of Ithuriel's spear; and finally his expansion from plebeian disguise to "shape Starr-bright" and then to "Dragon grown, larger then whom the Sun Ingenderd in the *Pythian* Vale on slime, Huge Python" (X. 450, 529). Here, the balloon is blown up with the motifs of Book I—the urge to ascend, the oriental barbarism, the mineral plutocracy of Hell, the heavy suggestion of a physical presence never quite particularised; but in the fifth line it is pricked with the derisive collocation of sounds in "Satan exalted sat", and all his gas escapes in sibilance and near-rhyme:

> and from despair
> Thus high uplifted beyond hope, aspires
> Beyond thus high, insatiate to pursue
> Vain Warr with Heav'n, and by success untaught
> His proud imaginations thus displaid.

In *The Reason of Church Government* Milton had remarked that "Lucifer, before Adam, was the first prelate angel" (ii. 450); he is like the bad bishop in *Of Reformation* who, "when he steps up into the chair of pontifical pride", loses his pastoral responsibility and secularises his office: "then he degrades, then he unbishops himself" (ii. 373). The degeneration of popular rebel into tyrannical dictator is a naturally recurrent theme in public literature; but the difference between Milton's handling of it, and Shakespeare's, points to a 17th-century change in political feeling. Shakespeare was able by using actual past history to evade the insolubility of the conflict between royal right (whether divine or by birth) and usurping might. But it is clear from the fact of dramatisation, as well as from the facts of history and from medieval constitutional theory, that in the English view kings were not divine and their rights were merely human. Thus in *Henry VIII*, which was as far as Shakespeare could take the process without sedition and as far as it actually went in his lifetime, the usurping Wolsey, king *de facto*, is built up like Satan; "And when he falls, he falls like Lucifer" (III. ii. 371) because he has committed ecclesiastical treason against the king *de jure*. The king's right must be preserved, in the national interest. But Wolsey falls also because the ostentation of his *de facto* power trespassed on the mystical splendour of *de jure* majesty.

Divine right is latent in kingship; but only the king too weakly human to rule by his own right, and too inhumanly sophisticated to rule by popular assent, will try to make it explicit. As soon as he does this, divinity will be dulled by the light of mundane argument. This happened in Milton's lifetime. Like Shakespeare's kings, Satan is subject to undesirable foreign affectations, and treats his people as puppets, but the conflict is not between him and his peers or subjects, or within himself between man and king, but between himself and God as rival kings. His appeal for a volunteer—"whom shall we send In search of this new world" (II. 402)—is a parody of God's appeal, "Which of ye will be mortal to redeem Mans mortal crime" (III. 214), made effective before the divine parallel occurs in the poem by the reference to Isaiah's vision—

> Also I heard the voice of the Lord, saying, Whom shall I send, and who will go for us? Then said I, Here am I; send me.
> (vi. 8)

—and to the gospel texts of the sending of the Son and the

Comforter from heaven (e.g. *John* xiv. 26). The appeal unanswered, Satan *realises* his sovereignty, and so spoils its latent power:

> *Satan*, whom now transcendent glory rais'd
> Above his fellows, with Monarchal pride
> Conscious of highest worth, unmov'd thus spake.
>
> (427)

This is the exaltation which he had objected to in the Son:

> Who can in reason then or right assume
> Monarchie over such as live by right
> His equals?
>
> (V. 791)

and the tyranny usurped by Nimrod, "the first king" (*Eikon.* i. 494), "to himself assuming Authoritie corrupt, from God not giv'n" (XII. 64). Satan's establishment as king is heavily stressed: "Thus saying rose / The Monarch" (466). He receives from the peers the worship they withheld from their Creator:

> Towards him they bend
> With awful reverence prone; and as a God
> Extoll him equal to the highest in Heav'n:

They leave the council-chamber to confront the populace with a *coup d'état*:

> forth
> In order came the grand infernal Peers,
> Midst came thir mighty Paramount, and seemd
> Alone th' Antagonist of Heav'n, nor less
> Then Hells dread Emperour with pomp Supream,
> And God-like imitated State; him round
> A Globe of fierie Serephim inclos'd
> With bright imblazonrie, and horrent Arms.

Milton did not damn constitutional monarchy, but monarchy that was blasphemously absolute and undeserved:

> I confess many eminent and famous men have extolled monarchy; but it has always been upon this supposition, that the prince was a very excellent person, and one that of all others deserved best to reign; without which supposition, no form of government

can be so prone to tyranny as monarchy is. And whereas you resemble a monarchy to the government of the world by one Divine Being, I pray answer me, whether you think that any other can deserve to be invested with a power here on earth, that shall resemble his power that governs the world, except such a person as does infinitely excel all other men, and both for wisdom and goodness in some measure resemble the Deity? and such a person, in my opinion, none can be but the Son of God himself.
(1*st Def.* i. 113-4)

His last, and bitterest argument against the monarchy he knew, in England and Israel, was its appeal to the masses:

And I say, people of England! keep ye to these principles, and ye shall never want a king. Nay, after such a fair deliverance as this, with so much fortitude and valour shewn against a tyrant, that people that should seek a king claiming what this man claims, would show themselves to be by nature slaves and arrant beasts, not fit for that liberty which they cried out and bellowed for . . . now again intoxicated and moped with these royal, and therefore so delicious because royal, rudiments of bondage, the cup of deception, spiced, and tempered to their bane. . . .[1]

The devils are gullible like this. When the result of the council is announced "with Trumpets regal sound . . . all the host of Hell with deafning shout, return'd them loud acclaim", responding to the "sounding Alchymie"—tinkling cymbal, glittering casket—of state. Milton had experienced this in England as reaction: no sooner was the hedge of divine absolutism uprooted than the masses forgot its thorns and yearned for the flowers of regalia.

But because the people proved to be "a herd confus'd, a miscellaneous rabble" (*P.R.* III. 49) incapable of rational political behaviour, their leaders had to replace *de jure* sovereignty with some correspondingly stronger *de facto* government, lest anarchy befall, or monarchy return. Hence the acclaim of Cromwell, who embodied Milton's ideal of kingship:

For therein stands the office of a King,
His Honour, Vertue, Merit and chief Praise,
That for the Publick all this weight he bears.
(*P.R.* II. 463)

[1] *Eikon.* i. 482-3; cf. *Rdy. Way,* ii. 135-8.

It is an Elizabethan ideal, echoing Henry V before Agincourt:

> Upon the King! Let us our lives, our souls,
> Our debts, our careful wives,
> Our children, and our sins, lay on the King!
> We must bear all.
>
> (IV. i. 226)

But Henry could reject his own regalia at the same time:

> And what have kings that privates have not too,
> Save ceremony—save general ceremony?
> And what art thou, thou idol Ceremony?

Writing under a sovereign of unusual *de facto* strength and *de jure* splendour, about kings, and for them, on a stage shaped to ceremony, Shakespeare could afford to pooh-pooh the tide of pomp: "Why, what is pomp, rule, reign, but earth and dust?" "Vain pomp and glory of the world, I hate ye." "Take physic, pomp." He could remain constitutionally uncommitted. Milton, subject to a monarchy so weak that it staked all on right, and lost, was forced to commit himself to naked power. For the Commonwealth found a Henry V in Cromwell, and in his second defence of the people Milton bows to the absolutism he had abjured as idolatrous in his first:

> supreme power should be vested in the best and wisest of men. Such, O Cromwell, all acknowledge you to be; such are the services which you have rendered, as the leader of our councils, the general of our armies, and the father of your country. For this is the tender appellation by which all the good among us salute you from the very soul. Other names you neither have nor could endure; and you deservedly reject that pomp of title which attracts the gaze and admiration of the multitude. . . . But since, though it be not fit, it may be expedient, that the highest pitch of virtue should be circumscribed within the bounds of some human appellation, you endured to receive, for the public good, a title most like to that of the father of your country . . . the title of king was unworthy the transcendent majesty of your character. For if you had been captivated by a name over which, as a private man, you had so completely triumphed and crumbled into dust, you would have been doing the same thing as if, after having subdued some idolatrous nation by the help of the true God, you should afterwards fall down and worship the gods which you had vanquished.
>
> (i. 288-9)

The subjunctives show him worried, equivocal almost as Marvell; but the very form, of panegyric directed to proof of a case, shows him far more deeply committed than still-possessing Shakespeare, or less-to-be-lost Marvell had to be.

This committal to leadership gives illicit value to Satan's *führerlichkeit* in Book I and confuses the political satire in Pandemonium. Satan is the devils' Cromwell, "on whom . . . The weight of all and our last hope relies" (II. 415). Milton might even be satirising Cromwell. But his nervous sermon after the council attributes genuine virtue to Satan:

> Nor fail'd they to express how much they prais'd,
> That for the general safety he despis'd
> His own: for neither do the Spirits damn'd
> Loose all thir vertue; least bad men should boast
> Thir specious deeds on earth, which glory excites,
> Or close ambition varnish't o're with zeal.
>
> (480)

As a result, only Moloch appears in a single light, patently a Blimp: "My sentence is for open war; of wiles, more unexpert, I boast not—them let those contrive who need, or when they need, not now": it never is time for intelligence. It would not matter that the others are parti-coloured if we agreed with Milton's valuation of their colours: but we aren't likely to. Beezlebub is unsympathetic as the jackal of Satan. He dismisses the plans of Mammon and Belial sarcastically:

> Advise if this be worth
> Attempting, or to sit in darkness here,
> Hatching vain Empires.

But the makeshift resilience recommended by Mammon and Belial is more constructive than the intrigues of Satan. Milton knew this:

> War has made many great whom peace makes small. If after being released from the toils of war, you [Cromwell] neglect the arts of peace, if your peace and your liberty be a state of warfare, if war be your only virtue, the summit of your praise, you will, believe me, soon find peace the most adverse to your interests.
>
> (*2nd Def.* i. 295)

So although he condemns Beelzebub's counsel as devilish and

malicious (379, 382), he presents Beelzebub himself as a Cromwellian figure:

> with grave
> Aspect he rose, and in his rising seem'd
> A Pillar of State; deep on his Front engraven
> Deliberation sat and publick care;
> And Princely counsel in his face yet shon,
> Majestick though in ruin: sage he stood
> With *Atlantean* shoulders fit to bear
> The weight of mightiest Monarchies;

Belial, on the other hand, is at first commended as "in act more graceful and humane . . . he seemd For dignity compos'd and high exploit"; but immediately condemned as "false and hollow . . . for his thoughts were low; To vice industrious, but to Nobler deeds Timorous and slothful". We have seen why Milton disliked Belial; here he caricatures him with effeminate gestures and timbre, a habit of word-play ("worse, worst"), his voice trailing with the paranoiac passivity of stricken conscience through labyrinths of suasion. Yet he is the only speaker to recognise both the physical and the moral facts of the situation: "To suffer, as to doe, Our strength is equal, nor the Law unjust That so ordains". Milton says he recommends "ignoble ease, and peaceful sloath"; we might call it adaptation to circumstances, springing from the deep resourcefulness that his metaphysical suppleness of language suggests:

> for who would loose,
> Though full of pain, this intellectual being,
> Those thoughts that wander through Eternity,
> To perish rather, swallowd up and lost
> In the wide womb of uncreated night,
> Devoid of sense and motion?

It is Shakespeare's Claudio speaking, without a sister's peril to make his intellectualism seem dilettante. A similar mode of exciting mental and emotional life is suggested by Satan's plan, reminiscent of Milton's own invocation:

> who shall tempt with wandring feet
> The dark unbottom'd infinite Abyss
> And through the palpable obscure find out

His uncouth way, or spread his aerie flight
Upborn with indefatigable wings
Over the vast abrupt, ere he arrive
The happy Ile?

But—the verse does make the moral distinction—the power is misdirected into political adventure:

what strength, what art can then
Suffice, or what evasion bear him safe
Through the strict Senteries and Stations thick
Of Angels watching round?

When Blake worked these cadences back into a fusion of heroic passion and subtle intellect in "The Tyger", he re-formed, unspoilt, the potentialities of Satan. Mammon is more confusing. At one level he presents a central problem in Christianity, how difficult it is to accept forgiveness:

Suppose he should relent
And publish Grace to all, on promise made
Of new Subjection; with what eyes could we
Stand in his presence humble, and receive
Strict Laws impos'd, to celebrate his Throne
With warbl'd Hymns, and to his Godhead sing
Forc't Halleluiah's; while he Lordly sits
Our envied Sovran, and his Altar breathes
Ambrosial Odours and Ambrosial Flowers,
Our servile offerings.

It is a degraded conception of heaven, yet not far from the Heaven of the poem; and we cannot help hearing in Mammon's honesty what Milton had said about the English court. When Mammon appraises the wealth of Hell and asks "what can Heav'n shew more?", he demonstrates his confusion of values. His key-word (281) is "composed", the composure of a plutocrat co-opted to government, wondering what all the political fuss is about:

All things invite
To peaceful Counsels, and the settl'd State
Or order, how in safety best we may
Compose our present evils, with regard
Of what we are and where, dismissing quite
All thoughts of Warr,

But this too echoes Milton's advice to Cromwell:

> if you think that it is a more grand, a more beneficial, or a more wise policy, to invent subtle expedients for increasing the revenue, to multiply our naval and military forces, to rival in craft the ambassadors of foreign states, to form skilful treaties and alliances, than to administer unpolluted justice to the people, to redress the injured and to succour the distressed, and speedily to restore to every one his own, you are involved in a cloud of error . . .
>
> (*2nd Def.* i. 295-6)

And the policy of Beelzebub and Satan does lead the devils into demoralised divertisements and aggresive war-games like the boys in *Lord of the Flies*.

It is a pity that the satire should be confused by historical valuations pressed on us *in propria persona*, for Milton's intimacy with high politics qualified him as no English poet has been since the early 18th Century. When he leaves the verse to do its own work the satirical revelation of base motives under high counsel is devastating. The grand style's sullen flexibility differentiates character and satirises its own misuse in political rhetoric: "Which if not Victory is yet Revenge", "Goe therefore mighty Powers, Terror of Heav'n, though fall'n—the sentences echo in the mind then collapse into vacuum: "More glorious and more dread then from no fall, And trust themselves to fear no second fate". But Milton's engagement, however destructive of this satire, is endearing. He was engaged with still significant problems: a positive liberal, impatient of democracy's slackness and disunity, he admires the drive and loyalty of totalitarianism, forgetful that the price is hell. Of course it is a *public* problem, but the context and the verse are public; and they enable us to see into the privacies that motivate our politics also. In spite of the confusion of values, what Milton writes to represent them is ultimately true to life. The lunatic heroics of Hitler raised him above the clever Belials and constructive Mammons as well as the stupid Molochs.

There are two minor causes of his confusion. The first is that Greek ethics were mediated through the Humanists so that "virtue" acquired the Roman hue of "manliness". Hence some conflict between secular virtues and the "theological virtues" of Christianity, which are not manly in the Roman or schoolmasters' sense. Satan's heroism is secular; but what of the Son's parallel self-sacrifice? Here is one root of the non-incarnational view of Christ, as Exemplary Man. The Renaissance hero was *homo antiqua virtute ac fide*, and the quarrel between orthodox (i.e. Humanistic) Christianity and naturalistic humanism is reducible to whether we would derive "virile" or "virtuous" from *vir*.

Secondly, the habit of hierarchical thinking allowed the scale of heavenly society to be transferred to Hell the same way up when it should logically be turned upside-down. Milton was not an uncritical hierarchist. In *Reason of Church Government* he opposed the equal, unifying globe and cube (which in the poem are Heavenly shapes) to the schismatical forms of pyramid, cone and spire (manifest in the flames of Hell, e.g. I. 223) as emblems of the bishops' "criminous hierarchy" (ii. 463-5). Of Satan and the devils, "the superior Fiend" (I. 283) is one of several little sneers added to the large mockepicry of the catalogue of devils:

> Say, Muse, their Names then known, who first, who last
> Rous'd from the slumber, on that fiery Couch,
> At thir great Emperors call, *as next in worth*
> Came singly where he stood on the bare strand,
> While the promiscuous croud stood yet aloof?
>
> (I. 376)

But Satan nevertheless is Prince of Hell not because he is the basest devil but because he had been the most princely angel. This illogical transference is our usual habit and in tragedy it convinces: Lear the supremely foolish king becomes the king of fools. Iago on the other hand we instinctively label devilish because his malice is not heroic like Satan's but almost purely evil. His viciousness merits the epithets "extraordinary and almost supernatural" which Milton ascribed to Cromwell's virtue; Iago, not Satan, represents the ultimate corruption of Cromwell's triumph over "that flame of ambition and that lust of glory which are wont to make the best and greatest men their slaves", into a demoniac freedom for selfless sin. But we don't respond to this. Though theoretically a negative quality, evil is significant only when apprehended in men, or on a scale parallel to the human, as a positive. Invert the scale and you meet the sentient sludge of science fiction, "*Gorgons* and *Hydra's*, and *Chimera's* dire", unjudgeable ooze of the unconscious. That is why Milton insulates Pandemonium from Hell proper of the narrative, with Parliamentary realism. It is cut off from absolute morality by the devils' metamorphosis and the book-change at one end, and by the acute fantasia of Hell's exploration at the other.

2. *Tartarus*

When the council ends, and Satan rises to go,

> at once with him they rose;
> Thir rising all at once was as the sound
> Of Thunder heard remote.
>
> (475)

This characterises the verse describing Hell in Book II: imagery of sound, remoteness, rhetorical figuring ("at once . . . at once"). Noise is the subject of the most elaborate imagery: a crescendo swells from when Satan "Breaking the horrid silence thus began" (I. 83) to when he crashes through Chaos into the quietness of space. The remotenesses and rhetoric weave a haze of idyllium so that we hear and see the devilry and ruin of Hell ironically muted, and distorted into fantasy. Thus Beelzebub's glance

> Drew audience and attention still as Night
> Or Summers Noon-tide air,
>
> (308)

The applause for Mammon's speech is like the "blustring winds" of a collapsed gale

> which all night long
> Had rous'd the Sea, now with hoarse cadence lull
> Sea-faring men orewatcht, whose Bark by chance
> Or Pinnace anchors in a craggy Bay
> After the Tempest:
>
> (286)

It is part of the delusion motif—Hell hiding its head in its own skirts. Unreality is suggested by haphazard irrelevance—"whose barque, by chance (or pinnace) . . .", as in *Paradise Regained* where Hell deceptively drifts into the wilderness as

> an aged man in Rural weeds,
> Following, as seem'd, the quest of some stray Ewe,
> Or wither'd sticks to gather . . .
>
> (I. 314)

When the council ends, the revival of the devils' spirits is circuitously likened to the shifting of storm-clouds from the mountain tops, so that the volcanoes of Book I are charmed into pastoral hills:

> If chance the radiant Sun with farewell sweet
> Extend his ev'ning beam, the fields revive,
> The birds thir notes renew, and bleating herds
> Attest thir joy, that hill and valley rings.
>
> (492)

But the devils are still the "bleating Gods" of Book I, and make Hell ring with muffled din:

> As when *Alcides* from *Oechalia* Crown'd
> With conquest, felt th'envenom'd robe, and tore
> Through pain up by the roots *Thessalian* Pines,
> And *Lichas* from the top of *Oeta* threw
> Into th' *Euboic* Sea.
>
> (542; 1674 ed.)

The mountains and pines of Book I are diminished, the classical names have lost authority and become waywardly esoteric. The gigantic effort of Book I—"Forthwith upright he rears from off the Pool"—is agonised and inhibited: "Through pain up by the roots *Thessalian* Pines".

What is being frustrated is the devils' attempts to follow their leaders. These follow Moloch in rage; others are philosophical like Belial but their arguments are specious with rhetoric:

> and reason'd high
> Of Providence, Foreknowledge, Will, and Fate,
> Fixt Fate, free will, foreknowledge absolute,
> And found no end, in wandring mazes lost.

Others play, like the troops of Aeneas before his descent into hell:

> Part on the plain, or in the Air sublime
> Upon the wing, or in swift race contend,
> As at th' Olympian Games or *Pythian* fields;

Something of what Milton intended to be the difference between Hell and Heaven may be sensed from the febrility of these lines compared with the unhindered verve of

> About him exercis'd Heroic Games
> Th' unarmed Youth of Heav'n,
>
> (IV. 551)

Again, when

> Others more milde,
> Retreated in a silent valley, sing
> With notes Angelical to many a Harp
> Thir own Heroic deeds and hapless fall
> By doom of Battel

the harmony "Suspended Hell, and took with ravishment The thronging audience". The pathos has to be set against the lovely accomplishment of

> That day, as other solem dayes, they spent
> In song and dance about the sacred Hill . . .
> And in thir motions harmonie Divine . . .
>
> (V. 618)

They are following the advice of Mammon to "seek our own good from our selves, and from our own Live to our selves, though in this vast recess" (252), so they descant on their own deformity in the chivalric tradition of Book I; but the vast recess swallows up the piping of their egos.

Other devils explore, revealing a more fantastic and literary hell than Book I's. Only the "frozen Continent" beyond Lethe is real—

> dark and wilde, beat with perpetual storms
> Of Whirlwind and dire Hail, which on firm land
> Thaws not, but gathers heap, and ruin seems
> Of ancient pile;

This was almost certainly logged by a Magellan or a Willoughby and it is followed by the Serbonian bog simile which is real geography and had its history attested by Diodorus Siculus. Even so the granular hail and sand are sterile and intractable, like the classical rivers, whose allegorical significance is carefully defined. There is apocryphal authority for this punitive kind of hell in the second heaven of the *Book of the Secrets of Enoch*:

> a very terrible place, and there were all manner of tortures in that place: cruel darkness and unillumined gloom, and there is no light there, but murky fire constantly flameth aloft, and there is a fiery river coming forth, and that whole place is everywhere fire, and everywhere there is frost and ice, thirst and shivering, while the bonds are very cruel, and the angels fearless and merciless, bearing angry weapons, merciless torture. . . .
>
> (x. 1)

But the details are drawn from Homer's and Virgil's Hades, Dante's Inferno, and redactions of Virgil—Spenser's Cave of Mammon, Sackville's induction to the *Mirror for Magistrates*, Fletcher's *Christ's Victory on Earth*, and the *Faust-book*. Rhetoric insists on the literary quality. From "the parching Air Burns frore" (594) to the end (628), the references to Lethe, Medusa, Gorgon, Tantalus, as well as *Enoch*, are set like gem-chips in a wire of rhetorical figures[1]: the Spenserian archaisms of "frore" and "wight"; polysyndeton as in "*Gorgons* and *Hydra's*, and *Chimera's* dire"; brachylogia in "Rocks, Caves, Lakes, Fens, Bogs, Dens, and shades of death"; unremitting alliteration

[1] I apply the Elizabethan jargon when figures of rhetoric are being used with conscious artifice and would have been recognised by readers educated as Milton was. The most reliable definitions will be found in Puttenham and (sometimes differing) Abraham Fraunce's *Arcadian Rhetoric* (repr. E. Seaton, Oxford, 1950) and Henry Peacham the Elder's *Garden of Eloquence* (2nd ed. 1593 repr. W. G. Crane, Gainesville, Fa., 1954); but it is safer to refer to Warren Taylor's variorum dictionary, *Tudor Figures of Rhetoric* (private ed. by Univ. of Chicago Libraries, Chicago, 1937), or the index to Veré L. Rubel's *Poetic Diction in the English Renaissance* (New York, 1941). I have an article on Milton's rhetoric in *MP* (1959), but I will define here the figures I mention most often in this book (cf. Chaps. 4 and 7). *Anadiplosis*: starting a line with the last word of the line before. *Antimetabole:* repeating a phrase the other way round. *Antonomasia:* referring to someone by epithet instead of name. *Asyndeton:* series of parallel phrases without conjunctions. *Auxesis:* arrangement of elements in climactic order of sense. *Brachylogia:* series of disjunctive words. *Climax:* phrases interlocked through series of parallel constructions. *Epanalepsis:* line beginning and ending with same word. *Epizeuxis:* words repeated adjacent to each other. *Parison:* series of phrases in parallel construction. *Ploce:* significant repetition of single word. *Polysyndeton:* series of words or phrases linked by conjunctions. *Prosonomasia:* using homophonous words close to each other with punning effect. *Traductio:* repeating a word in a different grammatical form. The terms of rhetoric have the advantage of indicating schemes where nowadays we recognise only tropes as "imagery". Schemes are non-metaphorical arrangements of language which usually tone by emphasis, adjacence, mimesis, etc., but they can have tropal effect, e.g. Pope's zeugma, "Or stain her honour, or her new brocade".

("dark . . . drearie . . . dolorous"); oxymoron in "burns frore"; epizeuxis and antimetabole in "the bitter change Of fierce extreams, extreams by change more fierce". So daedalian the medium that its cleverness is all we take in; its rhetorical and archaistic idiom frays the narrative texture; and even if the materials were not smothered by the medium their tremendous symbolic potencies would jostle each other out of the way. The *compages* alters the focus, makes Pandemonium realistic, gives Satan breath; it intellectualises "those flaming mountains, which to grosser apprehensions represent Hell" into a psychological disaster; and it outdoes the classics again on behalf of England and Christendom. But in the last resort Milton is simply glorying like a strong man to run a race. His syncretistic omnicompetence is a rehearsal of the literary power transmitted by his Muse, and the spiritual power imputed to him from Christ, to "lead Hell Captive maugre Hell, and show The Powers of darkness bound" (III. 255). It dismisses the devils, as at the end of Book I, with elegant effrontery, into fantasy.

3. *Chaos*

The contrast between the fluid desert of Chaos and the walled city of Heaven, the walled garden of Paradise, is obvious; and the whole movement of Milton and the reader in Satan up to Heaven may be regarded as a rite of passage in which our natural satanism is exorcised. But to discuss the voyage through Chaos as a type of the Jungian death-and-rebirth myth would be to trespass on the overt allegorising of the piece. Perhaps because it is fundamentally a rite and a psychological symbol, though, its surface allegory is inconsistent. Already in 1712 Addison could object to the "improbability" of the allegorical figures, though he admired the moral they drew. We are less certain of the laws of probability, and see Spenser closer behind Milton. But the difference between Milton and Spenser still hinders Milton's allegory from taking Spenserian effect. In the *Faerie Queene* it is clear from the start that any figure may "melt into allegory"[1] and back again at any time because the setting of the poem, and its style, are remote and fluid. Guyon is ferried across the Idle Lake by Phaedria in "A little Gondelay" (II. vi. 2)

[1] Tillyard, *Studies in Milton* (1951), p. 61.

a "little barke", a "shallow ship", a vessel so designed for voyages in poetic allegory that Keats and Shelley could use it too. Guyon's destinations in Canto xii are nominatively allegorical—the Gulf of Greediness, the Rock of Reproach, the Whirlpool of Decay and so on. The rhetorical style sheds over the Bower of Bliss the delusive haze of Book II's Hell:

> No tree, whose braunches did not brauely spring;
> No braunch, whereon a fine bird did not sit:
> No bird, but did her shrill notes sweetly sing;
> No song but did containe a louely dit:
> Trees, braunches, birds, and songs were framed fit,
> For to allure fraile mind to carelesse ease.[1]

At the other pole of allegory is the *Pilgrim's Progress*: all that is meant meets the eye at once through everyday realism; the allegory falters only occasionally when the realistic presentation runs on through little scenes too exigently allegorical to bear it, as in the House of the Interpreter.

Satan's voyage through Chaos lies between these poles. The rhetoric is simpler than Spenser's, much of it intended to represent confusion, as in

> Ore bog or steep, through strait, rough, dense, or rare,
> With head, hands, wing, or feet pursues his way,
> And swims or sinks, or wades, or creeps, or flyes:
> (948)

—though some more elaborate figures are used to mark stages in the journey:

> So he with difficulty and labour hard
> Mov'd on, with difficulty and labour hee;
> (1021)
>
> With tumult less and with less hostile din,
> That *Satan* with less toil, and now with ease
> Wafts on the calmer wave by dubious light
> And like a weather-beaten Vessel holds
> Gladly the Port, though Shrouds and Tackle torn;
> (1040)

But the rhetoric is not constant or elaborate enough to establish its own convention; it lapses, as in the lines above, into the

[1] A textbook classic of anaphora, auxesis, climax, collectour (concluding repetition of key-words).

poem's underlying realism. Satan is not floating in a soully shallop through mental chaos to a psychological landfall, but navigating an actual district of the poem's firmly-delineated cosmos towards the reader's living universe, and taking with him the physical presence, the ally-making generalship and the mundane associations that belonged to him in Hell. The Spice Island simile (634-42) expands from the fantasy of the devils' explorations into the world of 17th-century commercial geography and starts Satan off on a voyage that curves up to the outer shell of the universe in Book III and down to Eden in Book IV, with well-marked resting-places at the gate of Hell, the court of Chaos, the outer convex, the sun, and the cliff of Paradise. The whole voyage is related in maritime terms, many of them conventional, Spenserian, Virgilian,[1] but all realistic, and some (such as the Spice Islands and vulture similes) peculiarly accurate in their geography. There is a good deal of weird imagery as well—Lapland witches, "Ophiucus huge", the gryphon—but it is continuous with and on the full scale of the imagery of the realistic Hell of Book I (the fairies, Orion, classical monsters and Leviathan). So when we meet Sin and Death, and Chaos and Night, we are not so ready for allegory and rhetoric as if we had moved without change in the method of presentation from "*Gorgons* and *Hydra's* and *Chimera's* dire".

Allegory must rely on a convention, but here is a baffling confusion of analogues. Milton's Sin is Spenser's Error, "Halfe like a serpent horribly displaide, But th'other halfe did womans shape retaine" (*F.Q.* I. i. 14); she is related to Cerberus, Scylla and medieval witches; yet not Christianised like Gower's Sin (whose offspring are the Seven Deadly Sins), or dramatised like Giles Fletcher's Harmatia who is the daughter of Satan and Eve (*Purple Island*, xii. 27-30). Then Death is described like Phineas Fletcher's Sin, "A shapeless shape, a foule deformed thing, Nor nothing, nor a substance" (*Appolyonists*, i. 10), these terms being derived via Spenser's Death—"Vnbodied, vnsoul'd, vnheard, vnseene" (*F.Q.* VII. vii. 46)—from Virgil's Cyclops, "monstrum horrendum, informe, ingens, cui lumen ademptum"[2]

[1] Cf. Maia's flight in *Aen.* I. 301: "remigio alarum" (ed. and trans. H. R. Fairclough, 2 vols. 1916-18: Loeb).

[2] *Aen.* III. 658. This shows the limit of logic in classical references: in Book I it was Satan who carried Cyclops' wand.

Milton's rhetoric is more efficient than the Elizabethans'—

> The other shape,
> If shape it might be call'd that shape had none
> Distinguishable in member, joynt, or limb,
> Or substance might be call'd that shadow seem'd,
> For each seem'd either;

—but it adds nothing to the conception of Death and the conventionality throws us back on so many minor analogues[1] that we find it difficult to apprehend either Sin or Death as a distinct character in this poem. Macbeth's hell was more significantly opened and shut, and Virgil's[2] writhed with a Latin that makes Milton's language deserve the Humanists' contempt for the vernacular. Of Milton's expeditio for the figure of Death, "black it stood as Night, Fierce as ten Furies, terrible as Hell", Bentley objected that

> to make One Person *Death* to be as fierce as *Ten Furies* together, smells of trivial and common Chat: and then *Terrible as Hell* is quite ridiculous. The man did not attend, that the Scene here is Hell: so Death, according to Him, was no more terrible, than the Place he sat in.[3]

A few lines further on we have again "the true Milton":

> The Monster moving onward came as fast
> With horrid strides, Hell trembled as he strode.

Death is really monstrous now, and when he and Satan address for combat their textures are fully differentiated as unreal, and solid:

> So spake the grieslie terrour, and in shape
> So speaking and so threatning, grew ten fold
> More dreadful and deform:

but

> on th'other side
> Incenc't with indignation *Satan* stood
> Unterrifi'd, and like a Comet burn'd . . .

[1] E.g. Shakespeare's Death in *Venus and Adonis* (951 ff.), Sackville's Misery in the *Mirror* (xxxvii ff.).

[2] VI. 273:

> vestibulum ante ipsum primisque in faucibus Orci
> Luctus et ultrices posuere cubilia Curae . . .
> mortiferumque adverso in limine Bellum
> ferreique Eumenidum thalami et Discordia demens,
> vipereum crinem vittis innexa cruentis.

[3] Ed. *P.L.*, 1732.

The improvement is partly due to the intense interest of a father-son opposition. But the differentiation between them, and some Biblical sources for the episode, suggest that Milton was trying to construct an allegory subtler than any of his predecessors. The standard text is in *James*:

> Let no man say when he is tempted, I am tempted of God: for God cannot be tempted with evil, neither tempteth he any man: But every man is tempted, when he is drawn away of his own lust, and enticed. Then when lust hath conceived, it bringeth forth sin: and sin, when it is finished [RSV full-grown], bringeth forth death.
>
> (i. 13, 14)

The Old Testament sources of this text include the *Psalms*, where as we have seen the prayed-for fate of Irsael's enemies is a major source for Christian notions of Satan and Hell. Satan may be read into *Psalm* vii especially, where "the enemy" is single; and it is there that "he travaileth with iniquity, and hath conceived mischief, and brought forth falsehood". In the similar context of *Psalm* xlviii the kings are met at Jerusalem, like Satan "at th' Assembly, and in sight Of all the Seraphim" (II. 749), and they are astonished by the splendour:

> They saw it, and so they marvelled; they were troubled, and hasted away. Fear took hold upon them there, and pain, as of a woman in travail.

This is how Satan conceives Sin, to comfort him in the face of omnipotent holiness:

> All on a sudden miserable pain
> Surpris'd thee, dim thine eyes, and dizzie swumm
> In darkness,
>
> (II. 752)

It is an allegory of human *Angst*, fearfully rejecting the reality of spiritual goodness and love, and fabricating instead images of ideal self or ideal parent-lover figure in which to allay its own ambitions, fears and lusts: "Thy self in me thy perfect image viewing Becam'st enamour'd . . ." (see Plate II). The issue is death because reality is died to. Sin and Death are shadowy and temporary figures because they are, ultimately,

University Library, Cambridge

II Richard Westall

The Birth of Sin (1794)

unreal—figments of the "evil imagination" which, according to the Rabbis, man was created with. In the Old Testamant it is this *yetser ha-ra'*[1], the pretensions and abuses inherent in the human heart because it is human, that leads to self-deification and idolatry. Hence in *Paradise Lost* Satan, Sin and Death parody the Trinity. It is in relation to Sin and Death that Satan acts as disposer of the universe. Sin his begotten accepts his promise of glorification:

> thou wilt bring me soon
> To that new world of light and bliss, among
> The Gods who live at ease, where I shall reign
> At thy right hand voluptuous,
>
> (II. 866)

She parodies the submissive cadences of filial obedience given to the Father by the Son, and ironically emphasises its denial by Satan, Eve and Adam:

> Thou art my Father, thou my Author, thou
> My being gav'st me; whom should I obey
> But thee, whom follow?

When finally Sin and Death bridge Chaos they pervert the Son's creative "disparting" of Chaos from the World, and "Hovering upon the Waters" (X. 284) they abuse the potency and office of the Holy Spirit. So also, when Adam and Eve eat the apple their sensations are similar to Satan's at the conception of Sin: "They swim in mirth, and fansie that they feel Divinitie within them breeding wings . . . Carnal desire enflaming . . . in Lust they burne" (X. 1009), and so on to the issue of death.

The relationships between Satan and Sin and Death also have a purely theological function. The text from *James* is intended as a disproof of God's responsibility for evil, and in the poem Sin's account of her birth establishes Satan, to his astonishment, as the literal "Author of all ill" (II. 381). If nevertheless Sin be a created thing of real spiritual or physical substance (as Luther regarded it), it must still be ultimately of God's creating, particularly in the Miltonic universe created of

[1] The medieval Rabbis held that man was created with *yetser ha-ra'*, "evil imagination" planted in him, on the basis of *Gen.* vi 5, "every imagination of his heart was only evil continually"—a comment on the "sons of God" story which for a long time had superior status as a Fall-myth to the Adamic.

the substance of God. This is Monism. But for Sin to be in the last resort unreal, a beloved superstition, is to absolve God from responsibility except so far as he allowed to angels and men a share of his own creative thought. "Sin has not been sent upon the earth, But man of himself has created it" is the doctrine in *I Enoch*, the *locus classicus* for Fall theory.[1] The episode also dismisses the opposite heresy, Dualism. Dualism is inherent in any realistic conception of Satan, but Milton avoids it as far as possible by emphasising the very efforts which demonstrate Satan's subordinate status: the godlike paraphernalia, titular extravagances, the antonomasia that refers to God as Enemy, Thunderer, Torturer. Pandemonium itself, and now the regal promises to Sin and Death, are desperate attempts of the creature to assert Dualistic equality with its Creator; and no objections to the quality of the heavenly power can blur the distinction between its inaccessible and self-existing permanence and the adscititious opportunism of Satan.

[1] The standard work on the Apocrypha is by R. M. Charles. Although the Apoc. was included in all 16th-century translations of the Bible, Protestant and Catholic, and in the AV of 1611, it was objected to by Puritans and came to be left out of the Bible in the 17th century. Yet it forms an important background not only to the origins of Christianity (most of the books were written between 200 B.C. and A.D. 100) but also to Protestant thought and especially to Milton's material: the books are argumentative, legendary, Pharisaic (or Scribal: opposing ecclesiastical law to the pretensions of politically ambitious priests and ecclesiastically ambitious princes), apocalyptic and pneumatological (much of what Milton is supposed by Saurat to have got from the Cabbala probably came from the apocalyptic books of the Apoc. which were the source of the 12th-century Jewish Cab.). Some Miltonic interests in the Apoc. are: (1) Original sin, with uneasy querying of its justice and Uriel's reply "How can you understand anything?"—*II Esdras*, iii; iv. 30. (2) Predestination: *II Esd.* viii. 1; ix. 21-22; *Wisdom of Solomon.* (3) Fall: generally in *I Enoch, Jubilees.* (4) Adam and Eve given dramatic character: several books. (5) Serpent identified with Satan: *Wis. of Sol.* iii. 24. (6) Angels: *I Enoch*, vi-xi—expansion of *Gen.* vi with Aazazel as villain and Michael (Watcher over good men and Chaos), Raphael (Watcher over spirits of men), Uriel (Watcher of the world and tartarus) and Gabriel (Watcher over paradise, serpents and cherubim) as heroes. (7) Devils the issue of miscegenation between angels and men (as in *Gen.* vi; cf. *P.L.* III. 461, etc.): *I Enoch*, xv. 8-9. (8) Election of Son of Man, before Creation: *I Enoch*, xlviii. 4. (9) Astronomical alteration of world after Fall: *I Enoch*, lxxx. (10) Things going from bad to worse after Fall (common theme *c.* 1600, cf. *P.L.* XII. 537): *II Esd.* xiv. 16-20. (11) Potted histories of Israel (cf. *P.L.* XII and standard Christian schemes of historical election to redemption): several books, especially *Judith* and *Ecclesiasticus* (or *Sirach*). (12) Heroising of the patriarchs: *Eccl.* xliv ff. (13) Idolatrous art productive of fornication, dissension, etc.: *Wis. of Sol.* xiv. (cf. *P.L.* I, XI).

The scene has inspired many illustrators of *Paradise Lost*[1] because of its dramatic grouping and the conjunction of exciting ambivalencies—Satan's incestuous potency, Sin's repellent allurements, Death's parricidal fury and his symbolising of the consummation and punishment of sexuality. But in the poem, of all the allegory, only the parodying of God comes through sharply. The Biblical sources are obscured by Homeric reference —"a Goddess arm'd Out of thy head I sprung" (II. 757)—and the significance of Sin and Death's insubstantiality is lost in the coarser convention of their being a bizarre joke. In popular woodcuts (such as Holbein's) of the Dance of Death and in emblems, Death is the skeleton, pitiably clad in rags or ragged flesh, that Milton and his literary sources describe: but the joke is always on his victims. It was usual for Christian poets to turn the joke back on Death, as in Milton's clockcase poem and Donne's "Death be not proud"; but to do this was still to treat the subject as in a cartoon. I think Milton had inklings that more could be done with it; but he failed, largely because the cartoon treatment was congenial to him. The grim smile, the repellent organic imagery and the wild exertion of his prose colour his Sin and Death, here and in Book X, as they colour the poem's other large allegory, the Limbo of Fools. Narrative allegory is essentially a polemical or didactic technique, so that when a poet who is trained in pragmatic polemic uses allegory for a literary purpose he is almost bound to write more coarsely than in his straightforward narrative. The area of Milton's mind which Sin and Death inhabited is defined by the line that joins Sin to St Peter in the anti-clerical passage of "Lycidas", and the Whore of Babylon (the Pope) in the *Appolyonists*:

> And in his hand two golden keyes he beares,
> To open heav'n and hell, and shut againe.
> But late his keyes are marr'd, or lost; for hell
> He cannot shut, but opes, and enters well:
>
> (iii. 16)

[1] The only scenes more popular than this are some involving Eve asleep or tempted (for their nude value), the expulsion from Paradise, and the heroic stance of Satan rousing the fallen angels. See C. H. Collins-Baker, "Some Illustrators of Milton's *P.L.*", *The Library*, 5th Ser., III (1948), 1-21, 101-119, with reproductions. I am much indebted to this article, and to Mr A. N. L. Munby for drawing my attention to it.

In this sort of context it doesn't matter how badly you write. Milton's failure to open up his inkling and present an immaterial Sin and Death far more real and dangerous than the figures he describes was of the same kind as his inability to take his human opponents seriously or see their point. Both failures symptomise a failure to understand his own soul. If you habitually crush your external enemies or disperse them in spittle of rhetoric you are likely to do the same to the enemies within. So Milton, dimly perceiving perhaps the common conflicts in him[1], instead of facing them, and turning away in the calm of understanding, aggravates their beastliness at the arm's length of narrative until he induces in himself enough horror to trample shuddering on what he now believes to be objective lumps of evil, when all the time they are just the lazy monsters of his own mind's ocean. "Which if not Victory is yet Revenge." It is a victory whose hollowness, at least in the external arena, Adam came to understand:

> with good
> Still overcoming evil, and by small
> Accomplishing great things, by things deemd weak
> Subverting worldly strong, and worldly wise
> By simply meek;
>
> (XII. 565)

Possibly Milton himself learnt it too, and internally: the Christ of *Paradise Regained*, armed with no trampling steeds, turns quietly away from temptations that Milton in *Paradise Lost* had brutalised in Hell. There are places even here when he seems to face and withdraw from his own monstrosities: tumescent Satan is restrained from combat by recognising Death as his son. But enough unrecognised conflicts go on: why should the "Sad instrument of all our woe" be a key hung from Sin's waist?[2]

[1] Sin is a classic example of what Jung calls "the Terrible Mother . . . above, the human, lovely and attractive half; below, the horrible animal half, converted into a fear animal through the incest prohibition" (*op. cit.* p. 113, etc.). Although there may be more direct anthropological explanations for some of these figures (e.g. in animal ritual), this is one of Jung's finest insights; we need it here especially because Milton's presentation of Sin as a character is so muddled.

[2] I don't know the source of this detail; it is not Biblical. Blake's illustration emphasises it. If you take symbolism seriously the key can only be permission to possess Sin.

This refusal to acknowledge strangers in the self is at the heart of Protestant monotheism. It was foreign to the Protestant spirit to multiply gods whether cosmic, political or psychic. In *Pilgrim's Progress*, Christian does battle with a variety of sins, giants, devils and deviationists, because Bunyan while rejecting metropolitan Papacy still felt as a rural Catholic; but the more sophisticated Protestant notion has always been of continuous single combat with the Evil One himself. This is the basis of the Puritan's sense of personal involvement in the cosmic struggle between good and evil. It is fatal to allegory and almost fatal to Theistic fiction as a whole, for with the imagination purged of all personifiable projections of both evil and good there remains nothing but the ultimate realities of God and Satan, imaginable only in the rapt vision of a mystic or the last ecstacy of a genuine Satanist.

Less can be said for Chaos. All that Milton himself need have said is in seven lines:

> Before thir eyes in sudden view appear
> The secrets of the hoarie deep, a dark
> Illimitable Ocean without bound,
> . . . .
> Into this wilde Abyss,
> The Womb of nature and perhaps her Grave,
> . . . .
> Into this wilde Abyss the warie fiend
> Stood on the brink of Hell and look'd a while,
> Pondering his Voyage;
> (890 . . . 910 . . . 917)

The simple, vast vision is split with rhetoric about the war of atoms, and followed by bathos: to compare Chaos with a battle is indeed "to compare Great things with small" (921), while to compare it with world-wide nuclear fission (924) is merely to say that chaos is like itself. The moral is ineffectually obvious. The court of Chaos (959 ff.) is the title-page to a titanic folio but adds nothing to the action, particularly as all the qualities personified by the courtiers have been actualised already—Confusion, for instance, is used as an ordinary substantive a few lines before (897) and both it and Tumult occur again before the end of the book (996, 1040), to say nothing of their adjectival forms. The "Anarch old" is something of a character. "If that way be your walk", he says, pointing to "the wilde expanse . . . Of fighting Elements" (1014), "you have not farr". But this is not significant characterisation any more than "Havock and spoil and ruin are my gain" (1009). Exhausted by his own Chaos, Milton collapses into chaotic writing on all sides—there is no point to the alliteration in "except whom God and good Angels guard by special grace" (1033); even Puttenham thought four alliterations excessive.

Our desire for chaos is less urgent than Lawrence's in 1928, but his essay on "Chaos in Poetry", pertinent to the whole poem, may be quoted to explain what happens next:

> Man must wrap himself in a vision, make a house of apparent form and stability, fixity. In his terror of chaos he begins by putting up an umbrella between himself and the everlasting whirl. Then he paints the underside of his umbrella like a firmament. Then he parades around, lives and dies under his umbrella. Bequeathed to his descendants, the umbrella becomes a dome, a vault, and men at last begin to feel that something is wrong.[1]

So, as Satan moves out of turmoil into order, Milton recovers. In the lines about the World as a star we are prepared for the immensity of Heaven and its gems and starry angels; but the vision is offered also on the scale of a woman's throat. Satan's "fresh alacritie and force renew'd" (1012) are spent in the story, and lose value in the reader's imagination, beside the glittering fragility of "th' Empyreal Heav'n" and "This pendant World".

[1] *Selected Literary Criticism* ed. A. Beale (1955), p. 90.

4

HEAVEN

1. *Introductory*

> I cannot enter upon subjects of so much difficulty as the SON OF GOD and the HOLY SPIRIT, without again prefacing a few introductory remarks.
>
> *De Doctrina Christiana*

TRYING to make it easier for us to palate the God of *Paradise Lost*, C. S. Lewis points out that "In the religious life man faces God and God faces man. But in the epic it is feigned, for a moment, that we, as readers, can step aside and see the faces both of God and man in profile."[1] This is to transcend the all-transcendent; however pious the motives may be it remains logically impossible to contemplate God—he ceases to be God as you do it. Therefore all objective discussions of God are absurd, and though they may be amusing their contact with reality is restricted to moments at which the listener may share a glimpse of the speaker's God. That is not a philosophical experience, but an aesthetic one. "What is offered to man's apprehension in any specific Revelation is not truth concerning God but the living God Himself."[2] This is the form taken by the most satisfactory literary revelations. This is not to say that devotional poems are the best or only possible religious literature. Donne's holy sonnets, Herbert's descriptions of his struggles with God, Hopkins' "terrible sonnets", are not images of God but of the relationship between the poet and his God. It is true though, that any presentation of God in narrative must be within the individual's vision of him. The poet must take responsibility for what he sees as God. Unless he does, the God

[1] *Preface*, p. 128. With my counter argument cf. Kierkegaard: "A religious poet . . . will seek to establish a relation to the religious through the imagination; but for this very reason he succeeds only in establishing an aesthetic relationship to something aesthetic." There are several versions of the statements in *Either/Or*, e.g. in the essay on "The Ancient Tragical Motive" (trans. D. F. and L. M. Swenson, 2 vols. 1946).

[2] William Temple, *Nature, Man and God* (1934), p. 322.

he presents will be open to theological and philosophical objections, as well as to literary criticism.

In the Old Testament God is a person: "Thus saith Yahveh", "And the word of Yahveh came unto me saying"; even the hellenised parts of the New Testament claim to be records of the experience that the writers have had of the living God in the resurrected Son or in vision. But the tendency in the art of Christendom has been to present God either Platonically or Homerically, or as a mixture of the two. Spenser's God is Platonic. In the *Faerie Queene* he confessed that the Holy City was "Too high a ditty for my simple song" of objective fiction (I. x. 55) so in the *Hymns* he described heaven and God in abstract patterns of rhetoric. Heavenly love, instead of being a present power in the universe, or a dramatic motive in the poem, is "Th'idee of his pure glorie" (283) which we "shall plainely see" some day in the eschatalogical future. Heavenly beauty is not the face of God but "th'aspect of that felicitie, Which they haue written in their inward ey" (284). Giles Fletcher's God in *Christ's Triumph after Death* is also "th'Idea Beatificall", the paradoxically eternal end and beginning of everything, eyeless all-seeing—a structure of the intellect alone. Yet the heaven he lives in is an aesthetic pattern of solids:

> About the holy Cittie rowles a flood
> Of moulten chrystall, like a sea of glasse,
> On which weake streame a strong foundation stood;
> Of living Diamounds the building was,
> That all things else, beside it selfe, did passe.
>   Her streetes, in stead of stones, the starres did pave,
>   And little pearles, for dust, it seem'd to have,
> On which soft-streaming Manna, like pure snowe, did wave.
> (38)

This wrapping of a concrete, aesthetically conceived heaven round an abstract God typifies the discordance of Hebrew myth and Greek metaphysics. The heaven comes from *Revelation*, almost word for word; yet the mystic of *Revelation* had no scruples about anthropomorphism:

> I was in the Spirit on the Lord's day, and heard behind me a great voice as of a trumpet, saying, I am Alpha and Omega. . . . And I turned to see the voice that spake with me. And being

> turned, I saw seven golden candlesticks; and in the midst of the seven candlesticks one like unto the Son of man, clothed with a garment down to the foot.

The importance of John's recording his vision so subjectively—"It happened to me"—is demonstrated by Fletcher in another poem of his series, *Christ's Victory in Heaven.* There he uses the mythological method consistently, managing to dramatise the Trinity as well as the angels and heaven itself into some appearance of cosmic action and immortal personalities. But Fletcher himself is not involved at all, so the effect is merely Homeric; religion is obscured in myth.

The *Paradiso* is consummated by a vision of the Trinity which, though Platonically geometrical in outline, is infused with more than ideographical potency by Dante's own passion:

> la mia mente fu percossa
> da un fulgore in che sua voglia venne.
>
> All' alta fantasia qui mancò possa;
> ma già volgeva il mio disio e 'l velle,
> sì come rota ch'egualmente è mossa,
>
> l'amor che move il sole e l'altre stelle.
>
> (xxxiii. 140)

The poetry makes the "tre giri di tre colori e d'una continenza" (116) adequate as symbols for the divine love and will that the poem is about, and even for the world outside the poem. Dante's God is hot as well as bright, a rose as well as a circle. There are difficulties, however, even with the *Paradiso.* The chief aesthetic difficulty is that the journey is not an action. Parts of it anticipate the consummation—the light imagery, the poet's own sensations, the explanation in Canto iii of the state of the blessed which Dante is to achieve—"è formale ad esto beato *esse* tenersi dentro alla divina voglia, per ch'una fansi nostre voglie stesse" (79). But it is difficult to remain interested in the Platonic cosmographying, the Aristotelian metaphysics and the Thomist theology that Dante discusses with Beatrice and the saints on his way up through "una ad una spiritali vita"—what have these to do with "l'amor che move il sole e l'altre stelle"? The religious difficulty in the poem lies in its chief aesthetic excellence, that we reach God only at the end. This is where Dante differs from *Revelation*. His God is immensely powerful but puts not forth his power—we do not see him immanent in any act, of creation, redemption, judgement. Except for the reader already at peace on the circumference of his will, he is not the still point of the turning world but the final point of an individual mystic vision.

This is perhaps the basic difficulty of Christian theology, that it cannot be mediated to any who have not themselves seen its God, even through Christ; for Christ is of only ethical interest unless he be recognised as God's Son. As Milton says in *De Doctrina*, "the disciples of the doctrine of Christ may fairly be required to give assent to this truth [*sc.* that God exists] before all others, according to Heb. xii. 6. 'he that cometh to God must believe that he is' " (iv. 15). The only answer to the question, "Who is the god of the Christians?" is Pothinus', "If thou art worthy, thou shalt know". The Reformation was partly an attempt to return to this position. It recognised the deficiencies in both the standard views of God: a Platonic theology can appeal only to men of intellect and education, an anthropomorphic one becomes in the hands of unmystical men a mythology; and neither is of much help in promoting individual morality or social justice. Yet though it strove to return to the simple ethical monotheism of the Hebrew prophets, the Reformation could not escape the contemporary influence of Greek metaphysics, Roman law and the Humanistic sense of history. It implicated the individual Christian in the divine process, but the process was as difficult to understand as ever. Thus Calvin, to us an iconoclast, saw himself as a practical anthropomorphist decrying intangible Catholic mysticisms:

> As for those who proudly soar above the world to seek God in his unveiled essence, it is impossible but that at length they should entangle themselves in a multitude of absurd figments. For God—by other means invisible—(as we have already said) clothes himself, so to speak, with the image of the world, in which he would present himself to our contemplation. They who will not deign to behold him thus magnificently arrayed in the incomparable vesture of the heavens and the earth, afterwards suffer the just punishment of their proud contempt in their own ravings. Therefore, as soon as the name of God sounds in our ears, or the thought

> of him occurs to our minds, let us also clothe him with this most beautiful ornament; finally, let the world become our school if we desire rightly to know God.[1]

But theology of a concretely manifest God is probably more intractable than Dante's. In Protestantism each man his own priest, deprived of the vicarious faith of componence in the Church as the mystical Body of Christ, has to work out his own salvation face to face with God; and for men of intellect not given to personal mysticism this means working out something like a sum in arithmetic.

Milton, convinced of the ethical and political truth of Reformation Christianity, was only casually a visionary of God. Of John Smith's categories of the religious he had been in his Idealist days and still was occasionally something of "the true metaphysical and contemplative man . . . who running and shooting up above his own logical or self-rational life, pierceth into the highest life". But he was never able to reach the mystic's consummation of "knitting his own centre . . . into the centre of Divine being"; at worst the Enthusiast's "sense of his own virtue and knowledge", at best the Rationalist's "glass . . . of reason and understanding",[2] as well as his Hebraic pragmatism, drew him back into the world of sense and argument. Typically of the English mixture of Jewish, Greek and Roman traditions, his normal approach to God was an attempt—like the Victorian doubters—to get him down to his own level for a debate. Milton did not enjoy the spiritual serenity or the environing peace or the worldly success which variously enabled the Metaphysical poets and the Cambridge Platonists to ignore the chaos of theology and find heaven in a vision or in themselves. He could not know Sir Thomas Browne's Dantesque heaven, for instance:

> where the Soul hath the full measure and complement of happiness; where the boundless appetite of that spirit remains compleatly satisfied, that it can neither desire addition nor alteration; that, I think, is truly Heaven: and this can onely be in the injoyment of that essence, whose infinite goodness is able to terminate

[1] *Commentaries on Genesis* trans. J. King (2 vols. Edinburgh, 1847), i. 60. Cf. Cudworth in Tulloch, *Rational Theology and Christian Philosophy* (2 vols. 1872), ii. 230-31.

[2] Powicke, pp. 98-9.

> the desires of it self, and the unsatiable wishes of ours. . . . Heaven, whose happiness consists in that part which is best able to comprehend it, that immortal essence, that translated divinity and colony of God, the Soul.[1]

Of other hexemeral poets, Grotius and Vondel had not presented God at all; most others just addressed him lyrically in invocations. Milton in this invocation approaches God in a mood which I think Sewell has caught:

> The immediate and satisfying consciousness of God, resulting from a confidence in God's special providence for England and for himself, had gone. The experiential proofs of God's favour had been found wanting. Little was left except a deep habit of mind expressing itself in an inadequate logical framework.[2]

But because he was not God-happy, something of the interest of devotional poetry does attach to the theologising of Book III.

2. *Invocation*

The paean to light forces problems on us. In the "Nativity Ode" the Son had been presented as

> That glorious Form, that Light unsufferable,
> And that far-beaming blaze of Majesty,

The indicative *that's* and the epithet "unsufferable" establish the "Form" as genuinely Platonic, something more than an ideograph; but here in *Paradise Lost* the light that Milton hails, though it suggest the Son—"ofspring of Heav'n first-born"—is coldly, even Scholastically presented. The analogue is Tasso's opening of *Le Sette Giornate del Mondo Creato*,[3] a didactic document

[1] *Rel. Med.* i. 49 . . . 51.

[2] *Study*, p. 111.

[3]
> Padre del Cielo, e tu del Padre Eterno
> Eterno Figlio, e non creato prole,
> Dell' immutabil mente unico parto:
> Divina imago al tuo divino esempio
> Eguale; e lume pur di lume ardente:
> E tu, che d'ambo spiri, e d'ambo splendi,
> O di gemina luce acceso Spirto,
> Che se' pur sacro lume, a sacra fiamma,
> Quasi lucido rivo in chiaro fonte,
> E vera imago ancor di vera imago . . .

of the Counter-Reformation, not the Age of Faith. This kind of writing seems to belong to the third stage in Ruskin's outline of the development of the false ideal in religious art:

> For a long time, when art was in its infancy, it remained unexposed to this danger [*sc.* of creating false images], because it could not, with any power, realize or create *any* thing. It consisted merely in simple outlines and pleasant colours; which were understood to be nothing more than signs of the thing thought of. . . . But as soon as art attained the power of realization, it obtained also that of *assertion*. . . . But a shadow of increasing darkness fell upon the human mind as art proceeded to still more perfect realization. These fantasies of the earlier painters, though they darkened faith, never hardened *feeling*. . . . In early times *art was employed for the display of religious facts*; now, *religious facts were employed for the display of art.* The transition, though imperceptible, was consummate; it involved the entire destiny of painting. It was passing from the paths of life to the paths of death.
>
> And this change was all the more fatal, because at first veiled by an appearance of greater dignity and sincerity than were possessed by the older art.[1]

Yet Milton's lines are not assertive. The metaphysical terminology, the querying ("May I express thee unblam'd?"), the adduction of Biblical authority ("since God is light"), the logic ("dwelt then in thee") invite us to share an intellectual effort to understand God in the world. It is, so far, very intellectual. Augustine's distinction between "the light which is God and the other light which God has made" is confused. Milton's affinities are with more speculative theologians. Flud had wondered whether "light is increate or created by an increate light". Plotinus used light to designate the creative, unifying energy that emanates from the One, the Father, the Good, the first person of the Neo-Platonic triad of hypostases. His authority, "God is light", is *I John.* If this was meant literally in the

1780 ed., London (I don't know of any modern ed. or a trans.). See Prince, *Italian Element in Milton's Verse* (Oxford, 1954). Milton and Tasso had Dante and Scholastic jargon in common, of course, as well as the figures of rhetoric; but a glance at Tasso is helpful in revealing the literal intent of some of Milton's apparently abstract or vaguely impressive words—*ardente, spiri, splendi, lucido* retain for the English reader more of the sensuousness that Milton was trying to use than their English equivalents.

[1] *Modern Painters,* Part IV, Chap. iv, Sec. 7. 5 vols. n.d. (1907: Everyman).

epistle or by Milton, it introduces Zoroastrianism, a Persian religion close to Judeo-Christianity in its mythology yet heretically Dualistic: the cosmic battle is between light and dark as equally divine aspects of Deity. So the learned reader is forced to ask, Is the God of *Paradise Lost* Ahura Mazdah, who is also Satan? or the One of primitive Neo-Platonism? or the Good of Plato? or the Johannine "light of the world"? or light as Newton saw it? The lines alone would merely stir inchoate lumber of the mind like this, but Milton passes swiftly enough to more orthodox suggestions for them to serve only as a gesture of fellowhip to the intellectual, whose worship must always be uncomfortable because his God, if he means anything at all, must mean so many complicated things. The "pure ethereal stream" which light may prefer to be called comes from *Psalm* xxxvi:

> the children of men . . . shall be watered with the fatness of thy house; and thou shalt make them drink of the river of thy pleasures. For with thee is the fountain of life: in thy light shall we see light.
>
> (7 *mg.*)

This has its difficulties too. The river, a fairly homely oriental metaphor, becomes the symbol of light as created life. But it is also a symbol for intellectual clarity, as in *Psalm* cxviii, "God is Yahveh, which hath shewed us light" (27). Bacon had brought the two together on the basis of the third verse of *Genesis*, saying that light as the first thing to be created was to nature and the material as knowledge is to supernature and the abstract or spiritual. But Milton descends lower, into his own soul. This passage is rendered liturgical and choric by the undulating rhythms ("The dark descent, and up to reascend" is typical). The reader is offered identity with Tiresias, Thamyris, Homer, Phineus, the nightingale and Milton himself as seers singing in the dark, striving to apprehend the unknowable and understand its unsearchable decrees. It is possible to grope and "feel thy sovran lamp" but not to see it, though profane and sacred poetry assist, the natural theology of the world, man's divinity, the regularity of the seasons, testify to the Creator's glory. A formalised version of Wordsworth's and Coleridge's *ichabod* odes, it is curiously penitential for an epic invocation. "Celestial light Shine inward" is a prayer for vision whereas Dante's corresponding prayer is for power to manifest the vision he has had:

> O divina virtù, se mi ti presti
> tanto che l'ombra del beato regno
> segnata nel mio capo io manifesti . . .
> (*Par.* i. 22)

The arrogantly intellectualised light of the first lines has been reduced through the splendid symbolic light of the *Psalms* to something indefinite, an only hope, as in the third collect, "for aid against all perils", at evensong: "Lighten our darkness, we beseech thee, O Lord". Even the dynamics of Platonism have gone: the Biblical mystics being caught up into heaven, Plotinus being drawn up by 'ερος, Dante by Beatrice, the medieval mystics somehow achieving the beatific vision for its own sake, have collapsed into the quiet ethical approach to God of Whichcote:

> The mind diverted from God wanders in darkness and confusion. But being directed to Him, soon finds its way, and doth receive from Him in a way that is abstracted from the noise of the world, and withdrawn from the call of the body; having shut the doors of our senses, to recommend ourselves to the Divine light, which readily enters into the eye of the mind that is prepared to receive it.[1]

In some ways this makes the transition to heroic narrative extra difficult. Not only will there always be a difference between what you see "Of things invisible to mortal sight" and what you manage to tell, but the suggestions of Platonism in whatever form dissipate the idea of an immanently active and personal God. Neither the "serene and lovely God" of John Smith nor its Deistic and Pantheistic derivatives—Newton's providential *primum mobile*, Wordsworth's impellent "motion and a spirit", Shaw's *élan vital*—has any more personality than a God who "is light"; and a God who can only be sensed intuitively cannot be justified in discourse. On the other hand the invocation which admits this confusion—and it is a confusion we all share—has set the episode in the framework of personal experience which is essential to the representation of God in literature.

[1] Powicke, p. 83.

The transition is conducted cautiously. It abolishes temporal sequence—"Now had the Almighty Father . . . where he sits . . . bent down his eye . . . past present future he beholds, Thus . . . spake"—for "in Eternity there is no distinction of Tenses."[1] The Father is steadfastly enthroned; then there is a vertiginous glance at "His own works and their works"; a glance back at the angels, abstract as "Sanctities", concrete as stars; then the Son, "radiant image of his Glory", a description which evokes his transfiguration and our experience of sunlight radiating from a mirror. The view goes down again to Earth, the distant "blissful solitude" suggesting the atmosphere of dream; then Satan in the present as he was at the end of Book II, his winged and footed scrabbling, his base mortality (weighed verbally in "the *dun* air") assuring the spirituality of Heaven; and finally "thus to his onely Son foreseeing spake". The crushing of language into this expressionless line is an attempt to amalgamate in one mould the vision and the word, past and future, Father and Son. It is the key to the celestial dialogue.

3. *The Godhead*

The Father's speeches accord only too well with the Argument; he "clears his own Justice and Wisdom from all imputation, having created Man free and able enough to have withstood his Tempter". It is more important to condemn this than to make allowances for Milton's difficulties or the historical conditions of theology. Dramatically, the argument is ineffectual —so far as the poem is concerned, man has not yet been created, has not sinned, and has not imputed injustice or folly to God; so that the speeches are a work of supererogation. From the religious point of view it is vicious: the poet's rationalisings purport to be the expression of Divine reason. The Father speaks as judge, counsel and plaintiff in one. The plaintiveness offends most—"So will fall, Hee and his faithless Progenie: whose fault? Whose but his own?" (95). The figures of debate, and the literally meant forensic metaphors, are symptoms of a legalism indigenous to Judeo-Christianity. Apart from its psychological origins, legalism will inhere in any primitivistic movement of the Church for practical reasons. The movement,

[1] Browne, *Rel. Med.* i. 11.

being towards ideal apostolic conditions, will take for its authority the Paul who had to justify Christianity to Jews and Romans; it will wish to strengthen its case against the accusation of anarchy by an appearance of lawfulness; and against the sneer of upstart modernity it will try to root itself in the Old Testament. Hence "the language of the Covenant" in the 17th Century, legal and sheik-like, which is Milton's language here.

But beneath all this lie intricate schemes of logical rhetoric:

> As if Predestination over-rul'd
> Thir will, dispos'd by absolute Decree
> Or high foreknowledge; they themselves decreed
> Thir own revolt, not I: if I foreknew,
> Foreknowledge had no influence on their fault,
> Which had no less prov'd certain unforeknown.
>
> (114)

This is the most concise statement of the problem and one of its "solutions" ever written. Milton has acquired factitious control over the concepts by control of the language that designates them. That control was needed. Compare Chaucer's translation of Boethius on providence with Hooker's redaction of the same commonplace:

> The engendrynge of alle thinges . . . and all the progressiouns of muable nature, and al that moeveth in any manere, taketh his causes, his ordre, and his formes, of the stablenesse of the devyne thought. And thilke devyne thought that is iset and put in the tour (*that is to seyn, in the heighte*) of the simplicitie of God, stablissith many maner gises to things that ben to done; the which manere whan that men looken it in thilke pure clennesse of the devyne intelligence, it is ycleped purveyaunce; but whanne thilke manere is referred by men to thinges that it moeveth and disponyth, than of olde men it was clepyd destyne.[1]

> The natural generation and process of all things receiveth order of proceeding from the settled stability of divine understanding. This appointeth unto them their kinds of working; the disposition whereof in the purity of God's own knowledge and will is rightly termed by the name of Providence. The same being referred unto the things themselves here disposed by it, was wont by the ancients to be called natural Destiny.[2]

[1] Book III, Prosa 6. *Poetical Works* ed. F. N. Robinson (2nd ed. 1957).
[2] *Ecc. Pol.* I. iii. 4.

Obviously the clarity of syntactical rhetoric and the stability of a uniform vocabulary had to be achieved before a native philosophy or science could start work (hence the Johnsonianism of Bacon). In the 17th Century rhetoric of this kind was still exercised chiefly in sermons.[1] The Puritans objected to the tropal rhetoric of High Church preachers such as Donne: they wanted to strip away conceits, images, decoration, to suit the plainness of their preferred ecclesiastism. Their preachers developed a schematic rhetoric that would carve Scripture and feed the congregation with marrow of divinity. They were not seeking emotive devices, or intellectual appeal—metaphysical conceits savoured of curious speculation; they wished to know the "truth". There is a stolid honesty about this that carries over into the Father's sermon—at least we know, what we don't usually from an Anglican pulpit, precisely what he is saying. We can see the way it will go: already the Puritan sermon had affinities with the rationalist's discourse and the academic exercise. After the Commonwealth the sermon moved away from rhetoric into the form recommended by Bossuet, "renfermant toute son éloquence dans le cercle d'une grande vérité réligieuse", while philosophical dialectic, its fortifying rhetorical regimen having worked, was able to soften into the sure-of-being-understood elegance of Shaftesburian dialogue. By the time *Paradise Lost* was published, the Father's speech was antiquated. That Milton should have made him speak so skeletally implies anxiety, as if he were trying to authorise the dogma by solidification; or perhaps, by making it so unequivocal, to abandon his own responsibility for it. For all his querulousness, the Father does not speak with a human tongue: he juggles with a limited number of arbitrary words, meanings and syntactical shapes. "They themselves decreed Thir own revolt" is followed twelve lines later by "they themselves ordain'd thir fall", and "I made him just and right" by "for so I formd them free". Every sentence sets a balance: "what praise could they receive? What pleasure I from such obedience paid?", "of freedom both despoild, Made passive both", "Both what they judge and what they choose", and so on. An extraordinary pattern of alliteration, prosonomasia and traductio on the words free-freely-all-fall-fault-failed-fell runs through the Father's

[1] See Mitchell, *English Pulpit Oratory, passim.*

whole speech and into his next: lines 95, 96, 99, 101, 102, 118, 122, 128, 129 actually end with parts of this series, forming a subdued rhyme-scheme. Within the sentences argument depends on traductio of the "foreknowledge-foreknew-unforeknown" type. The words accelerate into a continuous single sound. This effect is appropriate in a way for it represents the Father's speech as Logos, Alpha and Omega, I AM. Milton has got the better of language—"Only by the form, the pattern, Can words or music reach the stillness"—but by desecrating its nature. Ultimately his triumph is vain for he leads us into a corridor of verbal mirrors in which unbodied concepts are defined by their antitheses so all we can do is mark time with our lips. It had been done much better, in the Bible and by the Metaphysicals, and has been since, usually by relying on Dantesque imagery and human experience:

> Inside the room was a great steadiness, a core of living eternity. Only far outside, at the rim, went on the noise and the destruction. Here at the centre the great wheel was motionless, centred upon itself. Here was a poised, unflawed stillness that was beyond time, because it remained the same, inexhaustible, unchanging, unexhausted.[1]

That succeeds not merely because it uses the human reflection instead of the divine source, but because it is enclosed in an experiential context more immediate than Milton's.

Some details in the Father's first speech suggest that it was not originally designed as the theological mainspring of the poem's action but as a bastion against the intellectual assaults of Milton-in-Satan. I suspect a suture about line 95 between two versions, the first treating the angels' rebellion only, the second adapting it to the Fall of Adam (as Milton himself had been, politically, a Satan in the forties, a self-justifying God in the fifties, and perforce a submissive Adam after 1660). "Hee and his faithless Progenie" seems to refer to "man" two lines before; but the Father has just been looking down to view "His own works and their works" (59): "their works" can hardly be Adam and Eve's "Reaping immortal fruits of joy and love . . . In blissful solitude"; it must be the counter-creative activity of Hell. "Progeny" looks human, but it is used of devils (II. 430) and angels (V. 600) as well as mankind (XI. 107). The sub-

[1] Lawrence, *The Rainbow*, Chap. VI.

sequent "his . . . he . . . him" probably refers to Adam, but the sentence runs on into "all th' Ethereal Powers", who can only be angelic. The terminology of "allegiance", and later on "fealtie" (or "realtie") and "Treason" (204, 207), is more political than one would expect if it referred to Adam. The Father's reference to the "sole Command" that pledges man's obedience (94) presupposes the explanation of the Tree of Knowledge to be given at IV. 420. There is the familiar confusion between the "begetting" of the Son in V, which causes Satan's rebellion, and his glorification here which is the result of his sacrificial offer. The angels' hymn here makes more of the Son's victory over the rebels than one might expect at this stage, when the event has not occurred in the poem, and it is verbally very close to the description in VI. The theology of Book III is repeated in X and XI, where it is more immediately relevant to man. The eschatology is duplicated twice, in Book XII (451-65, 544-51). There are many small inconsistencies in the poem,[1] due to the overlapping of dramatic and epical versions, and to its having been written in anachronological order, as well as to mere absentmindedness. But what seems to have happened in the case of Heaven is that, having in the first three books conducted his quarrel with God through Satan, Milton found he could finish it on the right side only by bringing himself up against the impregnable rhetoric of dogma, and the historical fact of Christ's death. The preliminary speeches in Heaven represent submission to the intolerable fact that God should universally exercise both the monarchic absolutism Milton rebelled against on earth, and the omnipotence, freedom and incontrovertible rightness that he aspired to.

The Son's rhetoric is more flexible. His first reply picks up the Father's decree, "Man therefore shall find grace", and weaves lyrical patterns with it as if to beautify brutality:

> Oh Father, gracious was that word which clos'd
> Thy sovran sentence, that Man should find grace;
>
> For should Man finally be lost, should Man
>
> that be from thee farr,
>
> That farr be from thee, Father,

[1] See A. H. Gilbert, *On the Composition of "P.L.": A Study of the Ordering and Insertion of Material* (Chapel Hill, 1947). Sewell and Waldock agree, for aesthetic reasons, about the split in the poem here.

The dancing turns and repetitions suggest "the still point". The Father modifies his rhetoric into them:

> Man shall not quite be lost, but sav'd who will,
> Yet not of will in him, but grace in me
>
> Upheld by me, yet once more he shall stand
> On even ground against his mortal foe,
> By me upheld,
>
> To pray, repent, and bring obedience due.
> To prayer, repentance, and obedience due.

But this lyric note is interrupted by eschatological crunchings:

> Thou at the sight
> Pleas'd, out of Heaven shalt look down and smile,
> While by thee rais'd I ruin all my Foes,
> Death last, and with his Carcass glut the Grave:
>
> (256)

The poem's parody-scheme backfires for the Son's manner of speaking about Death is the same as Death's manner of behaving: "Grinnd horrible a ghastly smile to hear His famine should be fill'd, and blest his mawe Destin'd to that good hour" (II. 845). The derisive laughter of Yahweh will not carry over from *Psalm* ii into the Heaven of *Paradise Lost* without debasement of both poems. Masson thought it "worthy of remark that Milton . . . should have been thus careful to support his own invention absolutely, and to keep close to the words of the Bible" in this scene. But many such lines in *Paradise Lost* confirm Arnold's complaint in *Literature and Dogma* that so long as literary criticism of the Bible lags behind linguistic, archaeological and bibliographical scholarship, Bibliolatry will go on usurping faith and excusing brutality. Thus, the comparatively sensitive epilogue to the Son's eschatological prophecy—

> Thou wilt not leave me in the loathsome grave
> His prey, nor suffer my unspotted Soule
> For ever in corruption there to dwell

—is a paraphrase of *Psalm* xvi.10. But that psalm is superior as poetry, and its subject, prayer for more abundant life—"in thy presence is fulness of joy"—is not Milton's. The most elaborate piece of eschatology is the Father's about the last judgement, final conflagration and new creation:

Mean while
The World shall burn, and from her ashes spring
New Heav'n and Earth, (333)

We receive no sense of cleansing fire or new birth: the phoenix imagery, which comes alive at the end of *Samson Agonistes*, is here quite dead. The Son's lyricism is finally ruptured in the Father's summary of his plan:

So Man, as is most just,
Shall satisfie for Man, be judg'd and die,
And dying rise, and rising with him raise
His Brethren, ransomd with his own dear life.
So Heav'nly love shal outdoo Hellish hate,
Giving to death, and dying to redeeme,
So dearly to redeem what Hellish hate
So easily destroy'd and still destroyes
In those who, when they may, accept not grace. (294)

This is one of the most rhetorical passages in the poem, and the schemes are potentially lyrical. But there is no poetic grace in their handling, therefore no sense in the reader of theological grace. The theology is orthodox, but the coagulation of language makes "Heav'nly love" feel so much the same as "Hellish hate" that again the Father might be Ahura Mazdah.

It is sometimes remarked that the devils in Pandemonium, God in Heaven and Adam in Paradise use rhetoric of differing kinds which distinguish between the speakers' dramatic and moral position in the poem. The devils use rhetoric persuasively to put their own points of view, without regard for truth, as condemned in the *Gorgias*; the Father uses it to make a truism of the truth; Adam uses it to celebrate creation, including his own divinely rational power over language. But the least successful contrast is between the Father's rhetoric in Book III and Satan's. At the temptation Satan asks:

Of good, how just? of evil, if what is evil
Be real, why not known, since easier shunnd?
God therefore cannot hurt ye, and be just;
Not just, not God; not feard then, nor obeyd:
Your feare it self of Death removes the fears.
(IX. 698)

The superficial similarities to the Father's speech are obvious. The only distinction is that Satan's rhetoric is forensically superior:

> One fatal Tree there stands of Knowledge call'd,
> Forbidden them to taste: Knowledge forbidd'n?
> Suspicious, reasonless. Why should thir Lord
> Envie them that? Can it be sin to know,
> Can it be death? and do they onely stand
> By Ignorance, is that thir happie state,
> The proof of thir obedience and thir faith?
>
> (IV. 514)

This is neater as sheer rhetoric—the epanalepsis and erotema of the second line, for example—and more dramatic: "Can it be sin to know, Can it be death?" is a real spoken doubt, not a rhetorical question; and the tone is morally preferable to the querulousness of the Father when he speaks with a real voice. We are left with only two distinctions of rhetoric that support the thesis of the poem, that God is better than Satan: Satan is never lyrical, and rarely schematic. His rhetoric is Pandemoniac not Heavenly: forensic, flickering through ploce and traductio and erotema with suspicious speed; pragmatic, lacking the ceremoniousness that in places gives to what the Father (and especially Adam) says an aesthetic value. This is not enough to mark the vast gap that the poem supposes to exist between the minds of God and Satan. The fault seems to lie in rhetoric itself. For all its elaborations as a system it is not a flexible enough instrument for the dramatic function of distinguishing between characters. It if be argued that this is not drama but epic, the reply is, I suppose, that we have in *Paradise Lost* a demonstration of the unsuitability of the epic form, with its assumption of a consistent epic style, for the representation of moral distinctions.

What rhetoric can do in epic, though, is to relate the actions of morally similar characters to each other or to a common source by choric echo. The Son's speeches do this:

> Behold mee then, mee for him, life for life
> I offer, on mee let thine anger fall;
> Account mee man;
>
> . . . .
>
> on me let Death wreak all his rage.
>
> (236)

This is the spring of self-sacrifice which Adam and Eve draw on after the Fall to recover sanity and love. The central ploce on "me" is repeated on an even larger scale by Adam, and then by Eve: "first and last On mee, mee onely, all the blame lights due . . . on me, sole cause to thee of all this woe, Mee mee onely just object of his ire" (X. 831 . . . 933; cf. 738, 817, 824 ff.).

The circular structure of the scene in Heaven, the angels' encirclement of the throne, their circling dances, the reciprocating dialectic of the divine will, as well as the details of rhetoric and the abstract language, make the episode essentially theoretical, a chorus on the poem's action. Milton seems to have modelled it on his conception of *Revelation* as

> the majestic image of a high and stately tragedy, shutting up and intermingling her solemn scenes and acts with a sevenfold chorus of hallelujahs and harping symphonies:
>
> (*R.C.G.* ii. 479)

—God the central protagonist, the angels in the orchestra. But the Heaven of *Paradise Lost* differs from that of *Revelation* as Dante's does. Instead of enacting the divine comedy the Father postulates it. This presentation of the Father as Platonic Mind "Consulting on the sum of things" (VI. 673) while second causes work its bidding is typical of a rationalistic age which has rejected a personal, interventional Deity; and of an age (such as the post-apostolic) or a man (Milton) whose expectation of divine intervention has been disappointed. We sympathise with the 17th-century distaste for anthropomorphism; better Milton's providential Father than the capricious Jove of *Gerusalemme Liberata* (e.g. ix. 57) with all his rhetorical virtuosity. But "Eternal Providence" is alien to the Hebraic mannerisms of Milton's God; and it is as safe a refuge for complacent atheism as for disappointed faith. The Deistical result of 17th-century rationalism, obvious in Milton, is to deny the distinctive tenet of Christianity, that God is perpetually incarnate in man. The doctrine of incarnation is itself a poetic expression of faith; to versify the *Quicumque vult* and the XXXIX Articles is absurd. It is proper that confidence should be established in the immunity of God and the ultimate triumph of his will; but he should participate in the plot he controls. This can be done dramatically. Prospero, although acting as the providence of his island through a demiurge, is more deeply involved in the action than Ariel:

Ariel: Your charm so strongly works 'em
That if you now beheld them your affections
Would become tender.
Pros.: Dost thou think so, spirit?
Ariel: Mine would, sir, were I human.
Pros.: And mine shall.
Hast thou, which art but air, a touch, a feeling
Of their afflictions, and shall not myself,
One of their kind, that relish all as sharply,
Passion as they, be kindlier mov'd than thou art?
Though with their high wrongs I am struck to th' quick,
Yet with my nobler reason 'gainst my fury
Do I take part; the rarer action is
In virtue than in vengeance; they being penitent,
The sole drift of my purpose doth extend
Not a frown further. Go release them, Ariel;
My charms I'll break, their senses I'll restore,
And they shall be themselves.

(V. i. 17)

He claims through the echoes of his verse the priestly "power, and commandment . . . to declare and pronounce to his people, being penitent, the Absolution and Remission of their sins"; the power derives from Christ who was "not an high priest which cannot be touched with the feeling of our infirmities; but was in all points tempted like as we are, yet without sin" (*Heb.* iv. 15). It is now that Prospero drowns "this rough magic", the theory of his books, and becomes a man among men.

The descriptions that intersperse the Father-Son colloquy present a more incarnational Godhead, but still fail to reveal the heart of the doctrine. The Son's rhetorical modulations of the Father's theme of grace are realised visually between the speeches:

Beyond compare the Son of God was seen
Most glorious, in him all his Father shon
Substantially express'd, and in his face
Divine compassion visibly appeerd,
Love without end, and without measure Grace,
Which uttering thus he to his Father spake.

(138)

Rhetoric, whether its expertise appeal to contemporary taste or subsequently studied interest, demands theological training for its interpretation. But this imagery, ranging from intellectual to sensuous, asks only an experience of human love. It is the purest, most impressive anthropomorphism. The Son isn't really "Beyond compare": we are reminded of a painting, or a living face such as occasionally seen, having in it a compassionate sanctity which we call "radiance" because it is extravert and warm. A Dantesque effect, it serves characterisation and action by making the Son come alive. In Book VI where he is commanded to drive out the rebel angels the Paternal light strikes on his face like a blow:

> He said, and on his Son with Rayes direct
> Shon full, he all his Father full exprest
> Ineffably into his face receiv'd, (719)

so that he replies as if with effort: "And thus the filial Godhead answering spake". When he is sent to judge Adam and Eve,

> So spake the Father, and unfoulding bright
> Toward the right hand his Glorie, on the Son
> Blaz'd forth unclouded Deitie; he full
> Resplendent all his Father manifest
> Express'd, and thus divinely answer'd milde.
> (X. 64)

The enargia gives us a finer impression of spiritual power, and understanding of the atonement, than we get from all the theoretical exposition of Book III. Yet the Son remains God. He is not the Jesus-of-history but the Christ of the transfiguration in the synoptic gospels, "the fashion of whose countenance was altered" (*Luke* ix. 29, etc.), the Johannine Christ who is pre-eminently the Son of the Father, the Christus Victor of Aulén's "classic" theory of atonement.[1] Such attention to the godhead of the Son at the expense of the manhood of Jesus may be a mode of vicarious self-deification, or the Christian's substitute for Nietzschean hero-worship; but it helps in this context because the claim of Christianity to be more than an ethic rests on the dogma that the Jesus of history was the Son of God, and that the atonement takes place continuously in eternity. Any objection to the Son is not therefore that he is inhuman; but it might be that he is not sufficiently divine. Like Origen and Plotinus, Milton

[1] *Christus Victor: An Historical Study of the . . . Idea of the Atonement,* trans. A. G. Hebert (1931).

was privately, in *De Doctrina*, a subordinationist. He is tactful about this in the poem, but does present the Son as secondary to the Father, dependent on him as a reflection to its light-source. In the speeches the theological result of this becomes clear, that the divine sacrifice is vicarious, not a self-sacrifice of the Father-in-the-Son. It is easy to see from this dramatisation of theology why the Church has so fiercely opposed Arianism. All the psycho-mythic power of the gospel depends on its being God who suffers and rises again from the penalty of death that his own justice requires. Without this identity of judicial with suffering God, the Father is no more remarkable than Abraham offering Isaac, and the Son no more than a martyr. For the scene in Heaven to become "a high and stately tragedy", God must act Oedipus to himself. Even the angels' final paean to the Son, with which Milton identifies himself, strains after acceptance. Subordinationism is confirmed: "the strife of Mercy and Justice" is resolved outside the Father in him who "sat / Second to thee". The mistake is analysed in *Measure for Measure* (as in *Antigone*):

> *Angelo:* Your brother is a forfeit of the law,
> And you but waste your words.
> *Isab.:* Alas! alas!
> Why, all the souls that were were forfeit once;
> And He that might the vantage best have took
> Found out the remedy. How would you be,
> If He, which is the top of judgment, should
> But judge you as you are? O, think on that;
> And mercy then will breathe within your lips,
> Like man new made.
> *Angelo:* Be you content, fair maid.
> It is the law, not I condemn your brother. (II. ii. 71)

Angelo's excuse is Satanic, "necessitie, The Tyrants plea". Hooker makes the same mistake in theological discourse. Like Milton, he must find a rationale in the acts of God and therefore postulates something like the divine dialectic of *Paradise Lost*:

> They err therefore who think that of the will of God to do this or that there is no reason besides his will . . . he worketh all things *κατὰ τὴν βουλὴν τοῦ θελήματος αὐτοῦ*, not only according to his own will, but "the counsel of his own will". And whatsoever is done with counsel or wise resolution hath of necessity some reason why it should be done . . . (I. ii. 5)

Hooker insists on legalising all the divine operations by calling the rule of action, the self-imposed pattern of behaviour which God follows in order to achieve his ends, a law. This suggests that for him, as for Milton, even the salvific action of God was in accordance with law, rather than a passing beyond the bounds of law into mercy:

> O more exceeding love or law more just?
> Just law indeed, but more exceeding love!

Here in the Circumcision ode Milton, like the angels in *Paradise Lost*, acclaims the victory of ἀγαπη over law; but the carefully balanced rhetoric puts them back into an equation. Behind this and our objection lie two historical ideals of fatherhood: one in which the father is utterly reliable in his justice, but calculating even in his love; the other in which he is less predictable, but warm. The perfect father would be spontaneous and reliable; Milton's lacks a spontaneity equal to his reliability and it is because we are bound to see him—poetically and theologically—as an ideal parent that we object and cannot be soothed by theory.

The angels' hymn is a choric reiteration of what has passed. The Father is presented first as a negative abstraction—"Immutable, Immortal, Infinite" (373)—but in the following lines he is astonishingly brought to life:

> Fountain of Light, thy self invisible
> Amidst the glorious brightness where thou sit'st
> Thron'd inaccessible, but when thou shad'st
> The full blaze of thy beams, and through a cloud
> Drawn round about thee like a radiant Shrine,
> Dark with excessive bright thy skirts appear,
> Yet dazle Heav'n, that brightest Seraphim
> Approach not, but with both wings veil thir eyes.
> (375)

Reverently abstaining from an explicit simile for God, Milton implies it in this glimpse of the sun-bright edges of a cloud, as used in painting. But he keeps it supramundane by transferring our attention to the angels, and through their dazzlement makes God not an abstract celestial light but a power active in his own creation. In the description of the Son light again becomes tangible: "on thee Impresst the effulgence of his Glorie abides"

(387). The chorus ends with a contrast between the "Son of the Fathers might" whose actions are those of an epic hero, and "thy dear and onely Son" who "offered himself to die For mans offence". With the change the verse drops into a lament, with lyrical repetition of "thou didst not doome So strictly, but much more to pitie encline", and a final paean, "O unexampl'd love", in which the poet chorically identifies himself with the choric angels, and brings the episode in a circle from "Hail holy light" to "Hail Son of God, Saviour of Men".

The moments of reflected glory are the most valuable experiences in the episode. They link the invocation to the angels' hymn so that we have at least a framework of devotion. This mollifies the dogma of the speeches, placing it as the record of every believer's weary struggle to reconcile letter with spirit. As a struggle it models the whole poem, Milton *agonistes* on behalf of Christian doctrine. He achieves no mystical insight, but manages to recognise his own need for one to "come a light into the world, that whoseover believeth on me should not abide in darkness".

4. *The Image of Heaven*

"St John's description by Emerals, Chrysolites, and precious Stones, is too weak to express the material Heaven we behold." But having described the kind of Hell that Browne also found vulgar, Milton might have given his Heaven a corresponding magnificence of some higher kind. M. M. Ross has complained that the Heaven of *Paradise Lost* is already too Catholic, but the clouds of incense "Fuming from Golden Censers" (VII. 600), the golden altar at XI. 18 and "the golden Lamps that burne Nightly before" the Father (V. 710) come from the Jewish temple direct, not via a Roman cathedral. The real objection must be that these things are so much luggage in the attic, not drawn into any coherent plan for Heaven or the poem. Instead of making his Heaven thoroughly ecclesiastical or palatial, or on the other hand quite stripped of ornament, all of it a "profonda e chiara sussistenza dell' alto lume" (*Par.* xxxiii. 115), or like Dante moving steadily from one to the other, Milton havers between an apocalyptic heaven and an emblematic one. We have the golden pavement, harps, quivers, crowns, etc.: but they are mixed with a confused allegory about amaranth, the Tree of Life and the River of Life. The "river of Bliss through midst of Heavn Rowls o're *Elisian* Flours her Amber stream" (359). This is not the river of *Revelation*, but the *Paradiso*:

> E vidi lume in forma di rivera
> fulvido di fulgore, intra due rive
> dipinte di mirabil primavera.
>
> Di tal fiumana usclan faville vive,
> e d'ogni parte si mettìen ne' fiori,
> quasi rubin che oro circunscrive.
>
> (xxx. 61)

Dante has seized the advantage of plastic art—"Dipinte di mirabil primavera". Without pretending to be more than "di lor vero ombriferi prefazii" (78), the river and its drops that set like gems in gold along the banks give the reader a foothold in heaven. Milton's river does not. Rhythm makes it roll, but it has no distinct character. The reference to Virgil's Elysium doesn't help, for Virgil merely listed it with the Po (*Aen.* VI. 659). The amber is dim beside Dante's "fulvido di fulgore", and the living waters of Paradise.

Milton's inability to picture Heaven is admitted when Satan views Heaven-gate later in the book:

> The work as of a Kingly Palace Gate
> With Frontispice of Diamond and Gold
> Imbellisht, thick with sparkling orient Gemmes
> The Portal shon, inimitable on Earth
> By Model, or by shading Pencil drawn.
>
> (505)

Yet he is able to present Heaven through Raphael, who shows Adam the angels assembling "in Orbes Of circuit inexpressible... Orb within Orb" around "the Father infinite, By whom in bliss imbosom'd sat the Son" (V. 594). There is a masque-like impression of ordered movement, the planetary angels converging on the still centre of God's throne. Is it all done by rhythm: for the first dozen lines the syntax circles and drifts, then it tightens, and finally halts with the angels on "thus spake". This is the method used for the only satisfactory description of Heaven's geography, after the Creation:

So sung
The glorious Train ascending: He through Heav'n,
That open'd wide her blazing Portals, led
To Gods Eternal house direct the way,
A broad and ample rode, whose dust is Gold
And pavement Starrs, as Starrs to thee appear,
Seen in the Galaxie, that Milkie way
Which nightly as a circling Zone thou seest
Pouderd with Starrs. (VII. 573)

Milton's genius was for the syntactical manipualtion of given materials rather than making them new in metaphor. The difference between the Heaven shown in these books, V-VI-VII, and in Book III, though, is partly attitudinal. In Book III he is opening the clouds to actual Heaven; invention of his own must be irreverent as well as false. In the later books Heaven is displayed at second hand, from below, so that human experience of regal glory, the night-sky, and so on, can legitimately convey an image. Some connection between the Heaven of Book III and the others may be found in the dance of the angels after the Son's glorification in Book V, suggesting that this was its essence for Milton:

That day, as other solemn dayes, they spent
In song and dance about the sacred Hill,
Mystical dance, which yonder starrie Spheare
Of Planets and of fixt in all her Wheeles
Resembles nearest, mazes intricate,
Eccentric, intervolv'd, yet regular
Then most, when most irregular they seem:
And in thir motions harmonie Divine. . . .

(618)

The angels correspond to planets or stars throughout the poem. The correspondence had a serious meaning for Milton and his audience who readily translated astronomy into music and back again, seeing in both symbols of a cosmic harmony:

For there is a musick where ever there is a harmony, order, or proportion: and thus far we may maintain the music of the Sphears; for those well-ordered motions, and regular paces, though they give no sound unto the ear, yet to the understanding they strike a note most full of harmony.[1]

[1] *Rel. Med.* ii. 9.

Harmony is as dangerous as any ideal, as we saw when Milton admired the devils' concord. But the ideal has two poles. "At a Solemn Musick" evokes the positive "power Of harmony, and the deep power of joy" that Wordsworth recollects in "Tintern Abbey". Milton was still at this pole in 1642:

> Nor is there any sociable perfection in this life civil or sacred that can be above discipline; but she is that which with her musical cords preserves and holds all the parts thereof together. . . . And certainly discipline is not only the removal of disorder; but, if any visible shape can be given to divine things, the very visible shape and image of virtue, whereby she is not only seen in the regular gestures and motions of her heavenly paces as she walks, but also makes the harmony of her voice audible to mortal ears. Yea, the angels themselves, in whom no disorder is feared, as the apostle that saw them in his rapture describes, are distinguished and quaternioned into their celestial princedoms and satrapies, according as God himself has writ his imperial decrees through the great provinces of heaven. The state also of the blessed in paradise, though never so perfect, is not therefore left without discipline, whose golden surveying reed marks out and measures every quarter and circuit of New Jerusalem. Yet it is not to be conceived that those eternal effluences of sanctity and love in the glorified Saints should by this means be confined and cloyed with repetition of that which is prescribed, but that our happiness may orb itself into a thousand vagancies of glory and delight, and with a kind of eccentrical equation be, as it were, an invariable planet of joy and felicity. . . . (*R.C.G.* ii. 442)

In *Paradise Lost* the last hesitant image of "a kind of eccentrical equation . . . as it were an invariable planet" articulates into "Eccentric, intervolv'd, yet regular Then most, when most irregular they seem". But the astonished paradox of the prose is muzzled by antimetabole. He has moved to the pole of cosmic stability as Wordsworth did in the "Ode to Duty": "Thou dost preserve the stars from wrong". Neither personal depression nor Puritanism takes all the blame. It was partly that Milton had to escape the fatuity of this kind of celestial rhetoric:

> These thus in faire each other farre excelling,
> As to the Highest they approch more neare,
> Yet is the Highest farre beyond all telling,
> Fairer then all the rest which there appeare[1]

[1] Spenser, *Hymne of Heavenly Beautie*, 99.

So he forwent, in many cases, that "liuely shape of dauncing" recommended by Davies for "all ceremonious misteries. All sacred orgies and religious rights, All pomps, and triumphs, and solemnities".[1] Milton had recommended these festivals to the Commonwealth, but the people preferred maypoles. Turning to an audience of the dispersion, and writing to be read rather than heard, he felt I suppose that his main duty lay in reaching at one grasp to the formal reality that lay behind sensed manifestations of the divine. But it was mainly that he no longer enjoyed, as he had at the time of *Comus*, the passion of Plato and Dante which alone will vivify their kind of idealism.

[1] *Orchestra*, lxxvii. *Complete Poems* ed. Grosart, (2 vols. 1876).

5

THE WORLD

THE simile of the vulture (III. 431) positions Satan in the cosmos and plot of the poem as seen from the height of Heaven. He is travelling from the traditionally northern base of devilry,[1] connected by its "roving Tartar" with the oriental tyrants of Hell and the nomadic aggressors of Book XI, southwards to "Hills where Flocks are fed". Beneath the modern epical boast of map-reading these hills work inside the poem to indicate the pastoral scenery and symbolism of the gospels, and of Paradise: "*Ganges* or *Hydaspes*, *Indian* streams", were taken to be the Pison and Gihon that bound the Garden of Eden in *Genesis*. In contact with other devils and angels—Uriel, Gabriel—Satan remains splendid, asserting the cosmic scale of the issue between evil and good; but "alone bent on his prey" he is bestial, vulture or toad, like tragic villains in soliloquy. The episode in Heaven has made this alteration possible, its impervious perfection insulating the dark fantasy of Hell from the bright reality of the created world.

But Satan's discovery of the Limbo of Fools and the parable on hypocrisy in his deception of Uriel, seem—like the irruptions of anti-prelatical anger in "Lycidas" and when Satan leaps the wall of Paradise—discordant. We are apt to object to Miltonic satire on the widest grounds: that all vociferous protest coarsens the feelings of the subject, distorts the object, aims at symptom instead of disease; and of course all protestation as violent as this is directed as much at conflict within the protestant as without. But liberal gentility is just as personal and not at all times so useful. Milton's grim laughter can be cruel and stupid, but these are conditions more easily dissipated than the selfishness of a Browne:

[1] A prophetic tradition originally, e.g. *Jer.* iv. 6. Cf. Richard Barckley (discussing "vaine imitation of other countries fashions" with relevance to *P.L.* I, where also the devils are barbarians from the north): "there hath been an old saying, that all euils rise out of the North" (*Felicitie of Man*, 1631 ed., p. 327).

> I cannot laugh at, but rather pity, the fruitless journeys of Pilgrims, or contemn the miserable condition of Friars; for, though misplaced in Circumstances, there is something in it of Devotion.[1]

This tolerant equanimity is designed to preserve Browne's ego intact, at whatever cost, in an age when much more than habits of worship were at stake in the ecclesiastical conflict. Apart from the political implications of reformation, satire was more consonant with religion in the 17th Century than it is now because religion was more life-and-death—and not only on the extreme left wing. Joseph Hall was Milton's pamphlet adversary and a Juvenalian satirist, as well as a bishop. So in literature. A limbo of fools is not unexpected in the 16th-century satire *Julius Exclusus*—Erasmus wrote it probably, and his *Praise of Folly* was directed like Milton's Limbo against Scholasticism. There is another limbo in *Orlando Furioso* (xxxiv), which Astolfo visits under the aegis of St John the Evangelist who is patron of Milton's sun episode. And at the end of *Pilgrim's Progress* Christian sees the fate of Ignorance that he might realise "there was a way to Hell, even from the Gates of Heaven, as well as from the City of *Destruction*". Yet there remains a genuine religio-literary objection to this sort of thing in *Paradise Lost*. Romantic epic can absorb satirical explosions, and the fate of Ignorance is appropriate in a book about the practice of the Christian life. But in a poem geared to universal good and evil the Limbo is indecorous. The intensity of feeling is disproportionate to the dramatic value of the episode releasing it; and, congregated about Satan, it shifts guilt for the Fall from evil onto stupidity. This is a Humanistic motif and it has authority in the Bible's Wisdom books as well as Plato; but it runs smoothly on into Augustan rationalism. By associating himself with Pope's secular damnation of dunces Milton weakens his religious damnation of devils. The tendency is obvious in the verse:

> Here Pilgrims roam, that stray'd so farr to seek
> In Golgotha him dead, who lives in Heav'n;
>
> (476)

is a beautifully managed heroic couplet without rhyme.

[1] *Rel. Med.* i. 3.

Milton did some of his finest *writing* in this part of the poem. The allegory of the stairs to Heaven is unco-ordinated but look at the power of expression: "or aggravate / His sad exclusion from the dores of Bliss" (524) does more than all the episode it summarises. Satan's epical visit to the sun is not congruent with his dramatic address to it at the beginning of the next book, and Uriel's description of Creation is superfluous; but again the sheer skill of writing is astonishing, and most astonishing when most "Miltonic":

> Such wonder seis'd, though after Heav'n seen,
> The Spirit maligne, but much more envy seis'd
> At sight of all this World beheld so faire.
>
> (552)

Latinism *in excelsis*, as at 663—"His journies end and our beginning woe"—because it is exerting in a suitable context the peculiar control that Latin syntax assumes over the things designated by the words, disposing them in time and space. So we catch first wonder, then the higher and now sadly lost wonder of "Heav'n seen"; then the heart of Satan, "Spirit maligne", works on the wonder and transmutes it to envy; we catch that too, fleeting across his face, from the extended anadiplosis, and carry it forward to his envy of human love in Paradise; and suddenly Satan disappears altogether in the uninterrupted "sight of all this World beheld so faire", by the verse spread out so distantly below him and us. There is a curious passage later on where Milton allegorises hypocrisy. We think he is fumbling:

> And oft though wisdom wake, suspicion sleeps
> At wisdoms Gate, and to simplicitie
> Resigns her charge, while goodness thinks no ill
> Where no ill seems:
>
> (689)

But, the verse thus lulling our own suspicions, we are shocked awake to the power of hypocrisy by the brusque colloquiality that follows: "Which now for once beguil'd / *Uriel*, though Regent of the Sun . . ."

The brisk latinate stage-direction of Uriel's last line, "Thy way thou canst not miss, me mine requires", indicates what is happening. In this episode Milton was fulfilling the more naïve ambitions of the "Vacation Exercise", without much regard to their suitability in *Paradise Lost*: showing how well he knows his way about the universe, though blind. Satan's journey to the sun is magnificent cinema—the kinesthetics of his flight represented by free-arranged stresses, tenses shifting between past and present, and a shift in the visual image from Satan himself to the universe he is flying through. Worlds flicker past him—

> innumerable Starrs, that shon
> Stars distant, but nigh hand seemd other Worlds,
> Or other Worlds they seemd, or happy Iles,

—a technical device (antimetabole) repeated in his question about the worlds to Uriel:

> In which of all these shining Orbes hath Man
> His fixed seat, or fixed seat hath none,
> But all these shining Orbes his choice to dwell;

Against the full mysterious beauty of the universe Satan loses heroic stature.

The sub-plot of how Satan deceives Uriel and then betrays himself by grimacing in Paradise so that Uriel warns Gabriel and Gabriel has him arrested is unconvincing, distracting, and, in such a classical and supra-naturalistic poem, a sop to the reader's taste for melodrama. So the description of the sun functions chiefly as a more concrete image of Heaven. During Satan's flight it shines above all stars "in splendor likest Heaven". Its carbuncle, chrysolite, ruby, topaz are traditional emblems of the sun,[1] but with the other eight gems named they make up the twelve tribal stones of Aaron's breastplate (*Exodus* xxxviii. 17); in *Revelation* (as in *Pearl*) these ornament the wall of the New Jerusalem (xxi. 19). There is besides the philosopher's stone, converted here into a symbol of the imagination, able to "call up unbound In various shapes old *Proteus* from the Sea" (603) and thus to realise Heaven:

> What wonder then if fields and regions here
> Breathe forth *Elixir* pure, and Rivers run
> Potable Gold,

[1] The tradition goes back to the old lapidaries, e.g. Albert Magnus' *De Mineralibus*; see C. F. Kunz, *The Curious Lore of Precious Stones* (1913), pp. 67, 347, etc. and Joan Evans, *Magical Jewels of the Middle Ages and the Renaissance* (1921), pp. 23, 85, etc.

The symbol outshines the reality. Here is Dante's "lume in forme di rivera fulvido di fulgore", quite extinguishing the topography of Heaven, and accomplishing the contrast with Hell and Paradise that Heaven only suggested.

The sun is also allowed a creative potency that tends to usurp God's, so that Satan is almost justified in his heresy:

> The Gods are first, and that advantage use
> On our belief, that all from them proceeds;
> I question it, for this fair Earth I see,
> Warm'd by the Sun, producing every kind,
> Them nothing:
>
> (IX. 718)

Apart from Satan's address to the sun, it is the first thing Adam speaks to (VIII. 273) and he and Eve offer it qualified worship:

> Thou Sun, of this great World both Eye and Soule,
> Acknowledge him thy Greater, sound his praise
> In thy eternal course . . .
>
> (V. 171)

The authority of *Psalm* xix is countered with a reference to the Platonic *anima mundi*. Adam discusses the sun's astronomical function and cosmopolitical rank with Eve (IV. 660 ff.) and later with Raphael (VIII). The sun is mentioned ten times in Book X, where it is the instrument of change in climate after the Fall. It intrudes on Book XI with a sudden reversion to the Elizabethan style of the description of Creation:

> the cleer Sun on his wide watrie Glass
> Gaz'd hot, and of the fresh Wave largely drew,
> As after thirst, which made thir flowing shrink
> From standing lake to tripping ebbe, that stole
> With soft foot towards the deep, (840)

The sun is often personified as if Ovid were writing:

> On which the Sun more glad impress'd his beams
> Then in fair Evening Cloud, or humid Bow,
>
> (IV. 150)

> for the Sun
> Declin'd was hasting now with prone career
> To th' Ocean Iles,
>
> (IV. 352)

while now the mounted Sun
Shot down direct his fervid Raies, to warme
Earths inmost womb, (V. 300)

But here a more passionate and serious Ovid. Milton seems to have applied to the sun the *métier* for erotic poetry that first issued in his Latin elegies. Written through experience now, it has lost the sensuality of *In adventum veris* as well as the hysteria of *Epitaphium Damonis*, and become full, spendid:

and to each inward part
With gentle penetration, though unseen,
Shoots invisible vertue even to the deep
(III. 584)

when with one vertuous touch
Th' Arch-chimic Sun so farr from us remote
Produces with Terrestial Humor mixt
Here in the dark so many precious things (608)

Lawrence directs the sun's virtue at persons; Milton allows it to operate only on things. This avoids the uni-assertive extravagance of Lawrence's symbolism. Milton encloses phallic potency within the divine rationality; and his touch is surer, more procreative than Lawrence's. But, with Lawrence (and others, such as Hardy about the lush valley in *Tess*) having written, Milton's erotic characterising of the sun makes us all the more conscious that its virtue , which we value highly and more openly than he did, could be exerted by no other character in the poem, God least of all. The sun-poetry is magnificent, its direction admirable; but instead of attributing to God, at reverent secondhand, the power and the glory which could not be manifest in Heaven itself, it tends towards a rationalisation of sun-worship. This was constantly happening. Diodorus Siculus, for example, had said:

> Truly it is very apparent, that colours, odors, fruits, different savours, greatness of creatures, forms of things, and varietie of kindes produced by the earth, are made and procreated by the heat of the Sunne, which, warming the moisture of the earth, is the true and only cause of those productions.[1]

[1] *The History of D. S. Containing all that is Most Memorable and of greatest Antiquity in the first Ages of the World until the War of Troy*, trans. H[enry]. C[ogan]. (1653), III. xvii. 105.

And Montaigne:

> Of those [conceptions of deity] to whom they have given a body, as necessity required in that universal blindness, I should, I fancy, most incline to those who adored the sun.[1]

He quotes Ronsard's description of the sun as "L'œil du monde . . . L'esprit, l'ame du monde . . . Plein d'immense grandeur":

> forasmuch as besides this grandeur and beauty of his, 'tis the piece of this machine that we discover at the remotest distance from us, and, by that means, so little known that they were pardonable for entering into so great admiration and reverence for it.

It was a commonplace whose implications had so often been thought out by theologians—Calvin included—that Milton probably felt safe. Ultimately, he was christianising Plato's simile of the sun as the "Good" of the sensable world. But even in philosophy the analogy often obliterates the concept; in a poem where God himself, the source of celestial light, is presented, where the Son creates and comes to earth as judge, where archangels dine with men, the presence of an animistic viceroy is disturbing. Milton sacrifices the monotheistic Puritanism that his thesis requires to cosmographical ambition

[1] "Apology for Raimond de Sebonde", *Essays* trans. Charles Cotton (1685-6, etc., ed. and rev. W. C. Hazlitt, 3 vols. 1913; Bohn's Popular Lib.; originally 1893, Bohn's Standard Lib.), II. xii. 209.

6

PARADISE

1. *Satan in Paradise*

THE rest of the plot up to Book X could be summarised in Joseph Beaumont's words about Satan, "To Paradise he came, and brought his hell Into the earthly heaven."[1] Milton uses several devices to express what is really a spiritual or psychological experience, the insinuation of evil into good, in terms of epic action. First there is explicit statement about

> The Hell within him, for within him Hell
> He brings, and round about him, nor from Hell
> One step no more then from himself can fly
> By change of place:

Then Satan's admission, "Which way I flie is Hell; my self am Hell". These are supported with references peculiar to Hell in the poem. Satan's ambition "like a devilish Engine back recoiles Upon himself"—part of the gunpowder motif. When he leaps over the wall he brings the city with him, "as a Thief bent to unhoord the cash Of some rich Burgher . . . In at the window climbes, or o're the tiles." His leap over the wall is an emblem of transgression itself: "in contempt At one slight bound high overleap'd all bound", but this is not very successful for its seriousness is spoilt by the pun and dissipated by our interest in the mimesis which suspends the sentence for three lines as Satan sails through the air until he "sheer within / Lights on his feet". His entry in Book IX "involv'd in rising Mist" (75) through the underground river, and his approach to Eve as a city gallant to a milkmaid, is imaginatively much superior. But an emphasis on smell as Satan approaches the garden suggests the fluency of evil as well as his brutalism. The spicy scents drift down to his nostrils,

[1] *Psyche: or, Loves Mysterie. In xx. Cantos: displaying the intercourse betwixt Christ and the Soule* (1648): a kind of mystical epic.

> As when to them who sail
> Beyond the *Cape of Hope*, and now are past
> *Mozambic*, off at Sea North-East windes blow
> *Sabean* Odours from the spicie shoare
> Of *Arabie* the blest, with such delay
> Well pleas'd they slack thir course, and many a League
> Cheard with the grateful smell old Ocean smiles.

The simile returns us to the beginning of Satan's voyage when flying up through Hell he looked like the mirage of an East Indian merchant fleet trading for spice. But the heroic idyll is smashed with a grim recital of the plot of *Tobit* as if Satan's sensibility were corrupting the balms of Paradise into the sexual reek of "the fishie fume".

In the first of his three speeches in Paradise, Satan represents man struggling against God. Disdain (82), fear of mockery from his fellows, and distrust of his own motives (93 ff.) prevent repentance. God cannot be denied, but at least the world may be shared with him. The last part of this speech is a fine parody of the dream of spiritual coexistence. The third speech, where Satan declares his intention to corrupt man through the Tree of Knowledge, is merely a plot contrivance and probably derives from a dramatic version. When Satan says "But first with narrow search I must walk round This Garden, and no corner leave unspi'd" (528) he is a melodrama villain sharing his stage secrets with the audience. The second speech is the most successful: it does not advance the plot but it holds Satan and Paradise up to each other so that the nature of each is mirrored in the incompatible other. Adam and Eve have eaten supper, made love, watched the animals play, their innocence defined as unselfconsciousness; there is a breathless twilight, the sun sets, stars rise,

> When *Satan* still in gaze, as first he stood,
> Scarce thus at length faild speech recoverd sad.
> O Hell! what doe mine eyes with grief behold . . .
> (356)

We are identified with him in fascination with the scene so that his cry of destruction and grief comes as a genuine dramatic shock. He goes on to admire the man and woman, then to fondle them horribly—"Ah gentle pair . . ." His voice lisps as a snake: "League with you I seek, And mutual amitie so straight, so close", perverting the "happie nuptial League" of Adam and Eve in the previous paragraph. In the third act of *Adamus Exsul* Satan actually offers alliance with Adam, who spurns it. Grotius' instinct was right, for it is as a politician that Satan appears at his most irrelevant and uncomprehending in relation to the calm pastoralism of Paradise:

> Hell shall unfould,
> To entertain you two, her widest Gates,
> And send forth all her Kings;

The symbolic structure of *Paradise Lost* corresponds to Hobbes' sketch of poetry in general:

> As Philosophers have divided the Universe, their subject, into three Regions, *Cellestiall*, *Aeriall*, and *Terrestiall*, so the Poets . . . have lodg'd themselves in the three Regions of mankinde, *Court*, City, and Country, corresponding in some proportion to those three Regions of the World. For there is in Princes and men of conspicuous power, anciently called *Heroes*, a lustre and influence upon the rest of men resembling that of the Heavens; and an insincereness, inconstancy, and troublesome humor of those that dwell in populous Cities, like the mobility, blustring, and impurity of the Aire; and a plainness, and though dull, yet a nutritive faculty in rurall people, that endures comparison with the Earth they labour.[1]

As a pastoral culture Paradise is the traditional target of aggression from the civilised power of Hell; as a walled home, depending for existence on the observance of limit, it stands in contrast to the shoreless ocean of Chaos; as a garden it is distinguished from the super-nature of Heaven. It shares with all pastoral an elegiac note anticipating the Fall; but it differs from most pastoral in representing a theological and moral, rather than social or intellectual state of innocence. On the model of Christ's parables and New Testament paschalism, pastoral and homely material was recommended for use in the Puritan sermon. But it cannot have been easy for Milton to indoctrinate it because pastoral and elegy are upper-class genres and when, as often, united as pastoral elegy they become extravagantly "literary" expressions of illicit affection and death-wish. This is more obvious in the Romantic examples such as "Adonais"

[1] *Answer to Davenant*, Spingarn, ii. 55.

and "Thyrsis", but it can be examined in "Lycidas", *Comus* and Fletcher's *Faithful Shepherdess*. This is one reason why the Paradise that Milton presents is neither so naturally pastoral nor so elegiac as we might have expected.

Milton's description of Paradise has been used to exemplify "composition" as inferior to "imaginative creation" in an *aesthetic* argument conducted by Ruskin, and subsequently by Leavis and Wilson Knight.[1] But the virtue of the writing in its context has to be judged by more specific criteria. Even if we read it as a soul-state expression, though we admit that many poems deal with more interesting materials, display more intelligence or imaginative power in handling them, express more subtly various attitudes to them; there are few in which as here one mind's finest powers are so intensely consecrated that its own purification and ennoblement are imputed fully to the reader and every object near the poetry in space or time is glorified by it. The poet's reverence for his materials—art and nature, man and woman, Man and God—catches us up into a phase of reciprocating humility and dignity that is an apotheosis of humanity. Lines such as

> for blissful Paradise
> Of God the garden was, by him in th' east
> Of *Eden* planted;

have the supreme confidence of *Genesis*, and the simplicity:

> Out of the fertil ground he caus'd to grow
> All trees of noblest kind for sight, smell, taste;

"Flours of all hue." (256) is confident of the actual; "and without thorn the rose" reverently asserts the ideal. Again:

> thence united fell
> Down the steep glade, and met the neather Flood,
> Which from his darksom passage now appears,
> And now divided into four main Streams,
> Runs divers, wandring many a famous Realme
> And Country whereof here needs no account,
> But rather to tell how, if Art could tell . . . (230)

[1] *Modern Painters*, Part IV *passim*, especially Chap. xiv about the fields of medieval landscape; *Revaluation*, pp. 49 ff.; Knight's "The Frozen Labyrinth: An Essay on Milton" in his *Burning Oracle* (1939: a magnificent account of his response to Milton's poetry).

That art could tell of such things is ground for hubris, yet all hubris drains away in the fluent rhythms, the wondering tone; but the humility remaining is humility in the face of what man himself has created. Pride and humbleness, self-confidence and self-astonishment, absorb each other in faith, so strong that five and six books later Milton can weep for the loss of the Paradise he made as if it were an objective reality:

O how unlike
To that first naked Glorie.

(IX. 1114)

For still they knew, and ought to have still remember'd
The high Injunction not to taste that Fruit,
Whoever tempted:

(X. 12)

There are occasions in *Paradise Lost* where Milton's technical skill is not fully dedicated to its purpose, so that we can only appreciate it out of context, unless we are prepared to read the whole poem as good humanistic stuff and never mind the moral. But in Paradise, though we query its philosophical implications, there is an unusually sustained consonance between the idea and the symbolic expression of innocence.

2. *The Garden*

In presenting Paradise as a dramatic scene to an emblematic age Milton had to avoid the sort of abstractness and typological irrelevancies indicated by Vaughan's clauses about the Sabbath in "Son-dayes"—"Heaven once a week . . . Transplanted Paradise . . . Heaven here". Milton distinguishes Paradise from Heaven by proliferation of detail, classical allusion, natural sunlight; he only hints at the emblematic motifs; and he asserts the garden's actuality by reference to topical geography.

The traditional location and shape were based ultimately on the Zend word *pairidaeza*, a pleasure-garden elaborated in Persia from the oasis (Diodorus Siculus describes one of them). Thus it was essentially a life-giving place of refuge (the etymology is variously traced from the sense of grass, growth, or wall, enclosure). But in the West three stages may be observed in the literature of paradise. *Genesis*, with primitive respect for ancestral glory and the wealth to be had on the other side of the mountain, describes the first river of Eden, Pison, as that "which compasseth the whóle land of Havilah, where there is gold; And the gold of that land is good: There is bdellium and the onyx stone" (ii. 11). Mandeville, admitting he had never been there, reported that in the river Pison or Ganges "ben manye preciouse stones, and mochel of lignũ Aloes, and moche gravelle of Gold".[1] The third, Renaissance stage is found in Hakluyt, who reported truthfully that in the Persian Gulf "they found sand mingled with Gold", his margin pointing to "Golden Sand".[2] This coming true of dreams lies behind the hesperianising of Lyly and Greene, Marlowe, Jonson and Drayton, and Milton. Their ornate diction is identical with the travellers' prose—odoriferous and balmy, nectar and ambrosia, pearly streams, stately cedars and so on.[3] This correspondence of fact with fiction did not last long. The facts lost their glamour in familiarity and in the improvement of conditions at home; the fiction went on, deteriorating into fancy, shocking the Royal Society. But Milton crystallised the Renaissance moment of simultaneous wonder and confidence, by a classical authority and scientific definiteness. The materials are Ovidian, of course; he had used them in his own elegies: "Flumina vernantes lambunt argentes campos, Ditior Hesperio flavet arena Tago" (*El.* III. 45-6; cf. p. 30 above). But this was also, anyway at the time he wrote it, the language of actuality, not frigidly remote, though wonderful; and now he had christened and englished it through context and tone.

[1] *Voiage and Travaile* (1725 ed. repr. J. O. Halliwell, 1839), p. 304.

[2] Samuel Purchas, *Hakluytus Posthumus or Purchas his Pilgrimes* (4 vos. 1625, repr. 20 vols. Glasgow, 1905-07), x. 23; cf. vi. 108.

[3] See R. R. Cawley, *Unpathed Waters: Studies in the Influence of the Voyagers on Elizabethan Literature* (Princeton, 1940), pp. 8-11. Cawley establishes Milton's knowledge of the travel books I cite in *Milton and the Literature of Travel* (Princeton, 1951). See also A. H. Gilbert's *Geographical Dictionary to Milton* (New Haven, 1919); L. E. Lockwood, "A Note on Milton's Geography", *MLN*, XXI (1906), p. 96; E. N. S. Thompson, "Milton's Knowledge of Geography", *SP*, XVI (1919); E. M. Clark, "Milton's Abyssinian Paradise", *Univ. of Texas Studies in English*, XXIX (1950). The traditional background is treated in the general books on hexemeral literature, but I have not seen Sister Mary Corcoran's dissertation on *Milton's Paradise with Reference to the Hexameral Background* (Catholic Univ. of America Press, 1945). There is a bibliography of Renaissance landscape gardening in E. S. Rohde, *Old English Gardening Books* (1924).

Mandeville had remarked that "In the most highe place of Pardys, evene in the myddel place, is a welle, that casteth out the 4 Flodes, that rennen be dyverse Londes" (p. 304). Two centuries later a more reliable traveller saw irrigation systems of this kind at work in Morocco:

> The south part of east Fez is almost halfe destitute of inhabitants: howbeit the gardens abound with fruites and flowers of all sortes. Euery garden hath . . . a christall-fountaine enuironed with roses and other odoriferous flowers and herbes. . . . And well it may be called a Paradise. . . .
>
> Without the north, east, and south parts of the citie are great store of gardens, replenished with all kinds of fruite and with stately trees. Through the midst of these gardens, they deriue some small vaine of the riuer. . . .[1]

Milton suggests, by rhythm and personification, an emblematic value for the legend; confirms the fact by reference to osmotic pressure; and brings the whole thing under the direct creativity of God:

> for God had thrown
> That Mountain as his Garden mould high rais'd
> Upon the rapid current, which through veins
> Of porous Earth with kindly thirst up drawn,
> Rose a fresh Fountain, and with many a rill
> Waterd the Garden;
>
> (IV. 225)

On the other hand, Milton holds the realism under his poem's ethic. In "The Battel of the Summer Islands" Waller had drawn on travellers' reports and relied on his readers' familiarity with the Bermudas—"BERMUDA, walled with rocks, who does not know?". He goes on to describe

> That happy island! where huge lemons grow,
> And orange trees, which golden fruit do bear,
> Th'HESPERIAN garden boasts of none so fair;

He makes the usual references—"The lofty cedar", perpetual spring, "Ripe fruits and blossoms on the same tree live". In

[1] John Leo (Africanus), *A Geographical Historie of Africa* (trans. J. Pory, 1600, repr. as *The History and Description of Africa* by Robert Brown for the Hakluyt Soc., 3 vols, 1896), pp. 443, 474.

mocking the heroic manner Waller has secularised its materials: all mythological and dramatic significance is drained from the Fortunate Isles and Hesperian Gardens; the condition of the weather is reduced to a conversational joke—"For the kind spring, which but salutes us here, Inhabits there, and courts them all the year!"; and the evaluation implied by the description is mainly economic—the lemons are touchably large, the cedar fellable timber; all these things are "cates" which Nature pours out "with such a lavish hand". Marvell's tendency in his "Bermudas" is more sophisticated but similar:

> He [*sc.* God] gave us this eternal Spring
> Which here enamells every thing;
>
> . . . .
>
> He hangs in shades the Orange bright
> Like golden Lamps in a green Night.
> And does in the Pomgranates close,
> Jewels more rich than *Ormus* shows.

He may be mocking, but if so he is mocking a contemporary attitude, towards Creation as a pleasure-garden, a Mohammedan paradise such as Donne mentions in "Going to Bed" alongside "my America! my new-found-land", and Heylyn summarises from the piecemeal descriptions in the *Koran*:

> a place of all Delights, adorned with flowry Fields, waterd with Chrystalline Rivers, beautified with Trees of Gold, under whose coole shade they shall spend their time with amorous Virgins . . . and those to have their Virginities renewed, as fast as lost.[1]

This is why Milton's description of Paradise is different from Comus' speech on the bounties of nature. Milton offers the objects of sense-experience—"the smell of field and grove", "Grots and Caves of coole recess", fruits "of delicious taste"—at one syntactical remove; Comus tempts our greed with the imagined sensations of them. The hearer is invited to wallow in the lap of teeming Mother Earth as if she were a harlot—note the sexual connotations of "spawn innumerable", "the smooth-hair'd silk" of worms and so on, and the suggestions of

[1] Peter Heylyn, *Cosmographie in four bookes, containing the chronographie and historie of the whole world* (1652), III. 104 b. Purchas records an even more exotic paradise in *Purchas His Pilgrimage; or Relations of the World and the Religions Observed in all Ages* (1613; often bound as vol. iv of *Hak. Post.*), pp. 253-4.

economic value in the worms' green shop, the diamonds that "emblaze the forehead of the Deep" as if the sea were a maharajah. Comus' ruthless unchastity may be understood by observing the parallels and possible sources of his speech in the reports on Virginia's fertility: "But the Earth (fruitful Mother of Mankind) she is prodigiously prodigal, in fatnesse of the soile . . ." and the prospector goes on to catalogue the animal, vegetable and mineral resources of Virginia much as Comus does those of the world (including a dissertation on silkworms and the mulberry).[1] The purpose of his report is to recommend the land as ripe for economic exploitation.

Adam and Eve's sweet gardening labour seems absurd; but taken emblematically, as the slight references to it allow, it is a model of order in the commonwealth like the gardening in *Richard II* (III. iv; there are explicit references to Adam and Eve at 73 ff.). This is an anachronism, like Milton's psychology, because neither the garden nor the microcosm and macrocosm it represents should need pruning and weeding in innocence. But it is also, in part, like their meals, a sacramental expression of Christian love—love with ends beyond the good of either spouse (hence the disastrousness of dividing the labour in Book IX: it ceases to be a sacrament and becomes a task). The emblemism derives from the *Song of Solomon*: "Come, my beloved, let us go forth into the field . . . Let us get up early to the vineyards; let us see if the vine flourish, whether the tender grape appear, and the pomegranates bud forth" (vii. 11). This imagery comprehends the overt sexuality of love-talk in Donne's "Going to Bed" and *Lady Chatterley's Lover*; Milton adds the suggestion of procreation. Pruning the pampered boughs (IV. 214), leading "the Vine to wed her Elm" (V. 215) as if rearing children and giving them in marriage, Adam and Eve do not exploit nature but literally educate her. Spenser explains the doctrine:

> The antique world, in his first flowring youth,
> Found no defect in his Creatours grace,
> But with glad thankes, and vnreproued truth,
> The gifts of soueraigne bountie did embrace:
> Like Angels life was then mens happy cace;

[1] Purchas, *Hak. Post.* xix. 245. Cf. Hakluyt, *Principal Navigations* (1589, repr. 12 vols. Glasgow, 1903-05), vi. 164-73.

But later ages pride, like corn-fed steed,
Abusd her plenty, and fat swolne encreace
To all licentious lust, and gan exceed
The measure of her meane, and naturall first need.[1]

He goes on to describe mining as matricide. We need not insist on the continuing validity of Spenser's economic ethic. Milton dramatises the point in the contrast of Paradise with Hell. The devils dig and build for their own comfort and glory. Their condition is a symbol of the fallen soul's perpetual dissatisfaction with the resources of its own and external nature. Montaigne quotes Propertius, Plato, Lucretius on the topic, and adds, "the depravity and irregularity of our appetite outstrip all the inventions we can contrive to satisfy it". Spenser dramatises it in the Bower of Bliss,

goodly beautifide
With all the ornaments of *Floraes* pride,
Wherewith her mother Art, as halfe in scorne
Of niggard Nature, like a pompous bride
Did decke her, and too lauishly adorne,[2]

This explains also the relation between art and nature in Paradise: an equation that represents the omniprovidence of nature as she appears to the innocent contented soul. Greek and Renaissance philosophers and artists were sharply aware of a dichotomy between nature and art, and of the

[1] *F.Q.* II. vii. 16. Cf. Montaigne, "Of Cannibals" (*Essays*, I. xxx): "Neither is it reasonable that art should gain the pre-eminence of our great and powerful mother nature. We have so surcharged her with the additional ornaments and graces we have added to the beauty and riches of her own works by our inventions, that we have almost smothered her; yet in other places, where she shines in her own purity and proper lustre, she marvellously baffles and disgraces all our vain and frivolous attempts" (Florio's Elizabethan translation of this passage is noticeably more feeling than Cotton's proto-Augustan one). The doctrine might be rejected as sentimental, and an economist might reject Spenser's statement as an expression of the perennial unfounded fear that terrestial resources are running out—a useful chimera which spurs us to invention, adaptation and exploitation. But both statements are moral and can still be applied, for all our present wealth and ingenuity, to such activities as the manufacture of hydrogen bombs and fancy goods.

[2] *F.Q.* II. xii. 50. Cf. Heylyn's lyrical outburst over the Moroccan town of Fez: "A City so beautiful and well seated, as if Nature and art had plaid the wantons, and brought this forth as the fruit of their Dalliance" (*Cosmog.* iv. 33 b).

need to resolve it. The dichotomy became a symbol of human imperfection, hence of evil: in Spenser's Bower nature and art are rivals, "So striuing each th'other to vndermine" (59). In the end "Each did the others work more beautifie", but it is a beauty of *minauderie*. As the sterile woman in *The Waste Land* sits throned amidst the elegant vulgarities of a *recherché* Ovidianism, so the ingenious imitations of nature in the Bower of Bliss are products of the same discontent and impotence as the provocative antics of the naked damsels in the fountain. There are muscatels like ruby, grapes green as emerald, and other grapes of real gold, "So made by art to beautify the rest"; the water is crystal clear but its fountain made of crystal; there is real shrubbery but also ivy-leaves beaten out of gold. It is like the Golden Garden of the Incas with its "flowers and trees of gold and silver" described by Hakluyt.[1] There is a similar literary paradise in *Brittain's Ida*, and its significance is made clear by Fletcher's name for his in the *Purple Island*—the Garden of Vain Glory.

Conversely, for nature to behave artistically symbolised innocence. So the bower in Spenser's Garden of Adonis is "not by art but of the Trees own inclination made" (*F.Q.* III. vi. 44): "inclination" equates the physical posture of nature regarded objectively, and its co-operative tendency as apprehended by the innocent soul in contentment with God's provision for it. Nature's artistry is also a symbol of perfection because it reveals the designs of God. The plateau paradise in Drayton's *Endimion and Phoebe* is the scene of innocent but physical love between mythical but solid characters. There is a coniferous umbrella, occurring naturally but "thus divinely made" as in Paradise the natural canopy of the bower has been framed by "the sovran Planter" (IV. 691). Indeed, the more artificial nature's works appear, the more they "illustrate" the immanence of God. So in Drayton's poem the sylvan scene is beautiful, and significant because of its artifice:

> Which [sc. trees] Nature in such order has disposed,
> And there-withall these goodly walks inclosed,
> As serv'd for hangings and rich Tapestry,
> To beautifie this stately Gallery:

[1] *Navigations*, vii. 288.

> Imbraudering these in curious trailes along,
> The clustered Grapes, the golden Citrons hung,
> More glorious then . . .
> gorgious Arras in rich colours wrought,
> With silke from *Africke*, or from *Indie* brought:[1]

Here Drayton is being carried towards the economic extravagance that Milton avoids. Milton chooses static phrases—"vegetable Gold", "fruit burnisht with Golden Rinde," which simply equate nature with art, or balance them against each other. The "soft downie Bank damaskt with flours" (IV. 334) is not elaborated into the appearance of an ottoman. When the terms of art predominate—

> underfoot the Violet,
> Crocus, and Hyacinth with rich inlay
> Broiderd the ground, more colour'd then with stone
> Of costliest Emblem:
>
> (700)

—the reference is usually to the bower of Adam and Eve which had been deliberately made for them by God.[2] In the background is Ezekiel's vision of Adam's kingly splendour—"Thou hast been in Eden the garden of God; every precious stone was thy covering, the sardius, topaz, and the diamond . . ." (xxviii. 13)—as well as the amorously emblematic jewellery of the *Song of Solomon*:

> His head is as the most fine gold. . . . His hands are as gold rings set with the beryl: his belly is as bright ivorie, overlaid with sapphires. His legs are as pillars of marble, set upon sockets of fine gold:
>
> (v. 11)

In any other context the equation would deaden both its terms. It was asserted indiscriminately, of fallen nature, by

[1] Line 35. *Works* ed. Hebel, Tillotson, Newdigate (5 vols. 1931-41). In Marlowe's "Description of Seas, Waters, Riuers, &c" ("I walkt along a streame for purenesse rare"), trees growing beside the stream meet to form "a costly vallance ore a bed".

[2] Joan Evans illustrates a "George" of Charles II made of onyx, in which Milton's imagery is reversed: enamel represents flowerets, with precision and grace: *English Jewellery* (1921), Chap. V.

Browne for example—"all things are artificial; for Nature is the Art of God"[1]—and by Hooker: "Those things which nature is said to do, are by divine art performed, using nature as an instrument".[2] These are mere gestures at what would be nice. Intellectually Milton was no more perceptive about nature and art than these or any other systematic philosophers, because temperamentally he wanted a universal. The ultimate objective reality seemed to be Nature; the ultimate subjective one Reason. He could not be happy as a Naturalist or a Rationalist *tout court*, or like Thrasymachus and Montaigne a sceptic admitting the mergence of the terms. So he rationalised Nature and gave it the ideality of an artifact; and naturalised Reason, giving it the universality of immanence. This usual method begs the entire question of ethics, but permits an occasionally useful shuffling of the terms, and a more frequently useful patterning of the ideal. Thus, seeing that something is wrong with actual Nature and Reason, human and general, you postulate a Fall. This evokes two ideals: of education, as a means "to repair the ruins of our first parents" (*Educ.* iii. 464); and of Paradise and / or Heaven. The paradisal ideal can be useful in various ways, mainly by providing a sanctified arena for the projection of unrealised powers, and for the adjustment of imbalance (materialism or soulishness usually) in this life; hence although it can be an opiate it can also function as a privileged criticism of life, Sidney's golden world set against the brazen. It is this view of Paradise that makes Milton inconsistent. Looking back on life before the Fall he sees it not so much as a positive mode of existence in its own right, but rather a fulfilment of certain potentialities that he values but finds weak in this life—physical beauty, married love, human divinity; and a reparation of what he assumes to have been lost since. Thus, *τεχνη*, art, though now conventionally and with wide ethical implications opposed to *φυσις*, nature, must then have been inherent in nature. Milton's Paradise would have been much more complaisant if he had had the Metaphysical poet's confident intuition of the *φυσις* actually in *τεχνη* (the neurological basis of thought, for instance, and the physiological basis of soul-love as argued in "The Extasie"), and our knowledge of the *τεχνη* in fallen *φυσις*—the

[1] *Rel. Med.* i. 16.
[2] *Ecc. Pol.* I. iii. 4.

sine curves of a snail's shell or a fern. But such a Paradise would not have been true to *Paradise Lost*, or to any but the ideally intense moments of actual life. As it is, when describing nature as we normally experience it (in similes for instance) Milton writes naturalistically, and more so than the Augustans, who applied to *all* boskage the divinely-ordering title "grove", because to them the Fall had not really happened and nature was as good as it should be.[1] More significance inheres in such language when it is reserved, as Milton reserves it in *Paradise Lost*, to contexts in which the creative efficacy of God was operative and the perfection of nature could properly be assumed—in Paradise and at Creation. Here the standard Elizabethan inter-pretation of art and nature has a more than literary or geographical validity.

His re-creative and serious treatment of convention may be seen also in this, that he did not allow all the realities to steam away into idealism, allegory or wish-fulfilment. Camoens used the paradisal ideal—mostly derived from the *Koran*, apparently —as a reward. Marvell used it as a retreat. Spenser did not make the Garden of Adonis an acceptable chaste counterpart to the Bower of Bliss: although its topography is more natural than Milton's, its inhabitants are shades; while Venus and Adonis themselves unrealistically eternise a bewildering minute. The garden of the Temple of Venus is "a second paradise" (IV. x. 23) and nature is equated with art there too; but those of its inhabitants whom Spenser singles out as having "on chast vertue grounded their desire" are homosexuals. Drayton did not revive the Endymion myth because he was too explicitly allegorical. Milton simply names the trees, Drayton expounds their emblemism:

> *Phoebus* greene Laurell florisht in the shade:
> Faire *Venus* Mirtile, *Mars* his warlike Fyrre,
> *Minervas* Olive, and the weeping Myrhe,
> The patient Palme, which thrives in spite of hate,
> The Popler, to *Alcides* consecrate;
>
> (30)

The tradition of mishandling Paradise in this way goes back to the Greek Fathers. By Milton's time it had become part of that

[1] Cf. Davie, *Purity of Diction in English Verse* (1952), p. 43, and Willey, *18th-century Background* (1949), p. 35.

dreary world of title-pages and emblems that makes the 17th Century look, from outside, so musty and dull. The decay of Paradise as a symbol was not altogether a result of rationalism or Protestantism, or a healthy exile of the train of gods and goddesses. It was partly the symptom of an incapacity for making the old thing new. Just as drama degenerated back again into masque, and Spenser's *Epithalamion* gave place to Donne's, so myth was returned again to allegory and conceit because no one, until Milton, had the strength to give it new life in contemporary terms. The Garden of Eden was used often in sermons, and Metaphysical poetry, as an object-lesson; but not as a fable whose moral was inherent. Sometimes it was treated as large-scale allegory—by Phineas Fletcher as reformed England under attack from satanic Catholicism, for instance[1]; others interpreted the love of Adam and Eve like the *Song of Solomon*, as an emblem of Christ and his bride-Church.[2] Henry Hawkins, in his Catholic emblem-book *Partheneia Sacra*, emblemised and typologised every detail of the Garden of Eden so that it became merely beads to be told, an index of "al Graces; whence streame the littel rils and brooks watering the Paradice on al sides, and thence abundantly flowing to the rest of Mortals".[3] It adds a thin layer to our appreciation of the "Groves of Myrrhe, And flowring Odours, Cassia, Nard and Balme" (V. 292) to learn that myrrh is a prophylactic against devils and cinammon a symbol of incorruptibility.[4] Even so, Milton's attitude was not so aggressive as Heylyn's: "Some make *Paradise* to be a place of pleasure, and the four Rivers to be the four Cardinal Vertues; but these Allegories on the Scriptures are unwarrantable".[5] He suggests rather the permissiveness of Augustine: "allegorical interpretations may be suitably put upon Paradise without giving offence to any one, while yet we believe the strict truth of the history, confirmed by its circumstantial narrative of facts.[6]

[1] *Appolyonists*, i. 24 ff.; ii. 21ff.

[2] Man : woman :: Christ : Church. This was the standard interpretation of *Canticles* but Tulloch notes that Cudworth was very interested in it and was able to "heap(s) around it a multiplicity of quotations from diverse mystical authorities, amongst others from the 'masters of the Cabala' . . ." (*Rational Theology*, ii. 201).

[3] Rouen, 1633, repr. 1950 (Hand and Flower Press), p. 12.

[4] As Hawkins tells. Cf. the spice grove of paradise in *I Enoch*, xxxi-ii.

[5] *Cosmog*. III. 108 b.

[6] *City of God*. ed. Healey and Barker (2 vols. 1945), xiii. 21; cf. xiv. 12.

This is precisely Milton's method, and with it he remade the myth for Western Europe.

The topography is summarised in these lines:

> Thus was this place,
> A happy rural seat of various view;
> Groves whose rich Trees wept odorous Gumms and Balme,
> Others whose fruit burnisht with Golden Rinde
> Hung amiable, *Hesperian* Fables true,
> If true, here onely, and of delicious taste:
>
> (246)

The balance between nature and art lies in "odorous Gumms and Balme" against and within "fruit burnisht with Golden Rinde". Then as with the thornless roses we are led from actuality to myth: "happy rural seat" is almost laughably the England of Penshurst, Cooper's Hill and Appleton House; groves, dropping resin and spice, lead to the tropics, less familiar but still real (Virginia, Bermuda and the East Indies were news); but the parenthesis, "*Hesperian* Fables true, If true, here onely", with its slack syntax, drifts us away from geography to myth, until the last disjunctive phrase wrenches us back beyond myth, geography and home, to the Eden of *Genesis* and the beginning of this poem: "that Forbidden Tree, whose Mortal taste Brought death into the world". But the description starts again, into further detail, more baroque, setting the balance more acutely still so that at any moment the natural fecundity of the place, where "Nature boon Powrd forth profuse on Hill and Dale and Plaine", may spill over into a chaotic jungle of "enormous bliss", or the pleasing artifice of Nature—the lake's chrystal mirror—might petrify into the tinsel of a pleasure-garden. In either case innocence would be lost, to brutalism or sophistication. But for this book the balance is held, delicately adjusted in phrases like "vegetable Gold". Like the artifice of nature, the ethical balance it symbolises is really anachronistic, for it derives from the *δίκη* of the Greeks, manifest in Adam and Eve as *αἰγδώς* and the *σωφροσύνη* of their environment and way of life. But *δίκη* is the root of New Testament "righteousness", and *σωφροσύνη* the opposite of *ὕβρις*. An ideal moment of being would be more intense and passionate than this; but an ideal mode of continuous being is bound to be as classical Greek as the sculptural bodies of Adam and Eve and the πόλις they inhabit. The balance between reality and myth has a slightly different effect, suggesting that the state of innocence hovers between what is and what might have been. This is not mere nostalgia: human nature in its paradisal innocence is presented as having been superior to the imperfect nature we know since the Fall, but not yet matured and consummated as it might have been if Adam and Eve had, in the face of temptation, denied the serpent and affirmed their freedom; or as ours will be in renovation. Their innocence is a moment of potential: it must change: either develop into something richer, or be lost.

3. *Adam and Eve*

"Innocence" is a negative word, presupposing its positive. Children are innocent so far as they are ignorant, adults so far as they do not impute the evil they know. Lovers, pre-eminently, may stand naked, having been aware in the past of the possibilities of lust, disgust, distrust, flippancy, embarrassment, and so on, but now not discovering them. This kind of innocence, though it be passive, is not negative for it positively transcends nocence. Milton's difficulty is that strictly speaking Adam and Eve are not innocent for they have no nocence, intellectual or sexual, to transcend; so he has to present them as unconsciously transcending what we know to be evil. He mitigates the difficult by embedding them in the innocence of their habitation. They do not walk on to the stage but emerge from already-innocent Paradise as its phenomenal "Master work, the end Of all yet don" (VII. 505). The description sharpens to Spenser and Botticelli as Pan dances with the Hours when in the middle of a line the tone drops and Persephone gently presages the Fall but also, in the pain which it cost Ceres "To seek her through the world", the salvation of man. Then the expeditio of the Nyseian Isle and Mount Amara kaleidoscopes glittering patterns so that it is with a shock that the vision steadies, we are returned to the eyes of Satan who "Saw undelighted all delight", and out of the confusion of vegetation, myth, geography, emerge

> Two of far nobler shape erect and tall,
> Godlike erect, with native Honour clad
> In naked Majestie seemd Lords of all,

> And worthie seemd, for in thir looks Divine
> The image of thir glorious Maker shon,
> Truth, Wisdom, Sanctitude severe and pure,
> Severe, but in true filial freedom plac't;

At first entirely abstract, and with no active verbs, the language slowly proceeds to conventional physical details. The rhythm undulates sleepily, then rises in pitch until it is quivering at Eve's "sweet reluctant amorous delay" but at once her artfulness of love is checked by Milton's own bass voice declaring, "Nor those mysterious parts were then conceald". Yet even here the open "parts" are in effect concealed by "mysterious". The epithet is often glossed as "symbolic" (cf. "the Rites Mysterious of connubial Love" at line 742) but in both cases the word refers at once to the dark animal fact and the human significance. The materials are here waiting to be realised in either lust or love, by Adam and Eve, and the reader. Now Adam and Eve come to their wedding supper. Sensations are directly communicated—"The savourie pulp they chew, and in the rinde Still as they thirsted scoop the brimming stream"—for this is the proper office of sensation unqualified by art or reason. But even here there is danger. The verse sways from side to side—

> Under a tuft of shade that on a green
> Stood whispering soft, by a fresh Fountain side
> They sat them down . . .

—the words cease to have much meaning:

> To recommend coole *Zephyr*, and made ease
> More easie, wholsom thirst and appetite
> More grateful,

—when suddenly the line-ending catches up with us: "to thir Supper Fruits they *fell*". The compliance of the boughs becomes sinister, the side-long relaxation of Adam and Eve is a perilous declination from erectitude, and in a moment Satan's curses break in on us.

These are hints to the reader. The overall feeling we have about Adam and Eve in Book IV is of stability on the brink of change: it can, will fall, but it could be no more blessed than it is.

Milton partly establishes the condition as for an epithalamium, through the symbol of the bride who is for a moment virgin and matron at once. The verse describing Eve may have an actual as well as a literary Italian element in the "portamenti alti honesti" and "vezzosamenta altera" with which he had described Emilia, the girl he met at the Diodatis' (see p. 32 above). But there were no narrative examples to follow for Eve's character, I think. Epics had presented figures like Circe and the sportive damsels in Tasso's Fortunate Isle and Spenser's Bower of Bliss, or patient Penelopes, green maidens on whom knights could hang their honour; they had not offered anything like "the Virgin Majestie of *Eve*". Heroines were deteriorating in 17th-century narrative verse. *Brittain's Ida* is frankly pornographic. In *The Purple Isle* Fletcher describes Partheneia, who represents unmarried chastity, with succulent aestheticism:

> Her daintie breasts, like to an Aprill rose
> From green-silk fillets yet not all unbound,
> Began their little rising heads disclose,
> And fairly spread their silver circlets round :
>
> (x. 37)

This is not innocence, but the conventional *loucherie* of pastoralism. In pastoral the poet or his protagonists of the same class stand off a little way, as literate, sophisticate and aristocratic, from the primitivism of the pastoral characters which they envy, but patronise. This is what Satan does; it must be avoided in the direct presentation of Adam and Eve. Thus Sidney's country wenches in *Arcadia* are equally oxymoronic but the paradox is merely verbal:

> Upon their haire they ware garlandes of roses and gilliflowers; and the haire was so drest, as that came againe above the garlandes; enterchaunging a mutuall covering; so as it was doubtfull whether the haire drest the garlandes, or the garlandes drest the haire. Their breasts liberall to the eye . . . Their countenaunces full of a gracefull gravitie; so as the gesture matcht with the apparrell, it might seem a wanton modestie, and an entising soberness.[1]

[1] (1590 ed. repr. A. Feuillerat (Cambridge, 1939), III. ii. 2. This, and the quotation from Tasso below, and paintings, suggest that nakedness of the breast was less unusual, and therefore less exciting, especially in rural and low-class environments, than it has been since about 1830; so it was easier for Milton to present Eve's nakedness as primary and genital—that is, procreative—than for us, who would tend to concentrate on secondary and more aesthetic excitements. On the other hand it suggests that obviously

The flippancy of Sidney's oxymorons, the contemplative glee, show how firmly Milton in his description of Eve avoids pandering to the male desire to assuage its sadism on the modesty and its guilty masochism on the wantonness of a virgin. As Adam and Satan discover, Eve's naked majesty has more than sexual import.

Writing of Eve alone brings to notice another peculiar excellence of Milton's presentation, that although he lays more descriptive emphasis on Eve, she and Adam are a descriptive unity until Book IX. They share each other's naked innocence. Donne constantly affirmed this, but I don't think any other writer has dramatised it except Lawrence, and he, because of the rarity of such a thing, spoils the illusion of innocence by emphatic phallicism. Spenser achieved the Miltonic ideal in *Epithalamion*; but most writers were malely partial. There was the tradition of describing a woman's body as itself a paradise—*Venus and Adonis*, *Ovid's Banquet of Sense*, Donne's "Elegy xviii" and "Heroical Epistle", and the *Song of Solomon*: "A garden enclosed is my sister, my spouse . . ." This involved the commercial view of woman we have already seen rejected by Milton. Apart from the evasive Platonism of the Garden of Adonis and Temple of Venus, there were two naturalistic methods. One was the no-nonsense approach sometimes used by Donne. It always results in indignity for the woman. This does not matter in "Elegy xix", where he is writing as himself the master-lover: "As liberally as to a Midwife, shew Thy self" is a plausible joke of the genial bed; but in "Epithalamion made at Lincolnes Inne" it issues in the conceit of the bride laid naked "Like an appointed lambe, when tenderly The priest comes on his knees t'embowell her". The sacramental typology would not have appealed to Milton; and even in the mutuality of "Elegy viii"—

aesthetic features such as braiding the hair—the entwining of art with nature generally—would arouse that secondary kind of excitement more than it does with us; so that Milton's checking of artifice with plain nakedness ("Her unadorned golden tresses wore Dissheveld") was then even more important than I have suggested. Piero di Cosimo's profile of *La Bella Simonetta* (Musée Condé, Chantilly; repr. in R. Langton Douglas's ed. [Chicago, 1946] and in Berenson) shows the girl's face pleasantly open, her breasts bare (as often in his paintings, but here innocently bare); but her hair is heavily braided in serpentine plaits laced with pearl and her serpentine necklace is entwined by a live snake pointing its tongue at her breasts. The snake is supposed to symbolise the consumption she was dying of but aesthetically it is on the side of "art", the braids and necklace which threateningly emphasise her naturalness.

So kisse good Turtles, so devoutly nice
Are Priests in handling reverent sacrifice,
And such in searching wounds the Surgeon is
As wee, when wee embrace, or touch, or kisse.

—this conceit does not encompass married love—but only transmits the aching tenderness of the very moment of love's doing. Such a moment, even had Milton been capable of its transmission, would have shattered every other moment in *Paradise Lost*. We may hold that it should have done so, that once you admit the paradisal moments of human love you can't believe paradise is lost, or you can't want any other to be regained. Triumphant love is rare for genetic reasons, but no more than genius. But the Fall is a more domestic and dynastic alienation than the collapse of sexual passion; that usual decay, and the uncommonness of perfect love, are only two of the phenomena he is trying to account for. The second naturalistic method of presenting innocence, used more often in the 20th Century, is to assume the purity and beauty of love by insisting on the purity and beauty of the flesh which excites it:

Sideway his [*sc.* Adonis'] face repos'd
On one white arm, and tenderly unclos'd
By tenderest pressure, a faint damask mouth
To slumbery pout;[1]

It may be that Keats, anxious at this early stage to learn mere craft, had been affected here by Milton's description of the supper fruits, without realising that their sensuousness had only a local propriety. But it is probably just *Venus and Adonis*, and we revolt as from that poem: as literature it calls too much attention to its own mimetic skill, and as an imagined experience it disables itself because sexual love would be a perverse response to such meaty stimulus.

When we consider in this context the love-scene between Adam and Eve—

half her swelling breast
Naked met his under the flowing Gold
Of her loose tresses hid: (IV. 495)

[1] *Endymion*, ii. 403. Drayton details his Endimion, but without fleshliness. Rosemond Tuve discusses sensuous vividness as a criterion of decorum in *Elizabethan and Metaphysical Imagery* (Chicago, 1947).

—we can see that Milton has avoided pornography on one hand and idealism on the other; that he has still not descended to witty brutalism, not sensationalised the contact; but that he has struck a balance which is also part of the larger, theological balance of Paradise. The artifice of "gold" is almost rhymed against the sensuousness of "breast", as Yeats's nightingale opposes his "mackerel-crowded seas".

Adam and Eve share the artifice of eternity with Paradise. Their love is not urgent because they are perpetually in love. They process through the garden with a dignity immune to the pressure of lapsarian time: "So passd they naked on. . . . Thus talking hand in hand alone they pass'd. . . . Thus at thir shadie Lodge arriv'd, both stood, Both turnd. . . ." This is the point of the device which first names them: "*Adam* the goodliest man of men since borne His Sons, the fairest of her Daughters *Eve*" (324)—their children spring eternally from a syntactical union. The "Vivamus mea Lesbia" motif is found in most other paradises. In Tasso's garden Armida appears at first as frank as Eve —"Her breasts were naked, for the day was hot".[1] But she is a coquette, and Rinaldo her prisoner, so that "when her wooing fit was brought to end, She congee tooke, kist him, and went her way" (xxvi). The whole scene is a temptation to make the best of time. The virgin rose loses its innocence and dies in a day; so Tasso's bird of paradise sings,

> gather then the rose while time thou has,
> Short is the day, done when it scant began,
> Gather the rose of loue, while yet thou mast
> Louing be lou'd; embrasing, be embrast.
>
> (xv)

This is Milton's theme, but he makes it spiritual by channelling the conventional refrain into Satan's envy:

> Live while ye may,
> Yet happie pair; enjoy, till I return,
> Short pleasures, for long woes are to succeed. . . .
>
> (IV. 533)

Satire on the coy mistress theme is explicit when Adam and Eve consummate their love, as consummation not to be found

[1] *Ger. Lib.* XVI. x.

in the bought smile
Of Harlots, loveless, joyless, unindeard,
Casual fruition, nor in Court Amours
Mixt Dance, or wanton Mask, or Midnight Bal,
Or Serenate, which the starv'd Lover sings
To his proud fair, best quitted with disdain.

(765)

The courtliness of Adam and Eve does not vaunt. It is a habit of behaviour directed always at the honour of another, not of the self. It issues principally in their addresses to God, and to each other—"Daughter of God and Man, accomplisht *Eve*". In the late 16th and the 17th Centuries courtly modes of address were being adapted by the middle classes[1] (hence the conjugal use of Christian names and endearments remained less than genteel right into the 20th Century); similarly Adam and Eve domesticate cosmic seniority. Much of the semolina of bourgeois marriage that we regard as typically Victorian is to be found in Milton, as in the increasingly domestic plays of the 17th Century, and in Pope. But in Paradise it is not yet sticky. Adam and Eve realise the highest purpose of politeness, to recognise and celebrate the precise nature of the being addressed. This sets a standard of true courtliness by which to judge the chivalric bombast of Hell. When Adam goes to meet Raphael "His god-like Guest" (V. 351) he is himself "'our Primitive great Sire", a father-king to whom our attitude is implicitly directed by the fifth commandment; yet

without more train
Accompani'd then with his own compleat
Perfections, in himself was all his state,
More solemn then the tedious pomp that waits
On Princes, when thir rich Retinue long
Of Horses led, and Grooms besmeard with Gold
Dazles the croud, and sets them all agape.

Some critics object that Adam's ambassadorial qualities are not enough to excite dramatic interest in him so that his fall is not important to us. But any more definite characterisation of Adam would have made him fallen already. Waller makes Adam a Renaissance hero:

[1] See Wright, *Middle-Class Culture*, pp. 222-3.

> One! like the Author, whose capacious mind
> Might, by the glorious work, the Maker find;
> Might measure heaven, and give each star a name;
> With art and courage the rough ocean tame;
> Over the globe with swelling sails might go,
> And that 'tis round by his experience know;
> Make strongest beasts obedient to his will,
> And serve his use the fertile earth to till.[1]

But this is to forget the Fall. Milton's Adam, waiting for the Fall, is vehicle rather than character: the perfect form of manhood waiting for the introjection of personality. This cannot happen yet because they are beyond our fallen reach. But as they fall, Adam and Eve are humanised, to the level of identifiable domesticity. Dramatically it is a clumsy business; but that personality should coincide with sin is precisely the comment that the myth is trying to make: individuation is man's glory, and his peril.

Milton's consolidating power may be seen from the weakness, the aspiring superficiality, with which the ideal of marriage incorporated in Book IV had been stated before:

> A happy couple, he joying in her, she joying in her selfe, but in her selfe, because she enjoyed him: both encreasing their riches by giving to each other; each making one life double, because they made a double life; one, where desire never wanted satisfaction, nor satisfaction never bred sacietie; he ruling, because she would obey: or rather because she would obey, she therein ruling.[2]

Cowley's attack on false modesty as "The senseless rules, which first *False Honour* taught" (*Dav.* iii. 819), and his celebration of Love—

> There do'est thou sit (like Men e're Sin had fram'ed
> A guilty blush) *Naked*, but not *Asham'ed*.
>
> (ii. 80)

—lack both the personal intensity of Milton's manifesto, and the dramatic function of his presentation of Adam and Eve.

Nevertheless Milton's achievement is one of convention, eclectic and literary, not original and actual. He crystallised not

[1] "Of Divine Love", i. 27.
[2] *Arcadia*, III. xii. 4.

the finest moments of living but the finest hypotheses of idealism. So as an establishment of Paradise in this epic his work is supreme; but when we look back to it from beyond the Fall it is going to suffer in a way indicated by Newman. Because it almost escapes Newman's condemnation of literature as being the inevitably sinful history of fallen man, it falls on the other side:

> You may gather together something very great and high, something higher than any Literature ever was; and when you have done so, you will find that it is not Literature at all. You will have simply left the delineation of man, as such, and have substituted for it, as far as you have had anything to substitute, that of man, as he is or might be, under certain special advantages.[1]

In less comprehensive tragic poems, from *The Waste Land* to *Wanderer*, we find hints of a paradise latently more desirable than Milton's, and so a loss more poignant for being loss of that more local and specific bliss. At the end of this poem we feel sad not so much because the glory of Book IV has gone as because the wretchedness of Books XI-XII is actual. Aesthetically this is a fault; morally it is the poem's merit that it should abjure nostalgia and move unremittingly into the acceptance of loss. Not all is lost: the love of Adam and Eve, though sinful, is intensified by exile; and though they seem not to achieve the promised paradise within them, the poem itself does. The loss of importance that Paradise suffers across the Fall is similar to the loss of glamour and interest in one's childhood memories that occurs on the other side of growing up.

4. *Justitia Originalis*

The symbolising of innocence as a state of balance is confirmed by the scalar imagery of the poem's theology:

> no Decree of mine
> Concurring to necessitate his Fall,
> Or touch with lightest moment of impulse
> His free Will, to her own inclining left
> In even scale.

[1] *Idea of University*, Discourse VIII.

We should be happier about God's justice towards Adam and Eve if their will were not balanced, but unswayable, by whatever temptation. Yet an immutable will would make man either superhuman or subhuman. Theologians defined three different kinds of "freedom" to correspond with three states of being.[1] There was first the freedom of *non-posse peccare*, enjoyed by the blessed in heaven, perhaps belonging properly only to God. This is freedom from the necessity to choose. In *Paradise Lost* the Father declares that his goodness "is free To act or not, Necessity and Chance Approach not mee" (VII. 171). Secondly there was the freedom of unfallen man, *posse non-peccare*. This was the freedom to choose, imperfect relative to the divine freedom precisely because choice had to be exercised. Brunner defines it thus:

> the freedom of the origin is genuinely creaturely, a limited freedom, precisely in that which seems to make it especially free, the fact that it "can" do something. There is a kind of ability to do something which is not a sign of freedom, but of the limitation of freedom, of imperfection. Man originally possessed not merely the power of decision but the necessity for decision—this could not be the distinguishing element in the state of eternal bliss.[2]

All through the poem the necessity to choose is forced on Adam and Eve, by the balance of description, by their psychology, by Satan. Indeed, their innocence is most clearly defined by the possibilities of sin or apotheosis that it involves. Thirdly there is fallen man's slavery to sinfulness, and hence to political and domestic tyranny, as described in Books XI-XII. Milton believed that we retain a remnant of freedom in things indifferent and even in the performance of good actions; but in what matters, the ground of action, we are in a state of *non-posse non-peccare*, unable to act sinlessly. We are bound

> in that deprivation of righteousness and liberty to do good, in that slavish subjection to sin and the devil, which constitutes, as it were, the death of the will.
>
> (*De Doc.* iv. 25)

This system will not stand up to logical analysis, but it is itself a criticism of the word "freedom"; and it corresponds to life. For some people, inability to control their actions rationally or

[1] E.g. Augustine, *City*, xxii. 30; *Enchiridion*, xxviii.

[2] *Man in Revolt: A Christian Anthropology* (trans. Olive Wyon, 1939), p. 264.

ethically is the most apparent slavery. For others, though stronger-willed and more sophisticated, the slavery remains because there is always doubt as to the ultimate motive of action—they are aware of the danger of doing the right thing for the wrong reason. Even for the man whose will is most habituated to doing good and whose motives are pure as they may be, his involvement in other people's designs must tarnish all he does. The immediate ambition for the man of good will is the paradisal state in which his actions might be more clearly defined and issue in proportionate results unhindered by other people's counter-actions. The final ambition, expressed in most civilised notions of an after-world, is for some kind of rest, not from action but conflict: a state in which spontaneity need have no check because it can result only in excellence.[1] At some periods this seems most likely to be approached on earth by rational control, at others by emotional release. The phases meet in Wordsworth as "sovereignty within and peace at will, Emotion which best foresight need not fear Most worthy then of trust when most intense."[2] Adam and Eve belong if at all to the rational phase; but Milton's abjuring of Paradise, and the theology he was using, imply with Augustine that neither reason nor passion of themselves can avoid sinfulness; the search for innocent spontaneity must fail, and the search itself can be a retreat from the necessity to choose.

The Fathers had been interested in *iustitia originalis* since the time of Irenaeus. They probably knew they were really mythologising about the present condition of man; at any rate many of their differences seem much less significant than historians of theology have made them out to be.[3] There was one important shift of opinion, though. In Augustinian doctrine the primitive state of Adam was elevated to a higher peak of physical, intellectual and moral excellence than ever before. Scholars disagree as to whether Augustine himself thought of this excellence as

[1] Cf. Augustine, *City*, xiv. 19.

[2] *Prelude* (1805 version ed. Selincourt, 1933), XIII. 114.

[3] Here I rely mainly on N. P. Williams, *Ideas of the Fall and of Original Sin: A Historical and Critical Study*, 1927; F. R. Tennant, *Sources of the Doctrine of the Fall and Original Sin*, Cambridge, 1903; Rheinhold Niebuhr, *Nature and Destiny of Man*, 2 vols. 1943; see also S. H. Cohon, "Original Sin", *Hebrew Union College Annual*, XXI (1948). The most stimulating *interpretation* of original sin and the Fall is Kierkegaard's in *The Concept of Dread*; Niebuhr subsumes much of it.

natural or supernatural[1]; but in subsequent Scholastic thought[2] a distinction was developed between the "natural" and essentially "human" excellence and righteousness of Adam, residing in his *pura naturalia*, his *anima rationalis* alone; and a further *donum superadditum* which was essentially supernatural. This distinction tended to weaken the sense of original sin by making man's fallen state more "natural", a *defectus* from supernature instead of a *depravatio* of human nature; and it tended to sever the link between fallen man and God. At the Reformation the chief motives of religious thought were to bring individual men into closer relationship with God, and yet admit fallen depravity that grace might be more abounding. So the Roman Catholic distinction between *pura naturalia* and *donum supernaturale* was abolished by identifying them with each other. Adam's supernatural status was taken rather more literally, as superiority over the flux of irrational nature, and it was regarded as being proper to him, that which made him human. So when he fell it was not from a state of super-nature to nature, but from his own human nature to subhuman nature.[3] It was this Protestant view that enabled Milton[4] to treat Paradise realistically, to

[1] See Williams, p. 363.

[2] Aquinas can be ambiguous: "To Adam, as being the first man, was due a degree of perfection which was not due to other men"; but this is definite: "So it is clear also that the primitive subjection by virtue of which reason was subject to God, was not a merely natural gift, but was a supernatural endowment of grace". Or course it all depends what you mean by "natural"; unfortunately Adam was not *natus*. *Summa Theologica* (trans. Fathers of the English Dominican Province, 1911 . . .), iii. 305, 311.

[3] E.g. Calvin: "We ought to be satisfied with this, that the Lord deposited with Adam the endowments he chose to confer on the human nature; and therefore that when he lost the favours he had received, he lost them not only for himself, but for us all." Calvin does explicitly follow "Augustine and the school-men" in distinguishing between natural and supernatural gifts; but both are conceived of as "natural" in the sense of belonging essentially to mankind, not merely Adam: "the natural talents in man have been corrupted by sin, but . . . of the supernatural ones he has been wholly deprived. For by the latter are intended, both the light of faith and righteousness, which would be sufficient for the attainment of a heavenly life and eternal felicity". For Calvin the *supernaturale* in *donum supernaturale* relates to the object rather than the source of the *donum*. *Institutes* (trans. J. Allen, rev. B. B. Warfield, 7th [American] ed. 2 vols. Philadelphia, 1936), i. 273, 292.

[4] There are numerous references in the prose to Adam's *iustitia originalis* (e.g. *De Doc.*, *Tetrach.*) but it is considered as Man's normal state: no *donum* is superadded. Adam's free will, his "*natural* wisdom, holiness, and righteousness" (*De Doc.* my italics) are a consequence of his proper nature as a creature made in the image of God.

avoid Dante's hagiographical attutude to Adam and Eve, and to present the Fall dramatically, as a development of human nature anologous to our own experience rather than as a sudden reversion from god to man.

Miss Millicent Bell makes this point in "The Fallacy of the Fall in *Paradise Lost*"[1]. She shows that what most critics take to be causes of the Fall are human frailties in Adam and Eve which can only be its results. She concludes that Milton was "employing the somewhat intractable legend to characterize the state of fallen Man" under a system of "sophisticated philosophic monism" which "governs *Paradise Lost* and makes *felix culpa*, God's method of creating more good out of equal evil, the central theme". The identification of Adam and Eve with fallen man is not a peculiarity of Milton's but a characteristic of Protestant theology forced on it by taking the myth seriously. Neither is it true, for me, that Adam and Eve "are never purely Good, but fallen and capable of redemption from the start"; our first impression is of a balanced perfection, not the less perfect for being balanced. But it is true that this condition becomes less stable: the knife-edge between man's "disposition to do good" and his "liability to fall", as Milton puts it in *De Doctrina*, is sharpened through Books V, VII and VIII, especially where Adam's relations with Eve are concerned, and by reflection from the liability of even angels to fall away from God. At the very end of Book VIII, immediately before the Fall, Raphael warns Adam to "take heed least Passion sway Thy Judgement to do aught, which else free Will Would not admit". His use of the jargon of Greek psychology, which can apply only to the fallen soul, is an anachronistic; but it implies that the psychological make-up of man has "not changed" since before the Fall, that the sin of Adam is representative of as well as original to our sins. Augustine, in one place at least, would not admit this: he says that before the Fall Adam and Eve must have existed without perturbation, fear or desire, and that it was not necessary for reason to exercise restraint on the passions. Yet elsewhere he does admit that "Our first parents fell into open disobedience because already they were secretly corrupted; for the evil act had never been done had not an evil will preceded it. . . . The wicked deed, then,—that is to say, the transgression

[1] *PMLA*, LXVIII (1953), 863-83.

of eating the forbidden fruit,—was committed by persons who were already wicked".[1] To resolve this confusion it would be necessary to abandon the classical psychology, and also the notion that we possess only a "relic" of Adam's *iustitia originalis*; we should have to recognise, as Brunner says,

> that the *humanitas* which sinful man still possesses, and the *justitia originalis* which he has lost, both spring from the same source; this, however, is only possible by abandoning the historico-mythical form of the traditional doctrine, and by relating each human being both to his origin in the Word of God and to the Fall. And, on the other hand, we must conceive of the *Imago Dei* in a completely personalistic and actual manner, which means that we must do away with the Aristotelian idea of the *animal rationale*.[2]

Milton's psychology was too crude for him to accomplish the metaphysical part of this solution; but his poetry does modify the historico-mythical basis of the doctrine. He makes Adam and Eve move from careless innocence in Book IV towards a point at which they have to make a decision. This point lies in an area of acute anxiety which is already sin, properly considered—here Milton agrees with Kierkegaard as well as Augustine; and his treatment of the whole process is that recommended by Brunner, and Niebuhr:

> The relation of man's essential nature to his sinful state cannot be solved within terms of the chronological version of the perfection before the Fall. It is, as it were, a vertical rather than horizontal relation . . . the Fall is . . . a symbol of an aspect of every historical moment in the life of man . . .[3]

This relation may be found even in the scenic structure of the poem.[4] Paradise stands horizontally between Creation and Fall

[1] *City*, xiv. 13.

[2] Brunner, *op. cit.* p. 96 (I have rationalised the translator's punctuation). Brunner is concerned to abandon the distinction between *Imago* and *Similitudo Dei*. It can be argued that Adam and Eve fall from *Imago* by trying to acquire *Similitudo*, but this is a verbal doctrine deriving from *Gen.* i. 26. and Milton seems to avoid the argument at VII. 519, "Let us make now Man in our image, Man in our similitude", by simply quoting the verse.

[3] *Nature and Destiny of Man*, i. 285.

[4] Hence the danger of regarding the description as a mere topothesia, whether in ancient or modern critical terms. Tuve (*Imagery*, p. 102) suggests that in describing the Cave of Morpheus Spenser faced problems similar to Milton's here; but they were not complicated by dramatic as well as ethical exigencies.

in time and vertically between Heaven and Hell in space—a moment of time and poise.

5. *Satan and Gabriel*

The passage of time in epics had always been marked by elaborately animistic chronographias acting as "relieving" similes. The original motive for them, in primitive epic, was presumably to conjure times and seasons to reliability. Milton bends magic and convention to his own poem. Book IV carries us from noon—when Satan curses the sun—to sunset. The sunset is marked by two chronographias. The first separates Adam and Eve's supper and the playing serpent from Satan's cry of hatred and envy:

> the Sun
> Declin'd was hasting now with prone career
> To th' Ocean Iles, and in th' ascending Scale
> Of Heav'n the Starrs that usher Evening rose:
>
> (352)

The verse enacts the balance of Paradise. The second is based on *Aeneid* I. 522 ff. and works by Uriel's flight down a sunbeam to warn Gabriel, and then back again "On that bright beam whose point now raisd / Bore him slope downward to the Sun now fall'n / Beneath th' Azores" (590). Again there is a suggestion of balance, but the device functions mainly as an assurance of the smooth working of the divine laws of nature; a reminder of the physical position of Paradise in the world; and a contrast with Hell and the fallen world, whose endlessness and vicissitudes are modulated by no chronographias. The exquisitely adjusted verse lays quietness on our eyelids, broken only by "the wakeful Nightingale; She all night long her amorous descant sung; Silence was pleas'd"—where Hell was in uproar. "Now glow'd the Firmament With living Saphirs" where Pandemonium was lighted with naphtha flares. And where in Hell the moon was clouded, eclipsed and labouring here the "Apparent Queen unvaild her peerless light".

The episode at the end of the book makes a dramatic impact after the somnolence of the Paradisal afternoon, and insists on the involvement of Adam and Eve in cosmic politics—though the actual conduct of these politics, the need for sentries in Paradise, their failure to prevent Satan's approach to Eve, and God's release of Satan after his arrest, are absurd. The episode probably derives from a dramatic version. The reader sees Ithuriel and Zephon haling Satan to Gabriel, but Gabriel, speaking in the accents of Samson and Greek tragedy, unnecessarily remarks,

> O friends, I hear the tread of nimble feet
> Hasting this way, and now by glimps discerne
> *Ithuriel* and *Zephon* . . .

He makes an intelligent guess that the third figure "by his gate And fierce demeanour seems the Prince of Hell", and orders, "Stand firm, for in his look defiance lours". Every time these relics of Milton's early plans enter the poem they spoil it, not so much because they are ex-generic but because the genre they belong to is less serious than *Paradise Lost.*

Satan brings the technological and mountainous imagery of Hell with him into Paradise again: pricked by Ithuriel's spear he jumps up like exploding gunpowder; facing Gabriel's squadron he dilates "Like *Teneriff* or *Atlas* unremov'd" (987). The simile here is an interesting example of the continuity and complexity of Milton's ideas. The "careful Plowman" provides the usual mundane interval, but he is curiously detailed for this purpose, doubting "Least on the threshing floore his hopeful sheaves Prove chaff". I think he is intended to direct our attitude to Satan. In *Animadversions* Milton had scoffed at the Remonstrant's appeals to antiquity and allegorised them in the shape of an

> unactive and lifeless Colossus, that, like a carved giant terribly menacing to children and weaklings, lift up his club, but strikes not, and is subject to the muting of every sparrow.
>
> (iii. 66)

Then he declared that with the weapon of scripture "we shall not doubt to batter and throw down your Nebuchadnezzar's image, and crumble it like the chaff of the summer threshing-floors". This quotation from *Daniel* (ii. 35) relates both the colossus of the prose and Satan in the poem to Nebuchadnezzar's dream of the idol; so when a few lines later God hangs out the golden scales in Heaven the immediate reference is not so much to the *Iliad* (VII. 69; XXII. 209) as to Daniel's interpretation of the writing on the wall: "God hath numbered thy kingdom, and finished it. . . . Thou art weighed in the balances, and art found wanting" (v. 26). Thus the balanced frailty of Paradise is ultimately secure in the determination of God's will. Of course, Manicheeism lurks under this large symbol for Paradise. Like the war in Heaven, the argument between Satan and Gabriel is intellectually inconclusive; so is the war in man between what he "ought" and what he would. Milton, identifying "ought" with "good" and the less controllable kinds of "would" with "evil", is forced eventually to abandon his independence and bring a postulated omnipotence to the aid of his own "ought" and the world's "good". This is "faith". Its value depends on how fierce the struggle is, and how gentle the omnipotence.

The episode closes with an ominously brief chronographia: the Fiend "fled Murmuring, and with him fled the shades of night", taking us to Eve's falling dream.

7

ANTECEDENTIA

I. *Structure*

THERE is no accepted term for the deferred narrative which must occupy the middle of an epic that begins *in mediis rebus*. I shall call it—Books V-VIII in *Paradise Lost*—the *antecedentia*, using the word as a singular anglicism like "omnibus", to mean "what has happened already".

The antecedentia gives *Paradise Lost* a shape. A long central ridge, stretching from dawn to sunset, it suspends the poem's short dramatic period, and gives perspective to Hell, Heaven and Paradise on one side, and on the other the thunderous mutation of the world created in Book VII, the fate of the angels who rebelled in Book VI, the alienation of Adam and Eve who in the antecedentia are so sociable with Heaven; beyond is the decline into history. The σωφροσύνη of Paradise is applied to the specific condition of Adam and Eve in regard to knowledge, the apple, each other. And, through what they learn from Raphael of themselves, their status, and their involvement in the conflict of good and evil, Adam and Eve are drawn closer and closer to the point of decision: the antecedentia concludes with man and angel finally separating, "the Angel up to Heav'n . . . and *Adam* to his Bowre" and the exercise of informed free will.

Milton's antecedentia is more integrated with the action, and more sophisticated, than in most hexemeral poems. But that he should indulge in it at all brings *Paradise Lost* closer to its analogues. The War in Heaven reverts to the primitive angelomachias already surpassed in Books I and II by a more *engagé* treatment of the heroic; the Creation has no part in the action; Raphael's homiletics, though they wind the plot's spring, run it into diseconomy. This inflation is typical of epic and Milton was writing epic because he wanted to syncrete in it so many feelings and so much knowledge not strictly relevant to his central theme. But the central theme itself is not really an epical one; it cannot contain these Renaissance incidentals.

This is a major cause of disagreements about *Paradise Lost.* It is partly dramatic, partly lyrical; but our criteria of the dramatic have been made stricter by the novel and naturalistic drama, our idea of the lyrical is more personal and imagistic than Milton's. We have come to demand that if the work be mixed, its dramatic and lyrical phases shall closely reciprocate to form an "organic" whole like a Shakespeare play or a Lawrence novel. Milton's phases are not so intimately interrelated: partly because he did not have that kind of genius, but partly because he relied more than we can on the then obvious formal unity conferred by heroic verse and structure, and the obvious ideological relation between such themes as the Fall, Creation, War in Heaven, astronomy, scale of being, angelology. It probably does us no harm to relax our standards for him here: the specialisation of creative writing into "organic" wholes whose organisation must be entirely internal and autonomously literary, turns writing, and criticism, in on themselves.

2. *Men and Angels*

Eve's dream, Adam's comforting of her, and their hymn to the created world have been analysed by J. H. Summers.[1] An interesting symptom of Milton's anxiety about human nature, typical of Christian thought, is that while Adam attributes Eve's dream to natural psychological processes, Milton presents it in the plot as being Satan's influence. That is, although at the rational level Milton recognises the urgency of that invitation to darkness—"now is the pleasant time, The cool, the silent"—and Eve's nocturnal escapade as being naturally innocent, he cannot escape the superstition that such helpless potency is evil—as in waking life, as sexuality berserk, it would be. He just fails to draw this distinction, though Adam's dictum, "Evil into the mind of God or Man May come and go, so unapprov'd, and leave No spot or blame behind", is on the verge of a theory of the unconscious.

The incident has local dramatic value—the ordinary intimacies of sleep, tears, comfort are fresh after the heavy glories of Book IV; but it widens into a demonstration of cool self-knowledge and then, with the morning hymn, into a realisation of the place of man in creation. The hymn is a strophic version

[1] " 'Grateful Vicissitude' in *P.L.*", *PMLA*, LXIX (1954).

of *Psalm* cxlviii, the *Benedicite omnia opera,* as sung by the *Three Holy Children* of the Apocrypha.[1] It is a justification of Adam's call to observe "How Nature paints her colours, how the Bee Sits on the Bloom extracting liquid sweet" (V. 24), and a demonstration of how "In contemplation of created things By steps we may ascend to God" (511). As in the scale of being which Raphael is soon to describe, and the anaphoristic *gloria* sung by the angels before Creation (VII. 182 ff.), the steps are cut by rhetoric,[2] the *laudate's* descending from God through angels, stars, sun and moon, the four elements and the beasts, and returning to God as the source and end of all. There is a tendency for this sort of thing to die on your hands. Even the opposite notion of the world as a flux is contradicted in Fulke Greville's "The world, that all contains, is ever moving" by the rigidity of the rhetoric that expresses it. This does not happen in Milton's *Benedicite.* The dull verse "Praise him, sun and moon: praise him, all ye stars of light"[3] is so handled by

[1] Hence it fulfils the ambition recorded in *R.C.G.* "to imitate those magnific odes and hymns, wherein Pindarus and Callimachus are in most things worthy, some others in their frame judicious, in their matter most an end faulty. But those frequent songs throughout the law and prophets beyond all these, not in their divine argument alone, but in the very critical art of composition, may be easily made appear over all the kinds of lyric poesy to be incomparable" (ii. 479). Milton is trying here to sanction lyric poetry, but it shows that the preference for Hebrew literature over Greek stated by Christ in *P.R.* was not a sudden disillusioned revulsion from the classics. Also that the 17th-century attempts to paraphrase the *Psalms* were not all pitiable. Cf. Cowley's ode at *Davideis,* i. 482 ff., which paraphrases *Psalm* cxiv. The 18th Century lost much in having only Pindar, not David, as model for high lyric. Smart, Chatterton and Blake understood this.

[2] Ploce, traductio, surreptitious rhyme (172-184-191-196-204; 174-5-6), anti-rhyme (173-4).

[3] Even duller in its liturgical expansion. That one's heart should sink when the *Benedicite* is announced in church shows that it was not just Puritanism, least of all Milton's Humanistic and enthusiastically musical brand of it, that weakened the aesthetic of the English church. Ordinary Protestant Anglicanism, though firm and rich in its prose (mostly Cranmer's), has never produced—as the Puritans and Presbyterians did—poetic and musical vehicles of public worship worth replacing the Roman Catholic with. Of course the *Benedicite,* whether Milton's or the Prayer Book's, needed rewriting again in the 18th Century because the attitude to nature that it expresses was altered sometime between James Thomson and Wordsworth. *A Song to David,* "God's Grandeur" and some of Lawrence's poems are still truer now to the feelings and knowledge of the congregation. The argument against liturgical and theological revision is that God does not alter; but it is just for that reason that they could be revised, as men alter, without damaging him.

Milton that without in the least altering the total conception of the universe as fixed for ever firm and sure, he admits a lively fluidity. Because sun, moon, planets and stars are held in their courses by the figure of climax, and the planets related in their mobility to the dance of the angels and the harmony of the spheres, the easy cadence of "yee five other wandring Fires that move" can be enjoyed without the disruption that wandering elsewhere causes in the poem.

The interlude in Heaven where Raphael receives his instructions sets the paradisal balance again:

> and such discourse bring on,
> As may advise him of his happie state,
> Happiness in his power left free to will,
> Left to his own free Will, his Will though free,
> Yet mutable; (233)

Then, as if glad of release from celestial argument to mundane action, Raphael "Sailes between worlds & worlds" and "Winnows the buxom Air",[1] the parallel to Satan's mission. He alights and

[1] Raphael's flight, comparison to a phoenix, description of his plumage and his progress through the spice-grove, show how elements which look like incidental fancies of the poet are actually concretions of lore. In *de phoenice* Lactantius describes how the phoenix gathers spices for its nest (*Works* trans. W. Fletcher, [2 vols. Edinburgh, 1871], ii. 16-17). His description of the bird itself is like Milton's of Raphael: "her tail is extended, varied with yellow metal, in the spots of which mingled purple blushes". See Kathleen E. Hartwell, *Lactantius and Milton* (Cambridge, Mass. 1929). Kester Svendsen has incorporated several studies of Milton's knowledge of encyclopaedic material in *Milton and Science* (Cambridge, Mass. 1956). There has been little on his use of symbolic lore of the emblematic kind except Rosemary Freeman's pointing out in her *English Emblem Books* (1948) that the whale and anchor simile at *P.L.* I. 203 is an emblem motif (illustrated, e.g. in a 13th-century bestiary held by the Univ. Lib., Cambridge). But Milton was less interested than the Metaphysicals, and Elizabethans such as Sidney, in the emblematic and typological significance of his materials: his tendency was to expand and literalise. All the same he and his first readers would have been conscious of a latent significance in most living things, especially exotic ones like the halcyon, crocodile, myrtle; in all gems; and in certain bits of machinery such as compasses, scales, ladders. They would also have recognised some of his larger materials, including chaos, light, and the fall of Satan itself, as illustrated in emblems; and many of the classical myths (including Janus, Circe, Icarus, Bellerophon, Narcissus) would have been to some readers familiar as emblems rather than as literature. Most of the object lessons were obvious; but that cypress was an emblem of sanctity and agate a prophylactic against witchcraft we can only learn. The fullest single primary source is probably Geoffrey

> Him through the spicie Forrest onward com
> *Adam* discernd, as in the dore he sat
> Of his coole Bowre,

There is a subsequent reference to Alcinous but the primary analogues are the visit of two angels to Lot in Sodom, (*Gen.* xix. 1), and Abram's entertainment of angels in the plains of Mamre:

> he sat in the tent door in the heat of the day; And he lift up his eyes and looked, and, lo, three men stood by him: and when he saw them, he ran to meet them from the tent door, and bowed himself toward the ground . . . (*Gen.* xviii. 1)

In offering hospitality to Raphael, Adam and Eve expand the *à deux* relationship they had in Book IV; and the whole antecedentia reveals their responsibilities outside themselves, particularly to posterity. The dinner they eat together is a dramatic symbol of what Raphael is to talk about, the relation of man to nature and to spirit. We tend to think Protestantism dissociative; Milton thought it was Scholasticism that had severed divinity from humanity by hindering "all generous philosophy . . . with metaphysical gargarisms" (*R.C.G.* ii. 504), and that this was undemocratic, designed to "distract and stagger the multitude of credulous readers" with casuistry (*Prel. Ep.* ii. 422). In this respect his sensibility was, if anything, less dissociated than the Metaphysicals'.[1] He had a more elevated regard for human nature than they did. On the other hand, he was also more solemn about the supernatural ; he lacked their

Whitney's *Choice of Emblemes* (Leyden, 1586, repr. Henry Green, 1866), and the most useful secondary authority Green's *Shakespeare and the Emblem Writers* (1870).

[1] The theory of a dissociation of sensibility in the 17th Century propounded by Eliot in an essay on "The Metaphysical Poets" (repr. in his *Selected Essays*, 1932), was enlarged in a Tawnyesque treatment by H. Wendell Smith in *Scrutiny*, XVIII (1951-2), discussed in articles and correspondence either side, and criticised by Frank Kermode in *Kenyon Rev.* XIX (1957); he broadcast a potted version of this essay as "A Myth of Catastrophe", repr. in the *Listener*, 8 and 15 Nov. 1956. Owing to the nature of sensibility, to postulate its dissociation in the past can only be to relate an aetiological myth, for our view of it must be ethnocentrically distorted by our own and by our movement away from both even as we construct the theory. But we need myths; the question is whether it serves a useful function. What it most obviously serves at present is dislike of capitalism, constitutional democracy and the Reformation.

powers of minute perception and verbal synthesis, of seeing heaven in a grain of sand and saying so; he was affected more than they were by that deistical rationalism which by the time he came to write *Paradise Lost* was observing the distance between heaven and earth with increasing politeness. The huge scale of the poem exaggerated the distance. His efforts to narrow it are correspondingly violent; often he tries to naturalise the spiritual by sheer rationality, where the Metaphysicals had spiritualised the natural by intensity of feeling. It is the difference between a man who argues that the spirit must after all live through the body because he's not sure it ought to; and another who is not anxious about that but finds his bodily life becoming spiritual almost of its own accord, as, typically, one does in love.

Milton is most succesful when simply asserting the union of earth and heaven, body and spirit, rhetorically; least when he tries to demonstrate or argue about it. Thus in Adam and Eve's *Benedicite* and Raphael's first speech, on the need of all created things for food, the mobile active verbs and the dynamic schemes postulate a tension between animal and angelic superior to any dualistic clinging to animalism or soulishness at either end of the scale. The sacramental food that men and angel are going to eat together is most sensuously described (V. 341 ff.); the altar is natural, "Rais'd of grassie terf" (but Blake recognised the occasion as sacramental: the table in his illustration at Plate III has a chalice). Adam is "earths hallowd mould"; Eve is hailed as "Mother of Mankind, whose fruitful Womb Shall fill the World", linking her to both Mary and the "Earth all-bearing Mother" which yields their dinner. These are rather clumsy indications. Then:

> So down they sat,
> And to thir viands fell, nor seemingly
> The Angel, nor in mist, the common gloss
> Of Theologians, but with keen dispatch
> Of real hunger, and concoctive heate,
> To transubstantiate; what redounds, transpires
> Through Spirits with ease; nor wonder; if by fire
> Of sooty coal the Empiric Alchimist
> Can turn, or holds it possible to turn
> Metals of drossiest Ore to perfet Gold
> As from the Mine.

"So down they sat, And to thir viands fell", like "No fear lest Dinner coole", presents the communion of angel with men with good-tempered Flemish realism. But the alchemical analogy raises the same kind of discredence as the Scholastic theology it is meant to discredit. Milton is too anxious, and his anxiety seems to be as much about the stage-management of his epic as the relation between nature and spirit. But then we have Raphael's speech, the grandest affirmation since Book XXII of the *City of God* that man's origins in the soil are proper to him and as worthy a part of the divine order as his destination in heaven.

It is not a "degree" speech of the same order as Ulysses' in *Troilus*,[1] or Pope's in the *Essay on Man*,[2] or their medieval and 16th-century predecessors. There are no political overtones. The underlying principle is not static harmony but teleology—Adam and Eve are caught up in the universal animation they had celebrated in their *Benedicite* and which we have seen demonstrated in Raphael's flight to earth. Through the controlling schemes of climax and auxesis Milton departs from Aristotle in exhibiting creation as a series of interlocking escalators. Each feeds into the one above, each is assigned to one sphere of activity but is capable within that sphere of development from "body up to spirit" (represented rhetorically by the series of homophonous words that run from line to line within each class of being).[3] Each spiritual τελος is of a kind appropriate to its bodily εντελεχη. The sphere assigned to man includes

[1] Ulysses' speech is almost as schematic as Raphael's, but whereas Raphael is assuming order Ulysses is contrasting it with an actual state of disorder which he represents with violent tropes that swamp the schemes.

[2] Pope assumes order but it is the theoretical order of the *status quo* as defined by human reason, rather than the ideal order of divine creation; Pope does not *celebrate*.

[3] I.e. prosonomasia, ploce, traductio. Although what Raphael says is sound natural philosophy and physiology of the 16th Century he says it so artfully that the speech can be put into a diagram. The horizontal scaffolding runs thus:

green	.	.	leaves	.	breathes	.	.	.
.	floure	.	.	.	.	flours	fruit	.
.	.	.	.	Spirits	.	.	.	. Spirits
–	–	–	–	–	–	–	–	–
.	.	.	.	Reason	receives		reason	being
.	life	.	.	.	.	.	.	.
aspire	.	.	.	.	.	.	.	.
.	.	sense	whence	.	.	.	.	.

Heaven as well as Earth. He lives, as man, by virtue of the highest earthly efficiency of vital and therefore of intellectual powers, sharing with the angels a bodily form and a rationality which are of the same kind as theirs but less in degree of excellence. Hence the metabolism which already converts his material food to tenuous physiological "spirits" and so to psychological faculties may be expected eventually to convert it—as Raphael does—to an angelic body-soul. This means, in Milton's pneumatology,[1] that in apotheosis the human body would remain material but become decentralised, "Not ti'd or manacl'd in joynt or limb" (I. 426) but "live throughout Vital in every part" (VI. 344), each member or particle exercising all the powers of life, sensation, motion and control autonomously by a diffusion of the soul. There would be a corresponding increase in rational efficiency, for discursive intellection would give place to immediate apprehension.

This is a superb idea and I think that, in spite of its Pauline basis[2] and Thomist affinities, Milton concocted it for himself. In *De Doctrina* (I. vii) he argues logically—though probably from prior convictions which I will discuss later—that God cannot have created the world out of nothing. Therefore he created it out of his own substance, by withdrawing his vitality from it, moulding it into shapes, and re-infusing them with doses of his vitality appropriate to their natures. "Spirit" is therefore not a ghostly thing but the divine vitality by virtue of which all things live—*élan vital*. So in spite of the suggestion, also strong in Adam and Eve's *Benedicite*, of Platonic panpsychism, the Platonic separation of soul from body is explicitly rejected in favour of the Hebrew psychology, which identified them. Nothing exists except matter, infused with life in varying degrees. Since that vitality is divine, matter is intrinsically holy: "like the form and nature of the angels" it "proceeded incorruptible from God; and even since the fall it remains incor-

[1] Henry More and the pneumatology of Christian Platonism generally lie behind Milton's ideas (the scholarship is mulled over by R. H. West, *Milton and the Angels* (Athens, Ga., 1955). But Milton's treatment of the angelic is highly personal. Lewis and Rajan beg the question: *Preface*, Chap. XV; "*P.L.*" *and the 17th-century Reader* (1947), notes 5 and 7 on pp. 149-50.

[2] *I Cor.* xv. Milton's enlargement of the "spiritual" to *include* the physical places him, as I have suggested, in the Paul-Lawrence tradition.

ruptible as far as concerns its essence" (*De Doc.* iv. 180). Therefore the "spiritual" life of the angels, and of man in apotheosis, is still corporeal but more so—more vital, more highly organised and efficient.

Greek soulishness had bedevilled Christian, and scientific, doctrine for centuries[1]; Milton's rejection of it is admirable. His pantheism is a wonderful realisation of the ideal communion of all things and persons "in God". It implies in human relations reverence for the body because it is the stuff of God, and sympathy with all affections because they are the product of divine vitality acting in the divine substance. It implies a notion of the Church as indeed the body of God on earth, so that sacraments and symbols are actualised. It prohibits otherworldly escapism and gives, even in the fallen world, value to efforts at reform, relief and democracy. Theologically, it prohibits Idealism, makes mysticism unnecessary, and gives literal substance to the doctrine that man is created in the image of God. Blake's illustration comprehends all this (Plate III): flowers and their fruit in the foreground grow up into the frame, paralleled by Raphael's up-pointing wings and arms, and the beasts and birds of the middle distance. The hierarchy of Eve-Adam-Raphael is built into the design. But all this runs to waste in the poem. More conventional ideas of matter and spirit control the poem's effectual psychology; the good angels are

[1] I may seem to be making a fuss about this but so did Milton: "man is a living being, intrinsically and properly one and individual, not compound or separable, not, according to the common opinion, made up and framed of two distinct and different natures, as of soul and body,—but that the whole man is soul, and the soul man, that is to say, a body, or substance individual, animated, sensitive, and rational" (*De Doc.* iv. 188). Thus it is only when "we speak of the body as a mere senseless stock" that "soul" may "be understood as signifying either the spirit, or its secondary faculties, the vital or sensitive faculty for instance.—Thus it is as often distinguished from the spirit as from the body itself". He had reason to make a fuss. His pamphlet adversary Bishop Hall could still in 1621, in his popular *Meditations and Vows*, publish demoralising Senecan euphuism of this sort: "When I consider my soule; I could be proud, to thinke of how diuine a nature and qualitie it is: but when I cast downe mine eyes to my Body (as the Swanne to her blacke legges) and see what loathsome matter issues from the Mouth, Nostrils, Eares, Pores, and other Passages, and how most Carrion-like of all other Creatures it is after death; I am iustly ashamed to thinke, that so excellent a Ghest dwels but in a more cleanly dunghill" (1st Century, LXVII). Bodin, Rabelais and Montaigne (in "Apology for Raimond de Sebonde") had also attacked soul-divisions.

Huntington Library

III Blake

Raphael discoursing with Adam and Eve (1806)

actually Milton's, not Blake's; and the conception of superhuman apotheosis is incongruent with other parts of the poem. The first difficulty is that such an apotheosis should be offered at all to unfallen man, or offered as more than a symbol to us. It is a symbol, almost a hint half-guessed, for Paul. Milton typically inflates it, and so suggests an imperfection, at least an immaturity of created nature for Adam and Eve, and for fallen man a salvation that consists in more than a change of heart. Raphael's pretensions to scientific terminology and anagogical argument stress the difficulty. Even if the scent of flowers actually were more "refined" than petals, leaves, stalk and root, it begs the question to include scent in the "kind" or "class" of Vegetable. This doesn't matter; but the same question is begged of Man. The change from body up to spirit, whatever it may mean, is not just a change of status but, if "kind" and "nature" mean anything at all, of human being. Though it avoids soulishness, this is really only another sort of other-worldliness. Further, it is of no value in the poem. The Michelangelic solidity of Adam and Eve represents a perfection of complete human nature from which any change could only be a fall. The promise of change is played down anyway. Raphael is subjunctively vague—"may . . . perhaps . . . may . . . may". The Father in Book VII is even vaguer: he creates man as "a Creature who . . . might erect his Stature . . . and from thence Magnanimous to correspond with Heav'n" (506)—there is no active indicative verb and "correspond" is as indefinite as "become like".

The angels, as we meet them in the poem, are satisfactory. Aesthetically they are superior to most. They confute the Royal Society's strictures on poetic fictions by being corporeal. They are admirably adapted to social intercourse with men. Theologically it is good that they should so obviously be creatures, not gods. But so far as they represent the potentialities of human nature—and this is what they do in Book V—they are not adequate. The powers they manifest—fluidity, speed, strength—derive from their closeness to God (V. 476) and, so far as they go, are admirable. But these are no more than the powers manifested by Superman, or fairies, or Homer's gods and goddesses, or the *dei ex machina* of the masque (which Raphael, Uriel and Michael are descriptively associated with). Secondly, these powers are less than the power assigned to them in theory: only the chariot of wrath actually displays *élan* as such, "It self instinct with Spirit" (VI. 752), the wheels multitudinously eyed but one spirit ruling all (846-8). Some poetic tolerance must be granted here, for a poem full of angels like that chariot would be impossible. The third objection is unavoidable, though. The angels are supposed to be superior to man also in their powers of intuitive rationality. This is not demonstrated of them; and even if it were the distinction is false and degrading to man. Man is distinguished from animals not by substance or physical faculties or even by the faculty of ratiocination, but by his power to know himself. He needs no physical improvement to transcend this "cumbrous flesh" into memory, imagination and consciously initiated conceptual deliberation. But in neither Adam nor Raphael does this kind of spiritual life, properly so-called, flourish. They are capable of intellection, understanding, judgement; but they seem unable to get outside themselves and imagine. The transcendence of "reason" is occasionally implied. Man is "endu'd With Sanctitie of Reason . . . self-knowing" (VII. 507); and when Adam explains Eve's dream, speaking of the "many lesser Faculties" in the soul that "serve Reason as chief" (V. 101), and when Raphael warns Adam to "take heed least Passion sway Thy Judgement" (VIII. 635), they must be appealing to a faculty which can itself regard the "soul" and reason the soul's governor as objects—that is, a faculty which transcends reason, or a Reason which is self-transcendent. But this is only incidental. Whenever there is authoritative talk about psychology or ethics the language is Greek:

> Reason in man obscur'd, or not obeyd,
> Immediately inordinate desires
> And upstart Passions catch the Government
> From Reason,
>
> (XII. 86)

The finger wags on each word, separating the soul's "elements" beyond hope of integration, and implicitly separating soul from body. This is fatal to Milton's Hebraic integration of body-soul, to Adam's mortalism in Book X, to Raphael's notion of spirituality as a refinement of substance, and to the proper notion of reason as self-transcendent. Indeed, what we should regard as the "sanctity" of reason, its claim to more-than-natural power, is reserved to the fallen life. It is apparent in Eve's evil dream; when she eats the apple she is made aware of godhead (IX. 790), and when Adam shares it the dream-symbolism is re-enacted: they "fansie that they feel Divinitie within them breeding wings Wherewith to scorn the Earth" (IX. 1009). Above all, the devils, by a consistent use of Metaphysical imagery, represent themselves as aware of and exercising the faculty of self-transcendence. Belial asks,

> who would loose,
> Though full of pain, this intellectual being,
> Those thoughts that wander through Eternity,
> (II. 146)

This is a finer expression of spiritual power than any of the angels'. "Wander" of course suggest that their minds are not so much directing their transcendent power to some end as drifting in a world of unreality, whereas Raphael insists in Book VIII, and throughout the antecedentia, by his schematic rhetoric, that reason as intellect must be controlled by Reason as transcendent power. If it waver from direction towards the God who is its source it will cease to be a link between man and God and become like the devils', an aimless, self-centred escape from the real world into the vague horizons of the *yetser har-ra'*.[1] This is what we see happening in the rest of Book V. But Adam does not apparently possess this power at all. His fall is represented as a fall from the psychological ideal of Aristotle to the realism of Montaigne. It could have been presented more subtly, and more truthfully to experience, as a fall from Godward to selfward spirituality:

> man's distinctive endowment, his by the fact of creation, namely, the fact that he has been made in the image of God, is the presupposition of sin. Sin itself is a manifestation of the image of God in man.[2]

There is something of this in the "prompt eloquence" of their hymns; but not enough to outweigh the effect of Raphael's speeches and the activity of the angels.

[1] It happens that this is how Athanasius defined the Fall, as a slothful divagation from the beatific vision.

[2] Brunner, *op. cit.* p. 132.

Niebuhr has remarked,

> How difficult it is to do justice to both the uniqueness of man and his affinities with the world of nature below him is proved by the almost unvarying tendency of those philosophies, which describe and emphasize the rational faculties of man or his capacity for self-transcendence, to forget his relation to nature and to identify him, prematurely and unqualifiedly, with the divine and the eternal; and of naturalistic philosophies to obscure the uniqueness of man.[1]

In describing Paradise, Milton resisted the temptation of representing the pure as ethereal and disembodied. Here in Book V, and elsewhere theorising, he regresses into a dualistic idealism which contradicts the unifying naturalism that the theories seem to assert. This is partly because you can't really unify the cosmos, least of all in the biological terms which are Milton's basis here. But it was also, I think, because Milton was using these theories to serve his own interests rather than the poem's. The pan-psychism is more serious than that recommended by neo-classical critics such as Boileau and Cowley as a proper ingredient, along with the "marvellous", of poetry in general; the pantheism is more integral to the poem than Pope's in the *Essay on Man*; but the more you study these theories and note their dissonance with practice, the more obvious it becomes that they represent an indulgence of Milton's Buddhistic cast of mind, and other temperamental inclinations, of which the glorification of man-and-God in creation was a by-product. Thus the ultimate condition assumed in Raphael's speech is not so much of being rooted in the soil as sunk in the flux of nature, and nature sunk in the flux of God—the uniqueness of man denied.[2] Then there is a fondness for the ideally smooth and evolutionary, glossing the harsher facts of nature—"by gradual scale sublim'd" (483) sums up Raphael's apperception. There is a related preference in all Milton's writing for what is "more refin'd, more spiritous, and pure" over what is grossly corporeal: Raphael's digestive processes are antiseptically described; realistic organic activity is represented only in pejorative contexts (Hell's mountains, Sin's gestation, etc.). The pan-vitalism of the

[1] *Op. cit.* i. 4. See the whole of Chap. VI. of Vol. i.

[2] The psychology of panpsychism is understood in *Wisdom of Solomon*, xvii.

angels means little, in practice, to *Paradise Lost*; but hints of it run all through Milton's early prose, and it is exigent in *Samson*:

> Since light so necessary is to life,
> And almost life itself, if it be true
> That light is in the Soul,
> She all in every part; why was the sight
> To such a tender ball as th'eye confind?
> So obvious and so easie to be quench't,
> And not as feeling through all parts diffus'd,
> That she might look at will through every pore?
>
> (90)

The approval of matter is only presuppositionary—as the structure of Raphael's speech shows—to an ideal of material existence which is not human, either as we or Adam and Eve represent it, but angelic—a "soft And uncompounded . . . Essence pure" (I. 423). The personal importance of this to Milton may be judged from his solicitation of it even when—as in this quotation about the foulest devils in Hell—it is supposed to be "gross by sinning grown" (VI. 561). In the same place there is an anti-naturalistic contempt for man's "cumbrous flesh".[1] Finally, the most poignant evocation of the angelic nature is Raphael's explanation of how they make love:

> Whatever pure thou in the body enjoy'st
> (And pure thou wert created) we enjoy
> In eminence, and obstacle find none
> Of membrane, joynt, or limb, exclusive barrs:
> Easier then Air with Air, if Spirits embrace,
> Total they mix, Union of Pure with Pure
> Desiring; nor restrain'd conveyance need
> As Flesh to mix with Flesh, or Soul with Soul.
>
> (VIII. 622)

[1] A verbal motif associates the bursting of bowels, cracking of joints and obstruction of membranes, in opposition to angelic or soulish diffusion and unrestrained conveyance: *P.L.* I. 234, 426; II. 668 (Death) and the gestation of Sin; VI. 346, 587; the passage from VIII quoted below; *S.A.* 614. The body is sometimes dissected approvingly in the prose, but it is always the mystical body:

> Thus then did the spirit of unity and meekness inspire and animate every joint and sinew of the mystical body. . . . (*Of Ref.* ii. 377)

> he shall bring together every joint and member, and shall mould them into an immortal feature of loveliness and perfection . . . (*Areo.* ii. 89)

In *The Rainbow* Tom Brangwen uses angels as a marriage symbol: "*If* we've got to be Angels . . . and if there is no such thing as a man nor a woman amongst them, then it seems to me as a married couple makes one Angel . . . an Angel is the soul of man and woman in one" (Chap. V). Milton, once he has vented his personal worry about "exclusive barrs", expresses the ideal with lovely delicacy; but it is more than ideal or symbol: it is a fact. Presenting the fallen ideal, which should be a fact of unfallen life, as the fact only of superior angelic life, he spoils the love of Adam and Eve, and flees the very limitations of physical existence which make the act of love important.

Whatever the deepest causes may have been, it seems obvious enough that some of these peculiarities result from Milton's having been isolated, as a prodigy, in his family, and stood-off from the literary society of the mid-century; and from the difficulties of his first marriage. If we did not know of these things in his life, the poem's discrepancies would still make us surmise them. As it is, Milton's ascent, out of his deepest longings for enveloping unity, into a cosmic naturalism, and his declension in practice to a dogged dualism, is typical of Western soul-experience. Though some have more stamina than Milton, all decline eventually like the courtly poets' rose. Some fall back with Milton into stoic level-headedness. Donne, who had seen all innocence alive and bare, fell to thinking much on sin and death, "the centrique part" of his love-world drying to a bracelet of hair about the bone. Wordsworth, unable to bear alone on his mountain the weight of an ethic that postulated community, descended in the "Ode to Duty" and the *Wanderer* to a stoical, an ethic originated to make a virtue of isolation. Coleridge, his apprehension of "one omnipresent Mind Omnific whose "most holy name is Love" being from the start thinner than Wordsworth's, soon came to "see, not feel" the beautiful wholeness of a God-infused world. Others were hysterically vapourised: the problems Ibsen examined were personal but the only solution he could offer, as in *Rosmersholm* and *When We Dead Awaken*, was an infra-personal apotheosis; instead of transforming the drawing-room's iron cage his characters vanish out of its window. Others try to eternise the momentaneous in an esoteric system, which defeats its own object—Blake; and Yeats, who having heard the strange bird cry could escape from the derision of gerontion only by taking Plato and Plotinus for a friend. But neither the inevitability of *ichabod*, nor the insults of no-nonsense, "polite" or orthodox reaction should discourage poet or individual from perceiving and rejoicing in a not-impossible wholeness. Romantic literature is the record of its possibility. By observing that only aesthetic expression can immortalise it surely, we learn not to take for a rule of life what is actually a moment of living.

8

THE WAR IN HEAVEN

1. *Satire or Self-Parody?*

DR JOHNSON thought this episode childish, yet it thrillingly represented Milton to the 18th Century: "Such mystic visions send", prayed Thomas Warton to the genius of Night, as

> Milton knew,
> When in abstracted thought he first conceiv'd
> All heav'n in tumult, and the Seraphim
> Come tow'ring, arm'd in adamant and gold.[1]

In the Peace of the Augustans it must have appeared an enviably first-hand exercise in Homerics, not original but at least paraphrastic, when all they could manage was translation. Certainly Books V and VI contain the most obviously Homeric verse of the poem and because of Homer's prestige have been mistaken for the normatively "Miltonic". The true classical Milton is rather in lines such as "Precipitate thee with augmented paine" (VI. 280), and the Biblical, English Milton in:

> Such high advantages thir innocence
> Gave them above thir foes, not to have sinnd,
> Not to have disobei'd;
>
> (VI. 401)

The false norm is exemplified in the passage beginning "Now when ambrosial Night with Clouds exhal'd" at V. 639. Here we have the deep-breath temporal adverbs, the squashing of verbs into unrecognisable adjectival participles, the demonstrative "that", clausal inversion, moribund personification ("the face of brightest Heav'n" adjacent to "the unsleeping eyes of God"), parenthetic didacticism—"(for Night comes not there

[1] *Pleasures of Melancholy*, 66. *Poetical Works*, 5th ed. by R. Mant (2 vols. Oxford, 1802).

In darker veile)"—and the most conventional diction, "ambrosial, grateful, roseat", shot with scientisms like "globous". But is this even a false norm? As you look at it, in context, it appears that the true individual Milton is *using* the conventional vesture of a Homeric night-piece to shade the holy joys of Heaven and cloak the plotting of Satan. Warton, Gray and Johnson, as literary historians, were likely to miss contextual subtleties like this, and their own regard for the classics prevented them appreciating Milton's ambivalence. The question is whether, even for us, the episode succeeds as a satire on the Homerics it imitates. Stein is able to regard it as "a kind of diabolical scherzo, like some of Beethoven's—with more than human laughter, too elevated, and comprehensive, and reverberating, not to be terribly funny".[1] The evidence that Milton meant it so is plain. The battle is indecisive. The violent punning and the flyting between Satan and Abdiel are in the sarcastic manner of his prose. All the imagery of Hell is brought into Heaven—planetomachia (VI. 311), ruined mountains (194), flames, storm, hail, the "Horrible discord of madding Wheeles" (210) and applause like "the sound of waters deep" (V. 872). Satan's taste is already Babylonish with his

> Royal seat
> High on a Hill, far blazing, as a Mount
> Rais'd on a Mount, with Pyramids and Towrs
> From Diamond Quarries hew'n, and Rocks of Gold,
> (V. 753)

He parodies God like a juggernaut:

> exalted as a God
> Th'Apostat in his Sun-bright Chariot sate
> Idol of Majestie Divine,[2]

Archaic diction pushes the episode back into the "long and tedious havoc" of "fabl'd Knights In Battels feign'd": terrene

[1] *Answerable Style* (Minneapolis, 1953), p. 20.
[2] VI. 99. Cf. Nicholas Pimenta's account of a juggernaut in Trangobar: "so prodigious and innumerable were their Idols . . . that Superstition contended with Ambition; and the Colosses of their Idols were removed from place to place in Chariots as high as steeples, by thousands of men setting their shoulders to the Wheeles" (Purchas, *Hak. Post.* x. 207; cf. 274).

(78), battailous (81), weend (86), hosting (93), griding (329), foughten (410).[1]

But these conventions accumulate so wearisomely that they overwhelm their own point. Instead of consigning war to romantic epicism they back-fire as self-parody. So the heroic norm that Pope was to mock in *The Rape of the Lock* was as much Miltonic as Homeric. This is fine heroic writing:

> So spake the Sovran voice, and Clouds began
> To darken all the Hill, and smoak to rowl
> In duskie wreathes, reluctant flames, the signe
> Of wrauth awak't: nor with less dread the loud
> Ethereal Trumpet from on high gan blow:
> At which command the Powers Militant,
> That stood for Heav'n, in mighty Quadrate joyn'd
> Of Union irresistible, mov'd on
> In silence thir bright Legions, to the sound
> Of instrumental Harmonie that breath'd
> Heroic Ardor to advent'rous deeds
> Under thir God-like Leaders, in the Cause
> Of God and his *Messiah.* On they move
> Indissolubly firm;
>
> (VI. 56)

But (Voltaire's epithet) injudicious: it makes no *poetic* distinction between Heavenly and Hellish power. That is realistic enough —war does demoralise its own motives. But Milton's War is not realistic, and he seems to mock less at war's immortality than its inefficiency. We are hypersensitive about war; but so had Shakespeare been. The mockery of war is crude and external in *King John*. But in *Henry V* the king's heroics balanced by the realities that Pistol, Nym and Bardolph know about. In

[1] *Terrene* was an ME word; Shakespeare used it as an adjective, but this is the first recorded use of it substantivally, and Milton's only use of it at all. *Battailous* is a Spenserianism. *Weend* is used twice elsewhere in *P.L. Hosting* was quite archaic by 1667, belonging to old-fashioned verse and prose histories. *Griding* was a Spenserianism adapted from Lydgate; it had never been anything but poet. and arch. since the Middle Ages. *Foughten* is a Spenserianism, but the same phrase, "f. field", had been used by Marlowe, and Hobbes in his quatrain *Iliad*. Note also *onset* (98), a rare word, this particular usage apparently coined by Milton; it exactly translates OE *beaduraes*. Tuve (*op. cit.* p. 97) says that archaisms were held to constitute an apt figure in pragmatographia; but Milton had a more than theoretical notion of decorum.

Richard II the conventional epic diction—"With harsh-resounding trumpets' dreadful bray, And grating shock of wrathful iron arms"—has to compete with "the sweet infant breath of tuned sleep" (I. iii. 133). In *Henry IV* both the bright chivalric honour of Hotspur and the cowardice of Falstaff are disposed of, and we are not allowed to forget the wreckage of ordinary life between them. Milton's myth provided no peaceful antidote to war, only a greater power.

The technical failure is first apparent at the banquet in Heaven, held 200 lines after the dinner in Paradise, to celebrate the Son's glorification:

> Tables are set, and on a sudden pil'd
> With Angels Food, and rubied Nectar flows:
> In Pearl, in Diamond, and massie Gold,
> Fruit of delicious Vines, the growth of Heav'n,
> They eat, they drink, and with refection sweet
> Are fill'd, before th' all bounteous King, who showrd
> With copious hand, rejoycing in thir joy.
> (V. 632; *1667*)

Both meals are symbols of communion. But as a second demonstration of the substantiality of the spirit world and its physical interaction with the terrestial the meal in Heaven fails, because Milton abandons the humble simplicity of the meal in Paradise and, for very fear of quaintness and incongruity, turns Olympian. The phrase "refection sweet" shows how it might all have been done—the abstract word preserves the spirituality of the angels but does not damage their substantiality. Milton altered this passage in the second edition:

> the growth of Heav'n.
> On flours repos'd, and with fresh flourets crownd,
> They eate, they drink, and in communion sweet
> Quaff immortalitie and joy, secure
> Of surfet where full measure onely bounds
> Excess, before th' all bounteous King. . . . (635)

The scene is made still more concrete, and Olympian: "refection sweet" replaced by "Quaff", so that we are harked back to Horace's description of Augustus lolling in heaven (*Odes*, III. iii. 11-12) and Milton's imitation of it for Diodati: "Heroumque animas inter, divosque perennes, Aethereos haurit latices & gaudia Ore sacro" (*Ep. Dam.* 205).

Caedmon's *Genesis*, frankly political and amoral, has the genuine savage dignity of Homer; *Maldon* parallels the *Iliad* (100 ff. cf. IV. 445 ff.). The only way to civilise the heroic is to stand away from it. Pope managed this in his Homer, as Tillyard remarks[1]:

> A chosen Phalanx, firm, resolv'd as Fate,
> Descending *Hector* and his Battel wait;
> An Iron Scene gleams dreadful o'er the Fields,
> Armour in Armour lock'd, and Shields in Shields,
> Spears lean on Spears, on Targets Targets throng,
> Helms stuck to Helms, and Man drove Man along.
> The floating Plumes unnumber'd wave above,
> As when an Earthquake stirs the nodding Grove;
> And levell'd at the Skies with Pointing Rays,
> Their brandish'd Lances at each Motion Blaze.
>
> (XIII. 177)

Milton knew more than Pope about war[2]. But he could not be so academic because his battle was real and Raphael its narrator involved (inconsistently) himself; above all because whereas Pope was translating Homer for the 18th Century Milton was outdoing him inside an epic of his own. The civilising agent in Pope's lines is not the unavailing grandiosity of *Paradise Lost* but it is Miltonic—the rejective rhetoric of *Paradise Regained.* For example, Pope's particularly academic "Iron scene", which Tillyard notes as an addition to Homer, is actually Milton's:

> The field all iron cast a gleaming brown,
> Nor wanted clouds of foot, nor on each horn,
> Cuirassiers all in steel for standing fight;
> Chariots or Elephants endorst with Towers
> Of Archers, nor of labouring Pioners
> A multitude with Spades and Axes arm'd
> To lay hills plain, fell woods, or valleys fill,
> Or where plain was raise hill, or over-lay
> With bridges rivers proud, as with a yoke,
> Mules after these, Camels and Dromedaries,
> And Waggons fraught with Utensils of war.
>
> (*P.R.* III. 326)

[1] *English Epic and Its Background* (1954), p. 504.
[2] See Hanford, "Milton and the Art of War", *SP*, XVIII (1921).

The distance of prospect in *Paradise Regained* allows Milton to paint a picture magnificent but so formal as to leave him uncommitted, free then to reject not only the luggage of war but, in the next book, the very literature on which the picture was based—"Thir Gods ridiculous, and themselves past shame" (IV. 342). But in *Paradise Lost*, for all the ironical qualifications, literary ambition lures him into his own *mêlée*. He escapes once: Satan is wounded and

> A stream of Nectarous humor issuing flow'd
> Sanguin, such as Celestial Spirits may bleed,
> And all his Armour staind ere while so bright.
>
> (VI. 327)

The nostalgic and wondering tone of the last line, with its Shakespearean association, might have been the tone of the whole.[1] Milton should have abandoned his pretence of describing the War in terrestial terms and treated it all as science fiction. As it is, crude Homerics result in crude onomatopoeia[2] —a figure which becomes self-derisive when used to excess. He is sidetracked into mime bearing no relation to the morals stuck on to it.

The most serious result is failure to motivate Satan evilly. Satan's immediate motive for sin, the "begetting" of the Son, is ambiguous, vague (like the motives of Achilles) and confused by the ceremony after the war in time but before it in the poem when the Son assumes the office of Redeemer. God himself is confused. He says the rebels

> reason for thir Law refuse,
> Right reason for thir Law, and for thir King
> *Messiah*, who by right of merit Reigns.
>
> (VI. 41)

They have refused the Son as "Right reason" and as king; but it is not until after the creation of Man that the Son assumes the messianic office of anointed liberator, and reigns by merit of

[1] *John*, II. i. 315: "Their armours that march'd hence so silver-bright Hither return all gilt with Frenchmen's blood".

[2] In rhetorical theory, the excess of onomatopoeia compensates for the lack of tropes in pragmatographia, and is related to the use of archaisms, and enallage (Tuve, *loc. cit.*). This assumes an uncritical, descriptive treatment that contrasts with Shakespeare's.

his self-sacrifice. Satan's conspiracy and the invention of explosive, which take up most space, are indecorous. We are witnessing the birth of evil and all we see is Achaian warriors whispering in each other's ears and letting off cannon.[1] Hooker says of the angels:

> Impossible it was that ever their will should change or incline to remit any part of their duty, without some object having force to avert their conceit from God, and to draw it another way. . . . It seemeth therefore that there was no other way for angels to sin, but by reflex of their understanding upon themselves; when being held with admiration of their own sublimity and honour, the memory of their subordination unto God and their dependency upon him was drowned in this conceit. . . . The fall of the Angels therefore was pride.[2]

Milton makes Satan "allure" the other rebels and gives us the orthodoxy of the last sentence. But he does not give us any vision of the germinal defection of Satan himself, such as the birth of Sin provides in Book II and such as we have for Eve. It is true that Abdiel makes Satan state his reasons for revolt:

> That we were formed then saist thou? & the work
> Of secondarie hands, by task transferd
> From Father to his Son? strange point and new!
> Doctrin which we would know whence learnt: who saw
> When this creation was? rememberst thou
> Thy making, while the Maker gave thee being?
> We know no time when we were not as now;
> Know none before us, self-begot, self-rais'd
> By our own quickn'ning power, when fatal course
> Had circl'd his full Orbe, the birth mature
> Of this our native Heav'n, Ethereal Sons.
> Our puissance is our own. . . .
>
> (V. 850)

This perfectly represents the nature of Satan's prototypal sin—the creature's "blasphemous, false and proud" denial of his creaturely status on the ground of his own ignorance. Satan bases his argument, as we might, on a theory of mechanistic evolution. It is this that matters; yet it is just part of a debate with

[1] The gunpower motif runs Ariosto-Spenser-Drayton. I think Valvasone invented the cannon.

[2] *Ecc. Pol.* I. iv. 3.

Abdiel,[1] the emphasis on Abdiel's faithfulness rather than the nature of Satan's infidelity, while over the whole episode even this is obscured by the superficial political motives and military tactics.

Bunyan did not suffer these disabilities. Despite its allegory on one hand and realism on the other, *The Holy War* is in direct contact with both actual war and the central New Testament text:

> For we wrestle not against flesh and blood, but against principalities, against powers, against the rulers of the darkness of this world, against spiritual wickedness in heavenly places.
>
> (*Eph.* vi.12 *mg.*)

Bunyan discriminates crudely but effectively between the qualities and motives of the opposing forces by arming the Diabolians in a parody of "the whole armour of God"—helmet of desperation, breastplate of hardheartedness, sword of evil-speaking, shield of unbelief. Emmanuel's troops are led by the captains Credence, Good-Hope, Charity, Innocent and Patience, with appropriate standard-bearers and emblematic banners. Lacking Milton's historical attitudes and classical education, Bunyan can use the native, and Catholic, traditions of chivalry and allegory without the qualms of an educated Puritan, and so take advantage of the New Testament revision of war imagery.

A final cause of Milton's failure is the confusion which events had wrought in the 17th-century attitude to kingship. The mystique of kingship, so far as it ever existed off the stage and outside the immediate sphere of court patronage, had decayed by the time James I had reigned a few years. One reason for this was the Reformation dilemma:

> Foole and wretch, wilt thou then let thy Soule be tyed
> To mans lawes, by which she shall not be tryed
> At the last day? Oh, will it then boot thee
> To say a Philip, or a Gregory,
> A Harry, or a Martin taught thee this?

That is simply "Render unto Caesar", but Donne goes on to develop a theory that justifies the Revolution:

[1] Also a hexemeral convention: see McColley, *op. cit.* pp. 35-6.

That thou mayest rightly obey power, her bounds know;
Those past, her nature, and name is chang'd; to be
Then humble to her is idolatrie.

. . . . . .

So perish Soules, which more chuse mens unjust
Power from God claym'd, then God himselfe to trust.

Yet once the king becomes, whether in Hobbesian theory or the practice of 1649 and 1688, a constitutional monarch, emphasis falls on his consular qualities, as ruler. So Dryden called Cromwell "Prince", and Marvell wrote openly of the altered conception:

He seems a King by long Succession born,
And yet the same to be a King does scorn.
Abroad a King he seems, and something more,
At Home a Subject on the equal Floor.
(*First Anniversary*, 387)

The emotions previously lavished on the king now turn to the nation, changing from fealty to patriotism; government becomes a matter of providence rather than ruling. So, via Cromwell, Milton's God becomes confused with Satan. But whatever the his orical circumstances, Milton was too involved in Christian traditions and epic conventions to have resisted the coronation of God. The Church has always tried to shift back to "kingdom" the emphasis that Jesus, replying to hopeful messianists, laid on "heaven".

These days we either dismiss kingship as a symbol because it has no constitutional value in democracy; or overvalue it for the same reason. The real trouble is that kingship is only an intermediary symbol between the divine and the domestic. The God of the Old Testament is primarily Creator, contemptuous of kings; the New Testament analogy is Father. Only in very small and primitive communities can full religious and filial *emotions* meet in one man who actually is a priest-king. It can still happen in a family. But the political layer of existence is so important in Western civilisation that the monarchical absurdities of Books V and VI—the Son's sceptre, his "election" as viceroy, the power regalia—are symptoms of a constitutional and theological dilemma which has not yet been fully put aside; they cannot be read as symptoms of a peculiarly Miltonic idiocy. Donne and Herbert saw the dangers of confusing divine with human monarchy:

> That wee get not a slipperinesse
> And senslesly decline
> From hearing bold wits jeast at Kings excesse,
> To'admit the like of majestie divine;
>
> All worship is prerogative, and a flower
> Of his rich crown, from whom lyes no appeal
> At the last houre:
> Therefore we dare not from his garland steal,
> To make a posie for inferior power.[1]

But neither was able to perceive that the actuality of human rule was antecedent to the supposedly *a priori* theory of God's kingship. So Milton too admits the problem, but answers it only by extraverting the accusation of blasphemy, and repeating the usual upside-down *petitio*:

> Nor does it follow for all this that all kings, as such, are tyrants. But suppose it did, as for argument-sake I will allow it does. . . . "Then", say you, "God himself may properly be said to be the king of tyrants, nay, himself, the worst of all tyrants." . . . wish that blasphemous mouth of yours were stopped up, with which you affirm God to be the worst of tyrants, if he be, as you often say he is, the king and lord of such . . . Nor can you, without impiety and sacrilege, transfer this absolute power from God to a man . . .
> (*1st Def.* i. 54-5)

By an irony of Jungian reverberance, one of the sources for Christian notions of God as king is *Psalm* xlv. This is a royal epithalamion—"My heart is inditing a good matter"—so the poet celebrates the king's approach to his queen:

> Thou art fairer than the children of men,
> grace flows about thy lips,
> being blessed of God for ever.
> Gird thy sword upon thy thigh, O mightiest,
> in glory and in majesty.

[1] "To All Angels and Saints." Herbert's poem is an excuse to the Virgin that though he would like to pray to her "I dare not; for our King, Whom we do all joyntly adore and praise, Bids no such thing". It is not clear to me whether this king is God or James I.

> Long live the king! Prosper
> in succour of the loyal, the humble, and just!
> Dreadful is thy right hand in glory and majesty!
> Thine arrows are sharp in the heart of thy foes:
> nations fall before thee.
>
> Thy throne shall stand for ever and ever,
> for the sceptre of thy kingdom is just;
> thou lovest right and evil thou abhorrest,
> wherefore God thy God hath anointed thee with bliss
> above thy peers. . . .[1]

The misinterpretation of this as an allegory of Christ and the Church was due partly to idols of the mind—obsessive messianism, and a passion for typology—and partly to mechanical defects: misunderstanding of oriental metaphor ("fairer than the children of men" does not mean divine but, like "the fairest of her Daughters *Eve*", the most beautiful man that ever lived); a textual corruption of "Prosper in succouring the loyal" into "ride prosperously *because of* truth"; and a scribal error that deified the poet's patriotism into "Thy throne, *O God*, is for ever and ever." So the beautiful phallic regalia was militarised. Milton quotes the militarised version heavily when the Father sends out the Son to victory; and in *Animadversions* he had paraphrased it into revolutionary apocalyptic:

> Come forth out of thy royal chambers, O Prince of all the kings of the earth! put on the visible robes of thy imperial majesty, take up that unlimited sceptre which thy Almighty Father hath bequeathed thee; for now the voice of thy bride calls thee, and all creatures sigh to be renewed. (iii. 72)

2. *Victory of the Son*

The Legend of Artegall is background to the episode. But Spenser's definition of power as "the right hand of Justice" (*F.Q.* V. iv. 1) is too emblematic, metaphysical and political to work in a poem. In a poetic situation "the supreme of power" can only be Poesy—the truth apprehended in beauty. For Keats also it is a concrete but latent power: "'Tis might half-slumb'ring on its own right arm". By using instead of this the abstract

[1] Moffatt conflated with AV.

definition of Spenser, Milton invites argument which weakens the fable. When God says to the returned Abdiel, "the easier conquest now Remains thee . . . to subdue by force, who reason for thir Law refuse, Right reason for thir Law" (VI. 37), we are plunged into a pamphlet war. The doctrine rests on a fallacious universalisation of "reason" as "right"; and though Milton tries to put it in the form "Right is mighty" the verb can imply, with Satanic insidiousness, that to be weak is wrong, just as it does blatantly in "Might is Right". Niebuhr remarks that reason's

> universal judgements, its effort to relate all things to each other in a system of coherence, can be alternately the instrument by which the self-as-subject condemns the partial and prejudiced actions of the sinful self, and the vehicle of the self by which it seeks to give the sanctity of a false universality to its particular needs and partial insights.[1]

We know enough of God and Satan in the poem to realise that God has no motive for abusing reason, and he may be a symbol of Niebuhr's "self-as-subject" condemning the sinful self, while Satan constantly uses reason to sanctify his own ambition. But we also know enough of Milton to recognise the poetic manifestation of God's condemnatory power as only another version of Milton's personal attempts to smash deviational opinion for the sake of his own "particular needs and partial insights". Abdiel, facing Satan in battle now, draws God on to his side as a monstrous cat, who "with solitarie hand Reaching beyond all limit, at one blow Unaided could have finisht thee" (VI. 139); and gesturing to the innumerable Sons of Light jeers, "my Sect thou seest"! Embedded in the 17th Century, the conquest of the rebels loses all claim to universal validity.

Milton believed that

> in times of opposition, when either against new heresies arising, or old corruptions to be reformed, the cool unpassionate mildness of positive wisdom is not enough to damp and astonish the proud resistance of carnal and false doctors, then (that I may have leave to soar a while as the poets use) Zeal, whose substance is ethereal, arming in complete diamond, ascends his fiery chariot, drawn with two blazing meteors, figured like beasts, but of a

[1] *Op. cit.* i. 301-2.

> higher breed than any the zodiac yields, resembling two of those four which Ezekiel and St. John saw; the one visaged like a lion to express power, high authority, and indignation; the other of countenance like a man, to cast derision and scorn upon perverse and fraudulent seducers: with these the invincible warrior, Zeal, shaking loosely the slack reins, drives over the heads of scarlet prelates, and such as are insolent to maintain traditions, bruising their stiff necks under his flaming wheels.
>
> Thus did the true prophets of old combat with the false. . . .
>
> (*Apol.* iii. 129)

He is trying to prove "that there may be a sanctified bitterness against the enemies of truth" (p. 314); and in *Paradise Lost* he uses Ezekiel's vision again to sanctify the power of the "Chariot of Paternal Deitie" in which the Son rides "O're Shields and Helmes, and helmed heads. . . . Of Thrones and mighty Seraphim prostrate" (VI. 840). The Son, constantly imaged in light, represents the personified Truth of the prose. In the *Reason of Church Government* "the pure and powerful beams of God's word", that is, the Logos, defeat the Satanic "fenborn serpent" of prelaty with "the darts of the sun" (ii. 506). It was a convention in hexemeral epics to use Ezekiel's chariot to end the angelomachia, and it had been recognised that the Son's weapons were properly regarded as not military but the immaterial fire of the Logos. Ultimately, the Son's victory symbolises the necessity for divine intervention in the soul's strife: between reason and passion "War wearied hath perform'd what Warr can do" (VI. 695). But—a typical failure—Milton's language is not specialised enough to outshine the polemics and heroics which the action it describes is supposed to eclipse. It vacillates between Biblical spirituality and Homerics:

> Wheele within Wheele undrawn,
> It self instinct with Spirit, but convoyd
> By four Charubic shapes, four Faces each
> Had wondrous, as with Starrs thir bodies all
> And Wings were set with Eyes, with Eyes the Wheels
> Of Beril, and careering Fires between;
>
> (VI. 751)

With its sources in *Revelation* and *Ezekiel*, its tightened rhetoric and plain unrealism, this is impressive; but then Milton relapses into the classical vein:

> at his right hand Victorie
> Sate Eagle-wing'd, beside him hung his Bow
> And Quiver with three-bolted Thunder stor'd,
> And from about him fierce Effusion rowld
> Of smoak and bickering flame, and sparkles dire;

The poetry comes back when it is fed by the Bible, as the juvenile Latin for Young had been. The Son puts back the uprooted hills, restores the angels to their choric peace ("Stand still in bright array, ye Saints, here stand"), and repeats the sacrificial ploce on "me":

> stand onely and behold
> Gods indignation on these Godless pourd
> By mee; not you but mee they have despis'd,
> Yet envied; against mee is all thir rage,

The power he then puts forth is distinctly non-military:

> into terrour chang'd
> His count'nance too severe to be beheld
> And full of wrauth bent on his Enemies.

A change of expression in the face of the Son, in which alone the light of God can be seen, is a fine symbol for excommunication and has Mosaic support. But

> At once the Four spred out thir Starrie wings
> With dreadful shade contiguous, and the Orbes
> Of his fierce Chariot rowld, as with the sound
> Of torrent Floods, or of a numerous Host.

The "torrent" simile is casual, the ikon of "numerous Host" congruent. The following thirteen lines are again military, but once more Milton returns from Homer to Ezekiel:

> Nor less on either side tempestuous fell
> His arrows, from the fourfold-visag'd Foure,
> Distinct with eyes, and from the living Wheels,
> Distinct alike with multitude of eyes,
> One spirit in them rul'd, and every eye
> Glar'd lightning, and shot forth pernicious fire
> Among th'accurst, that witherd all thir strength,
> And of thir wonted vigour left them draind,
> Exhausted, spiritless, afflicted, fall'n.

The heavy rhetoric turns the incident to allegory. The rebels are not being killed, but overcome by the power of the Logos—infinite spiritual vigour is defeating conditional technical expertise. But here a last criticism has to be made. The chariot is to be used again in the next book for a creative purpose:

> About his Chariot numberless were pour'd
> Cherub and Seraph, Potentates and Thrones,
> And Vertues, winged Spirits, and Chariots wing'd,
> From the Armoury of God, where stand of old
> Myriads between two brazen Mountains lodg'd
> Against a solemn day, harnest at hand,
> Celestial Equipage; and now came forth
> Spontaneous, for within them Spirit liv'd,
> Attendant on thir Lord:
>
> (197)

This version reveals it as a phallic chariot, omnipotent genitalia with which the Son is "girt". Milton has made the mistake of confusing spiritual vitality, love-creative genius for life, with sheer potency and hence with a masculine eroto-motive force that is naturally as blindly destructive as creative. It is difficult to see how those careening spermatozoa are going to *create* anything; and they don't—the world is made by "th' Omnific Word", an equally potent symbol but one in which the power is rationally directed. The Son's victory could have been wrought in that way: "The heathen raged, the kingdoms were moved: he uttered his voice, the earth melted" (*Ps*. xlvi. 6). In Blake's illustration (Plate IV) the Son directs at the host of Satan a geometrical bow which is the couterpart of the compasses used to create the world by *The Ancient of Days*.[1] But the poem's chariot, for all its eyes ultimately symbolises destructive, not creative power; so that, when every allowance and interpretation has been made, we cannot accept the Son's conquest as a worshipful divine act. It does not, like that psalm, command us to "Be still, and know that I am God". It is not that our responses to all manifestations of power have been deadened by

[1] An isolated design. The original is at the Whitworth Art Gallery, University of Manchester, but it has often been reproduced. Like the Son in Plate IV, the Ancient of Days is kneeling on his right knee in an aureole, with his left knee high up, his left arm stretched down. The points of the compasses are parallel to the Son's arrows.

Huntington Library

IV Blake

Rout of the Rebel Angels (1806)

industrial totalitarianism. We can still appreciate the power of "Pity Like a naked newborn babe striding the blast Or horsed upon the sightless couriers of the air", the power of Prospero (though sometimes malicious), the power of Blake's tiger. But in all these the power is of weakness made strong (the lamb beside the tiger) as Milton presents it, prosaically, in Book XII. Further, they are not mechanical and, even if like Prospero intellectual, they are not disembodied intellect as the chariot's eyes are, but incarnate. Thirdly, their power is justified by their beauty, like the Poesy of Keats, And, although their power may be destructive, burning out the evil, it is eventually healing. This creative end that will justify the destructive means is not symbolised adequately by the Son's reparation of the uprooted hills, or in the lines

> Disburd'nd Heav'n rejoic'd, and soon repaird
> Her mural breach, returning whence it rowld.

All the emphasis falls on the ruin of the rebels in the preceding fifty lines. On a larger view, of course, this destructiveness is outweighed by the Creation in Book VII and by the grace of Books X-XII; but the destruction of Satan is no necessary premiss to creation, and as a premiss to grace it might, considering the nature of Adam and Eve, be regarded as *faute de mieux* rather than *felix culpa*. The basic difficulty is similar to that touched on in the discussion of Hell. Human experience and the Christian life may both admit the existence of "Satan" and hope for his elimination. But to contemplate an image of his partial destruction, or punishment, as having occurred before the world began is to indulge in the crudest autism. Unless deliberately related to the individual soul's combat with evil (as by Bunyan), it has no value in real life. Although the *Psalms* occasionally indulge in vicarious revenge on human enemies—"The righteous shall rejoice when he seeth the vengeance: he shall wash his feet in the blood of the wicked" (lviii. 10)—the canonical books of the Bible are reticent about the angelomachia; even the apocalyptic references are to the future, not the past. And if we do think about it apocalyptically we should be truer to our civilisation to think in terms of salvaging what is good rather than annihilating the Satanic. Yet when Milton comes to consider the final realisation of goodness in the world he reverts, in disregard of the connotations of "purg'd and refin'd" (XII. 548), to the hysterical imagery of chains and destruction that he found in the quasi-apocryphal books of *Peter* and *Jude*. He failed to understand the moral significance of aesthetic materials.

Yet how honest and complete, compared with our anxious self-regarding purity, to have expressed these blatancies as they arose in him, and to have had something in his stomach worth the purgation of *Paradise Regained*.

9

CREATION

1. *Structural*

THE invocation at Book VII is a good example of how difficult Milton's involvement in his poem makes it to reach critical decisions of a formal kind. The invocation is the most personal moment in *Paradise Lost.* So it cuts off the destructive from the creative manifestations of divine power, and breaks the antecedentia's homogeneity as reported narrative. The "barbarous dissonance" of devilry is arrogated to the poet's circumstances, the "evil dayes" are his, not Adam's. Against these personalia, the Creation is to be described with objectivity: so Urania is invoked; but why Bellerophon? It can only be because the invocation intrudes into the poem's structure the poet's anxiety about the presumptuous heroics of Book VI and the cosmography of Books VII and VIII. Bellerophon insures Milton against the sin of Adam and Eve, curiosity. On the other hand, as soon as we recognise this personal function of the verse, it takes structural effect. It edges the poem over its spatial middle towards the crisis at the end of Book VIII:

> More safe I Sing with mortal voice, unchang'd
> To hoarce or mute, though fall'n on evil dayes,
> On evil dayes though fall'n, and evil tongues;

are the most personal lines in the lyric; but careful rhetoric turns them choric, so that the evil tongue is Satan's; and the accumulated vowel of "fall" tolls from the invocation—"on th'*Aleian* Field I fall Erroneous, there to wander and forlorne"—into the second paragraph, "befell . . . befall . . . wandring" (43-4-50) and so out through the end of the poem.

The appalling latinate clumsiness of the preliminary colloquy between Adam and Raphael shows Milton's anxiety still operating. All sense of man-angel communion is lost as they circle nervously round each other's speeches, not to be regained by calling Raphael affable archangel or godlike guest. Confidence returns with the Creation narrative, which is different from any other sustained episode in the poem: it is written with exuberance; its events do not advance the action; no taint of sin inheres. For these reasons the episode was often treated alone in complete poems; and Milton may have composed it earlier than much of *Paradise Lost*[1] (a creation ode was planned for Act I of the third and fourth drafts of "Adam Unparadis'd") and so had to excuse it into the middle of his now graver subject. The six days are enclosed by the descent and reascension of the Son, counters to Satan's activity, and to the Son's violence in Book VI. There is a sense of release, Satan having dropped clean out of the poem into Hell for the time being; a relief that the poetry can now be unlimitedly magnificent and yet whole-heartedly on the side of the angels; and confidence that, though the poem's action may stand still, the incidents have the firmest Scriptural basis and are open to exciting Christian typology.

At first the Father is still a school-divine—"Yet farr the greater part have kept, I see, Thir station" (145)—but he gradually assuages this hectoring with gracious paternal dignity:

> My overshadowing Spirit and might with thee
> I send along, ride forth, and bid the Deep
> Within appointed bounds be Heav'n and Earth,
> Boundless the Deep, because I am who fill
> Infinitude, nor vacuous the space
> Though I uncircumscrib'd my self retire,
> And put not forth my goodness, which is free
> To act or not, Necessities and Chance
> Approach not mee, and what I will is Fate.

This points the orthodox analogy between Creation and Incarnation: the Father refers to his "over-shadowing Spirit" in the words of the Angel of the Annunciation[2]; the angels—"Glorie they sung to the most High, good will To future men, and in thir dwellings peace" (182)—rehearse their future carol to the

[1] As McColley claims.

[2] *Luke* i. 35. Cf. Hawkins, p. 245: "the Spirit of God, as we have it in *Genesis, did incubare super aquas* cover, as we say, or overshadow the waters: which was a work of the first Creation. So in the work of our Redemption, where the blessed Virgin, Maria by name, which signifyes the *Seas* also, it pleased the Eternal Word, leaving the delicious bosome of the heavenlie *Father* to descend into the *Sea*, of human miseries to take them upon him; and the *Holie-Ghost* likewise to overshadow her withal".

shepherds. When the Son rides forth comparisons to other events in the poem are gathered in a large implied simile. Like Satan he passes through the gates to gaze on the abyss but with creative purpose—

> The King of Glorie in his powerful Word
> And spirit coming to create new Worlds.

The link with the Incarnation is tightened by the distinctively Christian reference to the stilling of Galilee:

> Silence, ye troubl'd waves, and thou Deep, peace,
> Said then th' Omnific Word, your discord end:

There is no incongruity in the creative heroics—

> Nor staid, but on the Wings of Cherubim
> Uplifted, in Paternal Glorie rode
> Farr into *Chaos*, and the World unborn;
> For *Chaos* heard his voice:

The return from creation elicits a holy joy, elaborating the previous reference to *Psalm* xxiv: "The earth is the Lord's, and the fulness thereof; the world, and they that dwell therein . . . Lift up your heads, O ye gates; and be ye lift up, ye everlasting doors; and the King of glory shall come in".[1] Milton and God together watch their own creation in astonished glad innocence which clarifies the consummate technical skill from any taint of self-regard:

> The Heavens and all the Constellations rung,
> The Planets in thir stations list'ning stood,
> While the bright Pomp ascended jubilant.
>
> (562)

The glorious train is boosted upwards by varied staging of the operative verbs and prepositions ("up returned / Up to the Heav'n of Heav'ns . . . Up he rode / . . ."), by rhyme (553-5-7) and by assonance (558-9). With the procession the verse passes through the "blazing Portals" and spreads out horizontally, suddenly turning back our necks as the whole thing is viewed dizzily from underneath in the Milky Way.

[1] An appropriate reference: this was one of the psalms sung antiphonally at the holy convocation in the Temple on the seventh and last day of the Feast of Tabernacles, a harvest festival celebrating created nature.

CREATION

2. *The Hexemeron*

The six days of Creation here differ from Uriel's Lucretian exposition in Book III by being highly eclectic[1] but fundamentally Biblical: the main source is *Job* xxxviii-ix. As Newton remarked, the days' decrees are paraphrased direct from *Genesis*, "but afterwards he indulges a greater latitude of thought, and gives freer scope to his imagination".[2] The awesome boom of *Genesis* is made polyphonic, and the day-by-day progression opens out into daily more minute and sensuous particularity until on the fifth and sixth we are faced with the translation of God's inscrutable decrees into the objects of everyday experience. Yet each day also closes with a formal paraphrase of *Genesis*, like a refrain—

> The Waters thus
> With Fish replenisht, and the Aire with Fowle,
> Ev'ning and Morn solemniz'd the Fift day.
>
> (446)

The first creature is the unformed quintessence of light, described briefly from *Genesis* and *Psalm* xix. The second day's division of the waters that womb the world from the waters that flow inside it, by the shell of the outer convex, is described with an obscurity that results from an only half-successful attempt to combine scientific precision, cosmic grandeur and the Bible. At the time, the attempt was probably wholly successful because for a short while the language of poetry was the same as the language of science and both were exercised with reverence. The subsequent professionalising of both disciplines, rather than any 17th-century antagonism between them, has made us find dichotomies that were probably not there at the time of writing. For instance, about half the apparently "Miltonic" words in the passage 261-290—*transparent*, *elemental*, *diffused*, *circuit*, *convex*, *partition*, *distemper*, *satiate*, *genial*, *emergent*, *tumid*—were of late medieval or 16th-century usage. The more modern words are of just the same kind—real language, not poeticisms: *contiguous* (*N.E.D.* 1611), *embryon* (1592), *immature* (1599), *involved* (1607),

[1] Scholarship of the hexemeral background to the Creation episode is extensive and dull. Hallett Smith makes the point that Milton's poetry here is fresh in spite of the tradition: "No Middle Flight", *HLQ*, XV (1951-2), p. 161.

[2] Ed. *P.L.* (7th ed. 1770), note to VII. 339.

prolific (1650), *fermented* (trans. 1672), *capacious* (1634). *Circumfluous* (1638) has given way to *circumfluent*, but not because it is an unrealistic word. *Precipitance* is neater than the *precipitancy* from which Milton coined it, though the latter has survived. Milton's *expanse* is the first record of the word as we use it, substantivally, and it combines our connotations of large area, smoothness or liquidity, and stretched consistency, with Chaucer's adjectival sense of separation: the word is doing its full imaginative work within a coherent intellectual framework. Like most of Milton's coinages and neologisms, these are typically *a priori*, directed at the intellectual discrimination and definition of existing things and ideas, compared with the empirical inventions of Shakespeare.

On the third day, as the earth takes shape, the language narrows to common experience. The hills ascend like elephants getting to their feet, the waters congregate under surface tension like "drops on dust conglobing from the drie", the rivers are formed as if by rainwater running down a muddy lane: "And on the washie Oose deep Channels wore". But the image of the world cradled in uterine waters, though repeated through the episode, remains unrealised, just a Lucretian motif, so that its enormous symbolic power is wasted.[1] Similarly inspiration fails on the fifth day when the earth brings forth vegetation. Mother Earth is treated on the body-landscape analogy but without either gorgeousness or sensuality. The pubic "Bush with frizl'd hair implicit", though interesting as a symptom of unified sensibility, is too small-scale and facetious to take effect in the context.

Again on the fourth day, the heavens are spread with a too-fanciful conflation of Pliny (the sun as light-source), Lucretius, Galileo ("the morning planet gilds his horns") and alchemy (augmentation by "tincture", 367). The verse recovers only with a return to *Job* and Milton's own younger style—"the gray Dawn, and the *Pleiades* before him danc'd Shedding sweet influence".

The fifth day is a romp through air and water. It is doubly effective in that pristine world for we have lost twice over the innocent delight in stately play like this, and like the elephant who wreathed his lithe proboscis in Book IV: once, so far

[1] Cf. Shakespeare's economical but complete commital to the organic in such phrases as "procreant cradle".

as the poem is concerned, at the Fall, and again, so far as literature is concerned, about the time the poem was written. The Augustans were too refined, or coarse, for this; the Romantics, except Smart and Blake, too earnest—and unable to provide the huge context that will absorb and sanctify such sensuous riot; since then, there have been experts in exuberance like Hopkins, Dylan Thomas, Joyce; but on the whole we take literature too seriously to admit such insouciance, and our verbal play is introvert, conceptualised. Even here Milton attends to the detail of language, though. The sea-creatures either swim about "Or in thir Pearlie shells at ease, attend Moist nutriment, or under Rocks thir food In jointed Armour watch": the poetry of pearls and the romance of jousting are made real, and the single abstract word "nutriment" both appeals to the sensory imagination and makes a biological distinction between the nourishment of shellfish and the "food" of crustaceans.

On the sixth day the sensuousness is modified, as in Paradise, by metaphors of art that suggest the Creator's shaping hand. But it is the dead art of heraldry—"wings Display'd", the insects' "Liveries"—deriving from Du Bartas, from Lucretius who asserted that all animals literally rose out of Mother Earth,[1] and corresponding with Renaissance depictions of the event.[2] So the lion appears *couped* as on a crest, then *passant gardant* and *rampant* as on a shield. This is an anti-climax after the active feudalism of the lobsters, the uniformed fish, the swan's royal barge. There is a relapse into Bartasian homiletics, begun with "the prudent Crane" on the fifth day but now elaborated with the proverbially "Parsimonius Emmet" and political bee. The creation of man, and the warning not to taste the Tree of Knowledge (repeated by Raphael at the end of his narrative) are

[1] *De Rerum Natura* ed. and trans. C. Bailey (3 vols. Oxford, 1947), V. 795: "linquitur ut merito maternum nomen adepta / terra sit, e terra quoniam sunt cuncta creata" (cf. 821). Milton learned much from Lucretius about technique as well as content. The Penguin translator (R. E. Latham, 1951) notes that Lucretius enjoyed a similar temporary association of scientific with poetic diction.

[2] E.g. Michelangelo's creation medallion in the Sistine fresco, Uccello's "Creation" in the Chiostro Verde of S. Maria Novella, Florence. I am not suggesting Milton was influenced by such paintings. Coleridge, also objecting to the pictorial technique here, notes that Milton was not affected by plastic art: *Table Talk*, ed. H. N. C. (3rd ed. 1851), 7 Aug. 1832.

superfluous to Adam's description in Book VIII and what we already know. Didactic irritability weakens the myth. As a totem the Tree of Knowledge is absurd beside the trees that rise in stately dance, and amidst the creative operations of the Omnific Word the command not to touch it sounds old maidish. Milton has brought himself to the Augustinian crux: if you treat a God who is the morally ideal τέλος of rational life and also the efficient cause of all things, you must immediately introduce original sin to account for the checking of teleological development in actual life:[1] To do this by postulating a "Don't touch" from the Father and disobedience by the creature is not to solve the crux, for the prohibition is so little relevant to either creation or teleology. It becomes obvious here that the negative command is not the element of "discipline" necessary to rational life, as apologists claim. Discipline is a means to an end, the creative co-ordination of powers, as symbolised by the Son's compasses and Raphael's rhetoric.

What most distinguishes Milton's work here, though, is his freedom from Romantic empathy on one hand and Augustan contemplativity on the other. He participates as maker in the creation that his poetry celebrates. He was able to do this because his idea of God was still just personal enough, and his apperception of the universe had not quite lost symbolic content —as it had, for example, for Addison by 1712 when he ended a creation ode in the *Spectator* (23 Aug.) with this typical recovery from poetic loss to philosophic gain:

> What though, in solemn Silence, all
> Move round the dark terrestrial Ball?
> What tho' nor real Voice nor Sound
> Amid their radiant Orbs be found?

[1] Cf. Santayana, *Life of Reason* (5 vols. iii. *Reason in Religion*, 1905), p. 165: "The semitic idea of creation could now [Augustine having as a neo-Platonic idealist recognised evil as accidental] receive that philosophical interpretation which it so sadly needed. Primordially, and in respect to what was positive in them, all things might be expressions of the good; in their essence and ideal state they might be said to be created by God. For God was the supreme ideal, to which all other goods were subordinate and instrumental; and if we agree to make a cosmogony out of morals and to hypostasise the series of rational ideals, taken in inverse order, into a series of efficient causes, it is clear that the highest good, which is at the end of the moral scale, will now figure as a first cause at the beginning of the physical sequence."

In Reason's Ear they all rejoice,
And utter forth a glorious Voice,
For ever singing, as they shine,
"The Hand that made us is Divine".

The penultimate line is a paraphrase of Milton ("Lycidas", 180), but Milton was still able to *use* the music of the speres.

3. *The Use of Reason*

The calm clarity of Raphael's astronomical expositions in Book VIII are suitably postprandial and, when remembered against the tempting rhetoric of Satan in the next book, they assert the supremacy of reason even while they condemn "curiosity". Suggesting that the earth may be a planet, Raphael begins rhetorically—"now high, now low, then hid, Progressive, retrograde, or standing still" (126)—but then drops into a tone which celebrates and enacts what it argues: "Insensibly three different Motions move". It is a kind of writing not met with again until the *Prelude*, and the *Four Quartets*. When, though, Raphael brings God into the discussion his verse cracks under the strain:

> God to remove his wayes from human sense,
> Plac'd Heav'n from Earth so farr, that earthly sight,
> If it presume, might erre in things too high,
> And no advantage gaine.
>
> (VIII. 119)

Similarly when he agreed to tell the Creation story Raphael had warned Adam, "nor let thine own inventions hope Things not reveal'd, which th'invisible King, Onely Omniscient, hath supprest in Night" (VII. 121): the heroic antonomasia of God as "th'invisible King" is startlingly out of place. But what Raphael and Adam are trying to reject is not science so much as academicism—the unchecked "roaving" of fancy (VIII. 189; the dominant image of wandering is to culminate in the Fall), the search for knowledge "remote from use, obscure and suttle" (191), the sort of knowledge which will "no advantage gaine". Man's "own inventions"—his hypotheses—are not truth. The application of this is not restricted to those medieval Scholastics by whose "quaint Opinions wide" God may be moved to sardonic laughter,

> when they come to model Heav'n
> And calculate the Starrs, how they will weild
> The mightie frame, how build, unbuild, contrive
> To save appearances, how gird the Sphear
> With Centric and Eccentric scribl'd o're,
> Cycle and Epicycle, Orb in Orb:
>
> (VIII. 79)

The point is carried by the contrast between this parody and Raphael's tentative sketches of the alternative theories:

> Whether the Sun predominant in Heav'n
> Rise on the Earth, or Earth rise on the Sun,
> Hee from the East his flaming rode begin,
> Or Shee from West her silent course advance
> With inoffensive pace that spinning sleeps
> On her soft Axle, while she paces Eev'n,
> And beares thee soft with the smooth Air along,

Face-saving complexity of dogma is replaced by clarity and reverent doubt; and incidentally proves that the Copernician universe is as inherently "poetic" as the Ptolemaic.

We derive the class of information that Raphael offers from specialised textbooks, encyclopaedias and *Life* magazine. The telling and discussing done there, we look to art only for emotive suggestion, of the kind made about machinery and physiology in modern sculpture and in pylon poetry. It's no good lamenting this and begging for the poem of statement back again. Science and poetry have become separate modes of discourse. We can only make ourselves appreciate that Milton was supplying the 17th Century with instruction we use other media for. His verse was a more efficient medium than any English prose except Bacon's before the Restoration. It combines precision with explanatory vividness, and casts over the material not only the ethico-astrological significance pertaining to cosmology at the time, but a steady evaluating timbre superior to most later attempts (Sir James Jeans for example being mushy in comparison).

4. *Reason and Passion*

Adam's narrative of his own creation rounds off the antecedentia by returning us to Eve's in Book IV; and the discussion on sexual *mores* completes the theme begun in Book V when "at Table *Eve* ministerd naked". But the innocence is embarrassed now, Eve "blushing like the Morn", Raphael "Celestial rosie red, Loves proper hue". The uneasiness begins with the dreadful jostling of metaphorical corpses, pebble-mouthed latinisms and humble-pie circumlocutions, subjunctives and double-negatives, when Adam suggests:

> Therefore from this high pitch let us descend
> A lower flight, and speak of things at hand
> Useful, whence haply mention may arise
> Of something not unseasonable to ask
> By sufferance, and thy wonted favour deign'd.

This quaking false respect, not reverence, is what corrupts the poem's God and all the poet's relations with him. So the new-made Adam, who "sometimes went, and sometimes ran with supple joints, as lively vigour led" is not "The first Adam" of Book IV who might disturb globe-trotting madams and lie in the thought of girls at puberty. His dialogue with the Creator is a model of how communication lapses into banter when an aged don accosts an urgent young man with the twinkling eyes of patronage. The procreation of Eve is excruciatingly culinary ("a Rib, with cordial spirits warme, And Life-blood streaming fresh"), with none of the loving excitement of Donne's surgery; and their *prima nox* as rehearsed here is a joyless pastiche of Spenser's *Epithalamion* and the glories of Book IV. The embarrassment of the descriptive writing discloses the moral conflict in the subsequent discussion about passion and reason, the conflict that distorts the whole antecedentia, between a Humanistic urge to know—carnally and intellectually—and fashion the knowledge into active life, and a quietist submission to distant ignorance, "freed from intricacies, taught to live The easiest way, nor with perplexing thoughts To interrupt the sweet of life". Episode and discussion together run between these the gamut of clumsily pretended naïveté, smirking abasement, vulgarity, bad conscience, self-reproach. The essentials to be communicated—birth as creation, the data of sexuality, marriage as τέλος—

sink through the poet's anxiety. There is an Aristotelian pertinence about it all, but what did Aristotle know of Eden? When Adam confesses his feelings for Eve, Raphael answers like a disillusioned husband giving a young fiancé advice—"Oft times nothing profits more Then self-esteem"—that may have some validity in fallen marriages but should not make sense to Adam. Raphael tries to synthesise love and reason, but it is a mere verbalism. The verse of Adam's reply jumps like a cat on a roof:

> Neither her out-side formd so fair, nor aught
> In procreation common to all kindes
> (Though higher of the genial Bed by far,
> And with mysterious reverence I deem)
> So much delights me . . .

He is supposed to be "half abash't", but there is no reason why he should be. It is possible to be "sunk in carnal pleasure", but only at moments of intrinsically carnal activity which love may redeem from animality. When Raphael opposes this condition to a "heav'nly Love" which is the ladder-top of eros, he re-opens all the problems of his speeches in Book V and ignores the very completeness of love which Adam and Eve enjoyed in Book IV. Adam's disavowal of animality is priggish: "yet still free Approve the best, and follow what I approve". This determination to save himself and the concomitant refusal to give equal value to another personality is fatal to the moral of the piece; for the urgency that a woman's body as such may provoke can only be dedicated by esteem for the other-self inhabiting it. Theologically in any case, Adam's confession of "passion" before the Fall postulates a more than creaturely imperfection lying, as he says (534), in the nature of man and woman as gendered beings. Raphael's reply, "Accuse not Nature, she hath done her part", is merely the comfort of proverbial lore. The disparity of affection that Adam suggests between him and Eve, though it may exist in fallen marriages, is contrary to the mutuality of love demonstrated in Book IV.

You can get very angry with Milton for his obtuseness. But at least he is there to be angry with. This was probably the last piece of imaginative literature before *Jude the Obscure* to treat sexuality in serious practical detail. It continues to be more comprehensive and discussible, because so definite and ethical, than most things written since. His fundamental concern was Lawrence's, to assert the difference between male and female, self and not-self. The motives may have lain coiled in his own Belial complex; but the assertion is worth making because so rare in English literature, especially since its domination by the hyper-subjective and homosexual sensibility of the Edwardian period. One can see what he is getting at in terms of his plot—or perhaps reinterpret him, it is difficult to be sure because of the difference between our circumstances, knowledge *mores*, and his. The Fall results in a concupiscent act which is the symbol of its cause, a turning away from God towards another object of love and loyalty—ultimately to the self. So in Raphael's painting the serpent, which was often depicted with an angel's head, has Eve's; and the fruit is changed from phallic apple to pudic fig. She has fallen in love with herself and Adam is being tempted by his sinful image of her: he is looking at the snakes's head although the real Eve is offering him the fig.[1] Milton's Raphael uses the selfishness and idolatry that sexual love by its nature may easily fall into to warn Adam of the nature of all sin as self-occupied alienation. The chivalrous elevation of woman onto a pedestal, wrapping "an awe About her, as a guard Angelic plac't", is both idolatry and a selfish degradation of woman below the active importance of manhood. "In loving thou dost well, in passion not" (589) draws a correct distinction between giving of the self to an other, and subjugating the self to an affect which is not even the other personality but merely the enjoyable excitement she provokes.[2] The one is free yet generous—the magnanimity of ἀγάπη; the other bound, yet selfish. But so long as this is presented in the syncreted terminology of Christian Humanism it cannot take effect. Milton is not to blame for Aristotle, Paul, Augustine, nor they for the historicality of their ethics; but we have to recognise the multiplex relativism of Milton's conflation of them. Apart from that, all philosophies constructed out of assumedly stable units of language are more or less obtuse and absurd, Protestant Humanism more so because it rejected the analytical tech-

[1] Plate I. The design and plot are imitated from Piero di Cosimo's "Temptation". Raphael's Eve is modelled on his own Leda and anticipates his sketch of a Venus. See Clark, *The Nude*.

[2] Cf. Shakespeare's concern in *T. & C.* II. ii. 53 ff. and Sonnets 93, 137, 138, etc., where "the will dotes"

niques of Scholasticism (such as Occam's), but retained its own version of the Thomist synthesis. In this it was like the Roman Catholic Church. Montaigne, Bacon, Hobbes, were more "Protestant", anti-medieval, anti-Thomist, prima-principular than Hooker and Milton, and of them only Montaigne refrained from any kind of new-old synthesis. As a *Weltanschauung*, Christian Humanism was a product of anxiety for public stability at the Renaissance (Hooker its firmest proponent). An egotistically masculine philosophy, it failed most cruelly—because most influentially—to be true in intimacy. Its method was to impose big on little, the established ancient on the shifting new. It transferred an apparent cosmic hierarchy, a temporarily actual political hierarchy, and a supposedly analogical hierarchy of soul and body, to domestic life. Even Shakespeare escaped its tyranny only through the fantastic paschalism of the last plays, so that Imogen, Perdita and Miranda are his only properly feminine and marriageable heroines. But Eve as regarded here by Adam and Raphael is the ancestor of *Masterman Ready*'s Mrs Seagrave, and the Fairchild family's mother, women drained of sensuality and initiative. Eve does not let it happen to her, but others tried: it is what Mr Casaubon wanted to make of Dorothea, and George Eliot's model for him was the Milton in Raphael and Adam at Book VIII. But there had been another, thirty-five-year-old Milton, his Platonism solidified but not yet petrified into stoical Humanism, who could cry:

> Let not, therefore, the frailty of man go on thus inventing needless troubles to itself, to groan under the false imagination of a strictness imposed from above; enjoining that for duty which is an impossible and vain supererogating. . . .
>
> (*Div.* iii. 272)

10

THE FALL

1. *Tragic Notes*

MILTON'S last invocation fails to reach the devotional height of the first and second. His anxieties are too literary. Noting the danger of anti-climax compared with the great classical epics, which all end with a major battle, he claims that God's wrath over man is more "heroic" than Achilles' for Hector, Turnus' for "*Lavinia* disespous'd", and the quarrel between Neptune and Juno "that so long Perplex'd" Ulysses. Although the Olympian quarrel which sent Ulysses wandering the world for twenty years has some relevance to the ending of *Paradise Lost*, these comparisons justify the neo-classical opinion that

> the true Religion was not found to become a Fiction so well as a false had done, and all their Attempts of this kind seem rather to debase Religion than to heighten Poetry.

Then Milton tries to forestall Dryden's objection to an epic that ends on tragic notes by redefining true heroism as "the better fortitude of Patience and Heroic Martyrdom". This is true of Samson, and Paul, but it cannot apply to Adam and Eve until after the Fall and even then their patience is not heroic—neither like Samson's active, nor like Paul's a quality of joyous hope for the parousia.

The Metaphysicals were right: the Fall can only be a dramatic symbol, a metaphor, not an epic action. Milton clears his stage as for drama. Large ikons decrease, the actors' stature is reduced. More relics of an actually dramatic version survive here than anywhere else in the poem. There is a little piece of dramatic irony (more stagey than its counterpart at IV. 340) when Adam warns Eve of their "malicious Foe" who "somewhere nigh at hand Watches, no doubt" (IX. 256), as Satan, having crept round the garden, lies hidden. There are theatrical metaphors unusual in the later Milton: "So gloz'd the Tempter, and his

Proem tun'd" at the end of his first tempting speech (IX. 549); and Eve, sinfully embarrassed before Adam, "in her face excuse Came Prologue, and Apology to prompt" (853). She is acting a part, like Satan.

The shift into drama is incomplete and confusing:

> Revenge, at first thought sweet,
> Bitter ere long back on it self recoiles;
> Let it; I reck not, so it light well aim'd,
> Since higher I fall short, on him who next
> Provokes my envie, this new Favorite
> Of Heav'n, this Man of Clay, Son of despite,
> Whom us the more to spite his Maker rais'd
> From dust: spite then with spite is best repaid. (171)

The words spit and twist, revealing the weakness of a melodrama villain. Yet that kind of villainy seems absurd as agent to the Fall of Man. When Satan finds Eve alone, the heroic defiance of Books I and II falters again:

> Shee fair, divinely fair, fit Love for Gods,
> Not terrible, though terrour be in Love
> And beautie, not approacht by stronger hate,
> Hate stronger, under shew of Love well feign'd,
> The way which to her ruin now I tend. (489)

A figure of rhetoric—"stronger hate, Hate stronger"—is used to make Satan catch up again the confidence of hatred, and the speech ends with a scene-shifting couplet. This is not the expression of dramatic being but the external mimesis of an attitude. The words spoken by the character do less than the words Milton describes him with: "Active within beyond the sense of brute" (89); "Stupidly good, of enmitie disarm'd . . . then soon Fierce hate he recollects, and all his thoughts Of mischief, gratulating, thus excites" (465). Similarly with Adam and Eve: "To whom soon mov'd with touch of blame thus *Eve*" (1143) presupposes her whole speech. Their quarrel at the beginning of the episode is summarised by lines of this kind:

> And *Eve* first to her Husband thus began.
>
> To whom mild answer *Adam* thus return'd.
>
> To whom the Virgin majestie of *Eve*,
> As one who loves, and some unkindness meets,
> With sweet austeer composure thus reply'd.

To whom with healing words *Adam* reply'd.

Thus her reply with accent sweet renewd.

To whom thus *Adam* fervently repli'd.

So spake the Patriarch of Mankinde, but *Eve*
Persisted, yet submiss, though last, repli'd.

Instead of immediately representing through words what the character in these circumstances specifically feels and says, Milton consolidates description and speech into a pattern of this or that general posture. This slackens the tension, invites generalised response; sooner or later the reader must discard the poetry and make his own interpretation of the myth it sketches. It is appropriate enough as the action moves towards the Fall because "in Adam all die".

In the quarrel between Adam and Eve the drama tightens into domesticity. Eve suggests dividing their labour. Adam answers sententiously:

for nothing lovelier can be found
In woman, then to studie household good,
And good workes in her Husband to promote.

(232)

For solitude somtimes is best societie,
And short retirement urges sweet returne.

(249)

The Wife, where danger or dishonour lurks,
Safest and seemliest by her Husband staies,
Who guards her, or with her the worst endures.

(267)

Our response is confused because we recognise the verses' proverbial authority (the first is from *Proverbs* itself) but feel that Adam is relapsing into reasonable generalisation when he ought to be enforcing his will. Eve's second speech, of "sweet austeer composure", is superior to Adam's as dramatic poetry because it develops with her emotions within the actual situation, ending on the verge of self-induced tears—"Thoughts, which how found they harbour in thy breast, *Adam*, missthought of her to thee so dear?" (288): a model of how the pathistry of wives can subvert the rationality of husbands. Adam's reply is wordy, self-important, hurriedly trying to make amends and yet retain authority. Eve answers again with ominous "accent sweet" and now reveals her capacity for sophistry too, which parodies Adam's philosophy and prepares her for the reception of Satan's tempting quibbles:

> onely our Foe
> Tempting affronts us with his foul esteem
> Of our integritie: his foul esteeme
> Sticks no dishonour on our Front, but turns
> Foul on himself; (327)

In his last speech Adam recovers and speaks as, for Eve, the representative of God, using the Father's words and rhythms as she has used Satan's:

> within himself [Man]
> The danger lies, yet lies within his power:
> Against his will he can receave no harme.
> But God left free the Will, for what obeyes
> Reason, is free, and Reason he made right,

But his recognition of the balance in Paradise is anxious rather than faithful. If, as he admits,

> best are all things as the will
> Of God ordain'd them, his creating hand
> Nothing imperfect or deficient left
> Of all that he Created, much less Man,
> Or aught that might his happie State secure,

then Eve seems right to put perfection to the test:

> then wherefore shund or feard
> By us? who rather double honour gaine
> From his surmise prov'd false, find peace within,
> Favour from Heav'n, our witness from th'event.
> And what is Faith, Love, Vertue unassaid
> Alone, without exterior help sustaind?

Despite her Satanic tendencies, it is Eve who answers the question, Why did God place the tempting fruit within Man's reach at all? In *De Doctrina* Milton's orthodox answer is that the command was "a test of his obedience" (iv. 220). This seems ridiculous, but he elaborates:

> It was necessary that something should be forbidden or commanded as a test of fidelity, and that an act in its own nature indifferent, in order that man's obedience might be thereby

> tested. For since it was the disposition of man to do what was right, as a being naturally good and holy, it was not necessary that he should be bound by the obligation of a covenant to perform that to which he was of himself inclined; nor would he have given any proof of obedience by the performance of works to which he was led by a natural impulse, independently of the divine command.

The word translated as "would he have given any proof of" is *ostendisset*: not so much proof as a demonstration or declaration. Eve recognises that their virtue is nothing "unassaid"—it must be manifest by conquering temptation:

> It is not enough, for a rational being, that his relationship to the Other should be a fact. It must also be *intended*. It must be affirmed by his own will and choice.[1]

Without such affirmation "Fraile is our happiness". If Adam and Eve had not merely abstained from the Tree but abstained from it in the face of temptation they would have affirmed their relationship with God and, by tilting the precarious balance, have been on their way to the *beata necessitas non peccandi*.[2]

2. *Angst*

By making it the sequel to this unbiblical argument between Adam and Eve Milton has made the Fall deeper than it is in *Genesis*. There, it does not sound levels of the soul as deeply as

[1] John Macmurray, *Structure of Religious Experience* (1936), pp. 67-8.

[2] This orthodox Patristic doctrine is confirmed by ethical experience and by Milton's dramatic representation. The Liberal theologian's tendency is to regard the Fall as "the liberation of man from the beneficent determinism of Jehovah, and the birth—accompanied, indeed, by the throes of sin and suffering—of his capacity for true 'liberty'" (Willey, *17th-century Background*, p. 255). But "true" here means "as we know it" (the quotation marks round "liberty" admit but hide from the distinction); and the only liberty we know, the liberty to sin, is truer bondage for we cannot help it. Niebuhr admits that Man's "freedom is the basis of his creativity" but "it is also his temptation" (*Nature and Destiny*, i. 276): "We cannot, therefore, escape the ultimate paradox that the final exercise of freedom in the transcendent human spirit is its recognition of the false use of that freedom in action. Man is most free in the discovery that he is not free". This is Adam's freedom at the end of Book X; it is still a lesser freedom than he might have enjoyed had he grown up to godhead within "the beneficent determinism of Jehovah".

Oedipus, say, or Prometheus, or even Perseus and some of Jove's amours. It was an aetiological myth, not devised as an expression of experience but as an explanation of some of the exterior circumstances of man—mortality, labour, tool-using (of internal conditions, only shame of the body and fear of reptiles are explained). Most myths appealing to Western culture are more inward and passionate. Now before Christ this version of the Fall did not figure largely; the important version was the seduction of the daughters of men by the sons of God in *Genesis* vi. But with Jerusalem sacked, it was elaborated as a myth of despair in the apocryphal book *II Enoch* (1st Century A.D.), and used doctrinally by Paul. No doubt it appealed temperamentally to Paul (misogyny, etc.) but he used it negatively, to define the new man rather than dwell on the old: "as in Adam all die" is only an analogy for "in Christ shall all be made alive (*I Cor.* xv). The myth has a high didactic potential, but little poetic force; hence the elaboration of circumstances—Creation, angelomachia, etc.—and of themes such as *felix culpa*; and hence the variety of interpretations.

Spinoza held that the Fall stands for the necessary and beneficial attainment of adult self-knowledge. Coleridge that it stands for the corruption of intuitive *νοῦς* by the sophistical "*φρόνημα σαρκός*, or carnal mind . . . the wily tempter to counterfeit good; the pandar and advocate of the passions and appetites"[1]; or, as Wordsworth put it,

> There comes a time when Reason, not the grand
> And simple Reason, but that humbler power
> Which carries on its no inglorious work
> By logic and minute analysis
> Is of all Idols that which pleases most
> The growing mind.

He has to admit

> that danger cannot but attend
> Upon a Function rather proud to be
> The enemy of falsehood, than the friend
> Of truth, to sit in judgement than to feel.[2]

[1] *Aids to Reflection* (ed. H. N. C. 2 vols. 1843), i. 203, note.
[2] *Prelude*, XI. 123.

Coleridge claims that

> the Mosaic narrative thus interpreted gives a just and faithful exposition of the birth and parentage and successive movements of phenomenal sin (*peccatum phaenomenon; crimen primarium et commune*), that is, of sin as it reveals itself in time, and is an immediate object of consciousness.

But these interpretations are even more general and intellectual than the myth. The process and definition of sin implicit in Milton's version of the Fall—particularly its before and after—are subtler and more realistic. Milton intellectualises the actual temptation, as we shall see; but the quarrel between Adam and Eve is acutely psychological. It makes the Fall consist not in the usual list of sins—pride, disobedience, petty treason, murder, etc.—but in alienation (as defined at the end of the previous chapter). For all her clear-headedness, Eve is ready to lead herself into temptation. Speaking with that Satanic rhetoric, it is clear that she values temptation not so much as a chance to affirm virtue as a chance to become important to another person and to establish her own superiority. It is a kind of vanity. Jeremy Taylor remarks,

> There are some men more in love with the temptation then with the sin. . . . They resolve they will not commit the sin, they will not be overcome, but they would fain be tempted. . . . *It is impossible that any man should love to abide by a temptation for a good end. There is some little sensuality in being tempted.* . . . I doe not say, that to be tempted is always criminal, or in the neighbourhood of it; but it is the best indication of our love to God, for his sake to deny its importunity, and to overcome it: but that is onely, when it is unavoidable and from without, against our wils, or at least besides our purposes.[1]

It is in just these circumstances that Coleridge's carnal sophistry begins to corrupt the *νοῦς*; hence Eve's rhetoric. So, as discussed in Part 6, before the actual eating of the apple they have arrived in that condition of *Angst* which Augustine and Kierkegaard saw as the ground of sin. This has its equivalent in secular psychology. A child's unease at its parent's disunity tangles its emotional ties with them into a complex which will affect its relations with other people in the "fallen" world (Eve's feelings

[1] *Op. cit.* pp. 148-9.

about Adam, as soon as she has eaten the apple, are very complicated). The complex is untied by regeneration—being born again, through backward confessional re-enactment, into primal simplicity: "For Hades' bobbin bound in mummy-cloth May unwind the winding path". Milton prepares the ground with astonishing realism. Before their quarrel, Adam and Eve emerge, with less stateliness than usual, into a more mundane light than before,

> Then commune how that day they best may ply
> Thir growing work: for much thir work outgrew
> The hands dispatch of two Gardning so wide. (201)

They have begun to explore the possibilities of their existence and are finding them a little beyond their reach. Hence—at the level of common sense—Eve's suggestion. Her slight despair at the garden's fertility, and her desire for children, are significant:

> but till more hands
> Aid us, the work under our labour grows
> Luxurious by restraint; what we by day
> Lop overgrown, or prune, or prop, or bind,
> One night or two with wanton growth derides
> Tending to wilde.

She puts efficiency before community. Thus the limits of their physical powers, the scope of their foresight, and the richness of their environment,[1] have combined to bring them to the moment of choice.

3. *Falsehood*

The poignant domesticity turns ironic when Eve leaves Adam and re-enters an epical arena for the Fall:

> Thus saying, from her Husbands hand her hand
> Soft she withdrew, and like a Wood-Nymph light
> *Oread* or *Dryad*, or of *Delia*'s Traine,
> Betook her to the Groves, but *Delia*'s self
> In gate surpass'd and Goddess-like deport . . .

[1] It is a common Christian notion that earthly life is a heat for the race of Heaven but Milton held it more fiercely than most. Cf. *Areo.* ii. 75: "This justifies the high providence of God, who, though he commands us temperance, justice, continence, yet pours out before us even to a profuseness all desirable things, and gives us minds that can wander beyond all limit and satiety."

The expeditio of classical ikons is repeated to describe where she works—"Spot more delicious then those Gardens feign'd Or of reviv'd *Adonis*, or renownd *Alcinous*", or of Solomon (439) the uxorious idolater of Book I; and for Satan, when he comes to her, "never since of Serpent kind Lovelier" (504). Here for the last time in the poem the ancient world's beauty flowers, imaging vessels of evil. Milton's classical ikons nearly all have this element of decay, in verse sounding "that note of high lamentation and prophetic mournfulness",[1] to indicate the transitoriness of that to which they are applied—the glory of Mulciber, Lucifer, Eve, before they fell. There is no condemnation of Eve's beauty: her beauty is what makes the Fall so sad. This is the distinction between sordid accident and tragic catastrophe. The fall of Eliot's typist works ultimately not as an expression of the poet's grief at beauty lost—she is given none to lose—but of disgust for the act by which she throws away the only thing she has got, virginity. Potential beauty is admitted by the sun's last rays but immediately denied because they touch not her but her drying combinations, distasteful fetich for her sexual parts. Eve goes to her fall not only in classical grace but with the full hindquartered sensuality favoured by painters of the 17th Century, Adam watching her reluctantly. She passes through an implied simile to Persephone—"Her self, though fairest unsupported Flour"—which refers to Book IV's central simile and to her lake-looking, for when Persephone was abducted by Dis she was gathering narcissi.[2] Thus Eve is at least Satan's match but her fall inevitable: men sin by reason of their conscious supereminence in creation. Satan from a distance regards her as a town gallant would eye a milkmaid,[3] bringing as before the urban values of Hell, and its artificial lustre—"Carbuncle his Eyes; With burnisht Neck of verdant Gold, erect Amidst his circling Spires"—as well as the beast's acuity of scent by which he first sensed Paradise: the apples "more pleas'd my sense Then

[1] E. E. Stoll, *Poets and Playwrights* (New York, 1930), p. 247.

[2] Cf. Bacon, *Wisdom of the Ancients, sub* Narcissus, Prosperpina.

[3] Behind Satan's reaction here lies also the Rabbinical theory, brought in from *Gen.* vi, that the Fall was caused by Satan's lust for Eve (cf. *P.L.* X, 580). This was one of Browne's *Errors* (ii. 18-19). There was also the Talmudic interpretation of *Gen.* iii as an allegory of the discovery of sexual potency, the Tree being recognised as a phallic symbol. These interpretations again show the inadequacy of the *Gen.* iii myth.

smell of sweetest Fenel, or the Teats Of Ewe or Goat dropping with Milk at Eevn". But as the temptation begins, sensuousness and classical imagery fall away. The few, conventional tropes are based on rhetoric. They stem from the simile of Satan as "som Orator renound in *Athens* or free *Rome*" (670) so efficient that "Into the Heart of *Eve* his words made way" (550), "his words replete with guile Into her heart too easie entrance won" (735), "in her ears the sound Yet rung of his perswasive words", and so on. This metaphor was the motto of Renaissance rhetorical theory. Just as a kiss might literally unite two souls, eloquence could distort the intellectual spirits of the hearer—especially if a woman; and Satan was a notorious casuist.[1] His argument, though elegantly disposed in debating figures, circles round a few key-words:

> Queen of this Universe, doe not believe
> Those rigid threats of Death; ye shall not Die:
> How should ye? by the Fruit? It gives you Life
> To Knowledge: By the Threatner? look on mee,
> Mee who have toucht and tasted, yet both live,
> And life more perfet have attaind then Fate
> Meant me.

Eve drifts round the circle of traductio after him:

> Fruits . . . taste . . . forbids . . .
> Knowledge, knowledge, . . . Forbids . . .
> taste . . . forbidding . . . unknown . . .
> unknown . . . forbids . . . know, Forbids . . .
> forbids . . . Death . . . Fruit . . . die . . .
> dies . . . knows . . . death . . .

[1] See Andrewes, *Apospasmatia Sacra* (1657: posthumus lectures on *Gen.* i-iv), pp. 254-7. Similar rhetoric to Milton's is used in Quarles' emblem of the Temptation (I. i). Cf. Milton on the methods of the Remonstrant, who "as if he had the surety of some rolling trench, creeps up by this means to his relinquished fortress of divine authority again, and still hovering between the confines of that which he dares not be openly, and that which he will not be sincerely, trains on the easy Christian insensibly within the close ambushment of worst errors, and with a sly shuffle of counterfeit principles, chopping and changing till he have gleaned all the good ones out of their minds, leaves them at last, after a slight resemblance of sweeping and garnishing, under the sevenfold possession of a desperate stupidity . . ." (*Animad.* iii. 43).

Her concluding lines tinkle with failure to decide:

> For good unknown, sure is not had, or had
> And yet unknown, is as not had at all.
> In plain then, what forbids he but to know,
> Forbids us good, forbids us to be wise? (756)

What should she do? Counter-attack? Satan's argument, granted its fundamental lie that the snake has eaten the fruit, is intellectually unanswerable (and has, for the reader, ambiguous "authority" for it is an honest paraphrase of *Genesis* iii. 4-5). Resist with haughty mysticism like the Lady in *Comus*? Eve is not benighted in a forest, she has no reason to suspect the serpent, and the serpent is not blatant like Comus. Retreat to Adam? Not at once. I have spoken of Milton's tendency to batter temptation when it would be wiser to walk round it. Eve is circumspect: she goes to the tree and only then but then at once retreats:

> Serpent, we might have spar'd our coming hither,
> Fruitless to me, though Fruit be here to excess,
> The credit of whose vertue rest with thee,
> Wondrous indeed, if cause of such effects.
> But of this Tree we may not taste nor touch;
> God so commanded, and left that Command
> Sole Daughter of his voice; the rest, we live
> Law to our selves, our Reason is our Law.

She is not denying an intuitive sense of what is good for her in favour of imposed law, but denying the logic of Satan's plausibility in favour of what she intuits to be right. I say "intuition" because here the command represents conscience, intuitive *νοῦς*, Right-apprehending Reason. Milton and Christian orthodoxy generally treat the promptings of heredity and conditioning as the voice of God. We, in theory, recognise the promptings for what they verifiably are; but in practising choice we too hypostasise them, as, for example, the intuition of a critical intelligence peculiar to us as individuals, or the intuition of "what our blood feels and believes and says" which "is always true".

The taking of the apple is passed over quickly because it is words that matter most. Milton has moved from the Reformation theologians' *Angst* to the Coleridgean sophistry. The two elements unite in the pervasive imagery of error. Satan had arrived via an underground channel, "involv'd in rising Mist" and glided about "Thus wrapt in midnight vapor". His carcase is arranged in "mazie foulds", "fould above fould a surging Maze", "In Labyrinth of many a round self-rowld". He leads Eve to the Tree of Knowledge like *ignis fatuus* which,

> Hovering and blazing with delusive Light,
> Misleads th' amaz'd Night-wanderer from his way
> To Boggs and Mires, and oft through Pond or Poole,
> There swallow'd up and lost, from succour farr.

At its most significant level, the sin of Eve and Adam is not—like Satan's—aspiration after godhead, but acquiescence to the chutes of circumstance. An easy course invites; the carnal reason persuades it is the right one, though end-directing reason sees no goal; we saunter down it and for a long time may be lost and dead to limited but purposeful realities. Thus Adam finds "all my evasions vain, And reasonings, though through Mazes, lead me still But to my own conviction" (X. 829), and he rightly accuses Eve of "wandring vanitie" (X. 875; cf. 1136, 1146, etc.). It is another treatment of the *Comus* and *Samson* themes: Satan and his tempting represent the "dim darkness" of "this leavy Labyrinth" and "the blind mazes of this tangl'd Wood" that led the Lady astray (278, 181); the snares and gins of Delilah, the tangles in Naeara's hair. We may feel Milton was denying a darkness which had more value than he realised. This seems true of "Lycidas" where his inexperience rejected an experience that he would have found to be more than merely sexual. But in *Paradise Lost* the Fall is a failure of adult responsibility.

The wrongness that irks us does not lie in Milton's presentation, or the myth itself, but in the orthodox interpretation of the Fall, linking it to the Crucifixion. Through these two symbolic acts Christianity demands a *negative* affirmation of love, faith, obedience. I don't know how this paradox came to be constructed: in the Old Testament the prime symbolic act is God's creation of the world; and the earliest apostolic doctrine linked this to another positive, the Resurrection: "God that made the world and all things therein . . . hath offered faith unto all men, in that he hath raised him from the dead".[1] Because of this we

[1] Paul at Athens, *Acts*, xvii (*mg.*).

cling to the one positive act in the episode, Adam's eating of the apple, regarding it with Eve as an unarguably good affirmation of their love. In fact, like all postlapsarian actions, it is infected by its sinful ground. The love it affirms is not free, for Eve has demanded it by dilemma. Before coming to Adam she has wondered whether to "keep the odds of Knowledge in my power Without Copartner?" (820) and decided against it out of a jealousy—"*Adam* wedded to another *Eve*"—which she rationalises as devotion:

> So dear I love him, that with him all deaths
> I could endure, without him live no life. (832)

The anti-rhyming couplet points her partiality and from then on she acts a part. Her apologia to Adam is a speech for a great actress, constantly proper to its speaker in cadence, reference and implied gesture, and hollow all through. "But strange hath bin the cause, and wonderful to heare": no Elizabethan dramatist caught just that tone of schoolgirl guilt. At line 877, her speech inflated "up to Godhead", she suddenly drops her voice and nears Adam with a coaxing lie: "which for thee Chiefly I sought, without thee can despise"; but ends with a threat, "Least thou not tasting, different degree Disjoyne us". She is a cosmic snob. Once their relationship has been falsified like this it can only decay. Milton does not make much of Adam's dilemma; neither had Grotius and Vondel; for though in theory Adam stood condemned for supposing "that it was a venial transgression to cleave to the partner of his life even in a partnership of sin",[1] in practice humanity must stand or fall as one. This, rather than noble love, is Adam's argument, "Submitting to what seemd remediless", drawn by the bond of physical nature, "fondly overcome with Femal charm". We still feel uncomfortable because at the moment of the Fall Milton's domesticating upholstery will not cover the myth's frame; it fits better again on the fallen side. Eating the apple makes Adam lustful. This is unbiblical, but it completes the corruption of their relationship which is Milton's theme—"Of thir mutual guilt the Seale". It is the proper antithesis to their innocence in Book IV: Adam's advances, nocent in the sense of "knowing", are "well understood Of *Eve*". They make love to soothe

[1] Augustine, *City*, xiv. 13.

themselves, not adore each other—"The solace of thir sin". Their ungracious motives and graceless behaviour wonderfully symbolise the loss of theological grace. They are hectic before, and afterwards their language shrill—"O *Eve*, in evil hour didst thou give eare To that false Worm" (1067). The big clumsy Indian fig-leaves, unlike the frail wreath usual in paintings, blot out "that first naked Glorie", and their iconography—Samson, India, America—involves Adam and Eve in the poem's Hell; so they hellishly burn and inflame with lust (1013, 1015, 1031), and shake (1131) with the passions that moved Satan on Niphates. Like Satan, Adam is "estran'gd in look and alterd stile". His speech now is flattened[1] by the medieval theologians' *tristitia post coitum*, and querulously deprived of the courtesies of Books IV and V:

> Would thou hadst hearken'd to my words, & stai'd
> With me, as I besought thee, when that strange
> Desire of wandring this unhappie Morn,
> I know not whence possessed thee;

Eve answers shrewishly, despising him:

> What words have past thy Lips, *Adam* severe,
> Imput'st thou that to my default, or will
> Of wandering, as thou call'st it, which who knows
> But might as ill have happ'nd thou being by,

Adam recognises the perennial tragic dilemma of man and wife, parent and child, ruler and mob:

> what could I more?
> I warn'd thee, I admonish'd thee, foretold
> The danger, and the lurking Enemie
> That lay in wait; beyond this had bin force,
> And force upon free Will hath here no place.

4. *The Effects of the Fall*

"Meanwhile" is a perspective and integrative stratagem. But having fallen Adam and Eve are no longer "visible" in the

[1] Note the use of idiom in this section (as in *P.R.* and *S.A.*): "first thoughts" (IX. 213) and "second thoughts" (101), "weal or woe" (133), "Bush and Brake" (160), "Against his better knowledge" (998), "Sooner or later" (X. 613).

cosmos they were created to inhabit, and the events that occur in it now seem irrelevant to them, they irrelevant to the cosmic actors. Thus the next issue, the effect of human sin on angelic virtue, holds dramatic promise, recognised in the phrasing: "dim sadness did not spare That time Celestial visages, yet mixt with pitie, violated not thir bliss"; but that poignancy is overwhelmed by heroics—the hasty excusing manœuvres of the sentries, the atmosphere of some Bronze Age camp ("Th' Ethereal People ran"), the unmoved empty impressiveness of an archi-episcopal God.

The vast sentences and clanging syllables of heroic narrative build the bridge over Chaos. It is a magnificent descriptive achievement, "the Mole immense wraught on Over the foaming deep high Archt" itself a symbol of Milton's special power over words. It is a limited power. The episode indeed contrasts with the quiet drama of Book IX and the pure Biblical paraphrase of the Son's judgement; but it does not connect with them. Though

> now in little space
> The Confines met of Empyrean Heav'n
> And of this World, and on the left hand Hell
> With long reach interpos'd; (320)

they do not meet in the reader's mind. The relations between man and universe seem to demand epic scale; yet the scale's own enormousness obliterates the relation it is designed to make. On this hither side of the Fall wit is stronger than will—Donne watching the sun go round the earth while he lies in bed with both the Indias of spice and mine; or riding away from the dawn of Good Friday and asking,

> Could I behold those hands which span the Poles
> And turn all spheares at once, peirc'd with those holes?

When Satan returns to Hell, excitement is wrought up by his finding it withdrawn and desolate, "As when the *Tartar* from his *Russian* Foe By *Astracan* over the Snowie Plaines retires". Following this, and ringing back to the end of Book I, the metamorphosis of the devils into snakes is thrilling. To be hissed off his own stage is a just climax to the villainous melodramatics that have typified Satan's behaviour since Book IV. But Waldock's recognition of the comic cartoon technique here is helpful.

Human being is polarised between obedience and rebellion, tenderness and aggression. Cartoons, like Orwell's seaside post-cards, are a safety-valve for the naughty polarities usually repressed—safe because openly childish, and in the end the naughtiness is engaged punitively on the side of good (the marauding wolf or cat metamorphosed by his own engines of torture). But we only need this safety-valve in art if in our lives there is a dissatisfying slackness or separation between the poles. The most therapeutic art adjusts an ideal tension between them. Cartoons stretch us for a few minutes but leave us slack, sad, raw. So in *Paradise Lost* this transfer to the pole of torture, shocking, temporary, and for only this one set of characters, Satan in particular, is structurally fit, but only because the poem needs relief from the repression of a unipolar God. We respond indeed, but with confusion. Satan's fate being comic we cannot sympathise with him, yet because he has shared our humanity we feel his fate unfair and want to sympathise. What we do through Milton to Satan is really what, crushed by the Fall, we should like to do to God.

The dispute between Christianity and tragedy opens here. Great English tragedy is ironically dipolar: god and devil die together into apprehended manhood, and it will happen again, again. Christian irony, as often in Greek tragedy, and Hinduism, is more of a practical joke. Whereas in Shakespeare the motive of revenge turns inward to self-annihilation and renewal, here it produces answering vengeance from outside itself, finally. The God-admitted (615-40) irony of Sin and Death coming as scavengers to an earth they think is their inheritance is not really irony but outward satire.[1] It indulges an autetic justice inferior as poetry because ugly and pitiless, and dangerous as myth because it may sanction correspondingly gross action in life. The vocabulary of God's speech—"draff, filth, yawning, hurl'd, obstruct"—and the disgusting organic imagery of the Sin and Death episode belong to Milton's pamphlets; the "great Python" which Satan becomes personifies prelaty in *The Reason of Church Government* (ii. 505).

[1] The development of religious damnation into secular satire is made plain by Marvell in "Tom May's Death": "'Tis just what Torments Poets ere did feign, Thou first Historically shouldst sustain" (95). The poem is a minor *MacFlecknoe*, *c.* 1661.

The change of the universe to Hellish discord is only cursorily related to Paradise. We re-enter the human situation gradually. Descriptive hints suggest Gethsemane[1] and Satan on the lake of fire: "with black Air Accompanied, with damps and dreadful gloom. . . . On the Ground Outstretcht he lay, on the cold ground" (847). The content of Adam's lament has been analysed by Svendsen[2]: it is a paraphrase of *II Esdras*, vii. 46-56, locked into *Paradise Lost* by echoes of Satan. Adam's first words, "O miserable of happie! is this the end Of this new glorious World" recall Satan's *me miserum*! when he enters Paradise (IV. 73; cf. also X. 842), and his apostrophe to Hell, "Is this the Region, this the Soil, the Clime" (I. 242). Adam uses Satan's image of recoil: "all from mee Shall with a fierce reflux on mee redound" (738; cf. 814). Yet mingled with these Satanic cries, Adam quotes God:

> God made thee of choice his own, and of his own
> To serve him, thy reward was of his grace,
> Thy punishment then justly is at his Will.

The struggle culminates in an echo of the Son's offer of redemption:

> On mee, mee onely, as the sourse and spring
> Of all corruption, all the blame lights due;
> So might the wrauth.

Yet it is difficult to feel, even when Adam cries "O Conscience, into what Abyss of Fears And horrors hast thou driv'n me", that this is a Hell as real as the poem's actual physical or mental Hell; or that the echoing of God is more than a rhetorical device, a technical manifestation of theological grace. Put beside the "great perturbation in nature" that Lady Macbeth stages, or Ophelia, or Lear, it is weakly abstract and external. It is not simply that the symbolism lacks vigour (e.g. the image of recoil is not in literature peculiar to Satan but general for the villains of Jacobean drama) but chiefly that the Hell Adam is in, and the Heaven he is moving towards, have no sufficiently

[1] Hawkins says, "I speake not of *Eden*, the Earthlie Paradice, nor of the Garden of Gethsemany" (*Parth. Sac.*, p. 11). G. Fletcher also equates them in *Christs Triumph after Death*, 14.

[2] *College English*, X (1949), 366-70.

physical quality for the connection to bear on. When Oedipus appears blinded the Chorus ask, as Adam does and as we may ask of him, why he is not already dead? But Oedipus has suffered the death of his crime: he is blind. The knowledge that Oedipus and the Chorus share that the tragic agony must reside "in the flesh and in the soul's dark memory"—"It must be so; such suffering must needs be borne Twice; once in the body and once in the soul"[1]— is satisfied. And when Oedipus takes himself back to the local moment of hell at which the tragedy began he is able, because of the revelation given now by catastrophe, to make clear the symbolic significance of

> That silent crossroad in the forest clearing—
> That copse beside the place where three roads met,
> Whose soil I watered with my father's blood,
> My blood—

The universal tragedy is given a local habitation. Adam's is not: he has merely been reduced in stature and made unhappy. He appears as the representative of men who suffer like this rather than as a man actually suffering—actor instead of character. This would matter less if, as in a mystery play (such as the first act of Bale's *God's Promises*, which is about *felix culpa*) or a Racinian tragedy, it were supported by the physical presence of actors on a stage. There is dramatic debris,[2] but no drama: just misery's sluggish whirlpool—Why was I born? Why don't I die?—stirred for 125 lines. The resolution, modelling the whole poem's theodicy, does not come by insight but submission: "Him after all Disputes *Forc't* I absolve".

Drama revives with Eve. Her first speech in reply to Adam has been analysed by Rajan. Her Adam-ward attitude is expressed in cadences that belong to her at this particular moment:

> Forsake me not thus, *Adam*, witness Heav'n
> What love sincere, and reverence in my heart
> I bear thee . . .

[1] Trans. F. Watling, Penguin *Theban Plays* (1947), 1320 ff.

[2] Conscience, Truth and Justice, occurring in this speech, were to be characters on the stage at this point in "Adam Unparadis'd". Lines 845-62 repeat what Adam has already said.

> bereave me not,
> Whereon I live, thy gentle looks, thy aid,
> Thy counsel in this uttermost distress,
> My onely strength and stay: forlorn of thee,
> Whither shall I betake me, where subsist?

> both have sin'd, but thou
> Against God onely, I against God and thee,

Her last sentence quotes the psalm where David repents of his murderous seduction of Bath-sheba.[1] It brings the focus back to domestic and historical, where alone sin can be committed and salvation achieved. Her penitence before Adam germinates his before God, and so atones for her tempting of him.

In their penitence they become plain wife and husband. No longer nagging, they still avoid the courteous antonomasias of Paradise. Instead of evensong they offer a confession in which for a few lines Adam speaks with the redeeming cadences of Eve:

> and there confess
> Humbly our faults, and pardon beg, with tears
> Watering the ground, and with our sighs the Air
> Frequenting, sent from hearts contrite, in sign
> Of sorrow unfeign'd, and humiliation meek.

Here are the pity and the beauty that, interrupted by a thousand lines of historical doctrine and dogma, revive again at the end of the poem changed then into something more terrible and brave. It is so poignant that Miss Sitwell can hear in the phrases the authentic sound of falling tears.[2] This is the danger of tears, as of all poignancy in art, and sacramentalism, that we do not respond to them quite as we respond to the emotion they signify.

The religious context, and especially the cosmic view of it that Milton takes, make it difficult to avoid this confusion. Adam and Eve are contrite; but by the time their contrition has been stated by Adam, described chorically by Milton, and received by the Son as incense in the infinitely distant Heaven of the next book, the original dramatic emotion has drained away

[1] *Psalm* li. 4. The next verse, "Behold, I was shapen in iniquity; and in sin did my mother conceive me", was a prime authority for the doctrine of original sin—another example of the extravagant metaphor of oriental lyric being hardened into dogma.

[2] *Pleasures of Poetry* (1st ser. 1930), p. 12.

from the words on the page.[1] Another difficulty is that contrition is properly felt only by one who has wounded another. But God is invulnerable, and Adam and Eve as yet know nothing of the crucifixion, so that the essential motive of contrition in Christianity—

> O weep, child, weep, O weep away the stain,
> Lost innocence who wished your lover dead[2],

—is lacking, though it applies at the human level to both of them. It comes to this, that all through *Paradise Lost* existential motifs are disintegrated by stretching out through the time and space of cosmic epic. This is most disastrous in Book X because the Fall is not really a cosmic myth. The patterns remain but we have to reconstruct them again on a smaller scale if they are to be of any practical value.

Thus we feel even more uncomfortable when the dramatic incident of Adam and Eve's Fall, sufficiently cut off from the earlier heroic context and re-established now at the end of Book X, becomes in Book XI, without invocation to another muse, the node of a theological discourse and then of a history of the world. This difficulty does not inhere in the fable so much as in its expansion. Paul used Adam as a doctrinal symbol; Milton makes him a living being and then treats him as a hostage to dogma. The style lapses accordingly. Adam and Eve now stand to pray, not as it might have been like Abraham who "stood before the Lord" but like Deucalion and Pyrrha after Ovid's flood. Then,

> To Heav'n thir prayers
> Flew up, nor missd the way, by envious windes
> Blow'n vagabond or frustrate: in they passd
> Dimentionless through Heav'nly dores; then clad
> With incense, where the Golden Altar fum'd,
> By thir great Intercessor, came in sight
> Before the Fathers Throne: Them the glad Son
> Presenting, thus to intercede began. (XI. 14)

[1] Milton's intention, of course, is quite contrary: he is trying to present an archetypal sincerity. But apart from the dramatic looseness, fashions in sentiment have changed. Contrition is dry: "A pain flamed in her womb, for him. 'I didn't think I should hurt you,' she said, laying her hand very lightly, tentatively, on his arm" (*The Rainbow*). Tears are regarded suspiciously, especially between husband and wife: see the confession of adultery at the beginning of Mary McCarthy's *The Company She Keeps* (1957).

[2] Auden, "Song for St Cecilia's Day", *Collected Shorter Poems* 1930-1944 (1950): a classico-theological ode, combining Botticelli and Kierkegaard.

The great antistrophe of their penitence has gone quaint. The reminders of the Limbo of Fools and the dwindling of the devils at the end of Book I are extraordinarily inappropriate, especially when compared with the poetic classic of this situation, "The Collar", where Herbert of the 17th Century suddenly but quite naturally becomes Samuel of the Old Testament, subsuming all the meaning of Aaron's long tradition into the present moment without drawing any further away from God. Milton's ecclesiastical opinions are intruding. He had complained that "Contrition, humiliation, confession, the very sighs of a repentant spirit" were "sold by the penny" in the churches (*R.C.G.* ii. 500); now he wants to assert the direct communication of Protestants with their one High Priest. But even the Bible-learned Puritan reader must be disappointed: where the reference might have been to those cryings-out of the psalmist to God in his desolation, it is—if anything—to the Petrine doctrine of marital obedience (*I Peter*, iii. 7, etc.).

The decay of the poetry prevents us claiming it as the poem's "crisis".[1] If there is a moment about which the poem balances, it may be the end of Book VIII. But here we experience no crisis, only a check in the poem's emotional movement: the last hundred lines of Book XII slide down from the end of Book X; in between, Books XI and XII try to open out the domestic Fall and personal reconciliation into a dimension where they lose their force.

[1] See Tillyard, "The Crisis of *P.L.*" in his *Studies*.

II

EXILE

1. *Transition*

IN Heaven, where time is not, the regeneration of Adam and Eve, the Incarnation, the eschata, could have been brought lyrically home in a way the punctualities of narrative must fail to do; and all the havoc of Books IX and X could have been purged with poetic grace. But Milton relies timidly on Biblical metaphor and repetitious dogma. The Son presents Adam and Eve's prayer as "firstfruits", swelling the primitive image into a 15-line conceit (XI. 22-36) to make it connect with the trees of Paradise. There is logical discomfiture: to the Son, the Father declares that man is expelled from Paradise by nature: "Those pure immortal Elements that know No gross, no unharmonious mixture foule, Eject him tainted now" (50); but to the Angels he quotes *Genesis*: "Least therefore his now bolder hand Reach also of the Tree of Life . . . " (93), though "dream at least to live for ever" is Milton's interjection. As Willey points out,[1] Milton has made both trees fallacious. He thus edges toward the potential value of the myth in New Testament terms, that the result of eating either fruit depends on motive: "He who finds his life will lose it" (*Mat.* x. 39); but he doesn't get there, and leaves us adrift between the two reasons for expulsion. The first is the more convincing dramatically for it accords with a standard image in the poem, as admitted by Belial:

> our great Enemy
> All incorruptible would on his Throne
> Sit unpolluted, and th' Ethereal mould
> Incapable of stain would soon expel
> Her mischief, and purge off the baser fire
> (II. 137)

But it does not accord with our impression of the physical Paradise that Adam and Eve inhabit. There was no suggestion

[1] *17th-century Background*, p. 259.

that either man or his food were spiritual (in Milton's sense) before the Fall; indeed, Raphael's dissertation on spirits arises from his power to digest food which if not yet "mortal" is certainly not yet spiritual. The solid ideality of Paradise, so satisfying in Book IV, is proving inadequate as the poem passes into actuality. The bliss of Adam and Eve before the Fall was too external. Eve makes the same mistake. She wants to go on living in Paradise "though in fall'n state, content" (180), as though Paradise were simply an environment. She is anxious about her garden: "O flours, That never will in other Climate grow. . . . Who now shall reare ye to the Sun"? Yet she admits the incongruous peculiarity of Paradise: "how shall we breath in other Aire Less pure, accustomd to immortal Fruits?" The failure to identify the spiritual is Milton's as well as Eve's. The physical and spiritual worlds are alien to them now but he fumbles both. The preying eagle and lion that they see in Paradise are clumsy auguries; the eagle alludes absurdly to the founding of Rome. When Michael descends, the references to Janus (past and future), Hermes (messenger of the gods powerful to quell the monstrous dog of hades), Jacob (who saw a field of angels in Mahanaim) and Elijah (rescued by a host of angels from dastardly assassination) all have point, but there is no homogeneity. The atmosphere is Homeric. Michael appears like Raphael's "St Michael" in the Louvre, or one of his St George's:

> Over his lucid Arms
> A militarie Vest of purple flowd
> Livelier then *Melibaean*, or the graine
> Of *Sarra*, worn by Kings and Heroes old
> In time of Truce; *Iris* had dipt the wooff;

Michael is not alien because spiritual, but as plenipotentiary. So again when Milton assembles the apparatus for a vision (a hill of contemplation like Spenser's and Bunyan's, homeopathic eye-bright, rue the herb of grace) what Adam sees is not a vision, but a demonstration of Milton's panoramic omnicompetence—"*Cambalu*, Seat of *Cathaian Can* . . ."—proof of his ability to have written all the other epics listed in the Cambridge Manuscript if he had wanted to.

2. *Hell on Earth*

We must distinguish though between the "vision" of Old Testament legend up to the Tower of Babel at the beginning of Book XII and the subsequent relation by Michael of the history of Israel and the Church. The latter fails; the former, though disappointing as a vision, has its own merits. It is far and away the most competent handling of the material with which world-histories traditionally began and hexemeral epics ended.[1]

Though the spiritual is fumbled, the fallen is realised. The medium is drab. Epic similes fall away. The few tropes are dry, abstract and harsh as in Jacobean drama: "compassion quell'd His best of Man" (XI. 496); "So maist thou live, till like ripe Fruit thou drop Into thy Mothers lap" (XI. 535). The ikons are sturdy, everyday:

> But prayer against his absolute Decree
> No more availes then breath against the winde,
> Blown stifling back on him that breaths it forth:
> (XI. 311)

Pharaoh's heart is "still as ice More hard'nd after thaw" (XII. 193). It is the medium of *Paradise Regained*, where the storm is "harmless, if not wholsom, as a sneeze" (IV. 458). The new style undulates. Adam sees a landscape, and

> thither anon
> A sweatie Reaper from his Tillage brought
> First Fruits, the green Eare, and the yellow Sheaf,
> Uncull'd, as came to hand; (XI. 433)

The verse is relaxed, not tightened yet by anxiety to be particular; the reaper, his work and its fruits are distant, but fully realised. Milton is writing closer to his own "swink't hedger" than the carefully patronised ploughmen of 18th-century verse. But when Abel sacrifices a sheep the language climbs back onto Homeric stilts:

> His Offring soon propitious Fire from Heav'n
> Consum'd with nimble glance, and grateful steame;

[1] Cf. the dream that Cowley gives David as "A *Prophesie* of all the succession of his Race till *Christs* time, with their most remarkable actions" (*Dav.* ii, Argument; see 460-781); and the Sistine Chapel fresco, which ends with the Flood as it begins with Creation.

It is too economical for its directive wit (the pun on "Consum'd", the contrast between swift downward fire and slow upward incense-smoke) to work; the failure is similar to that in so much Augustan writing, where the couplets make you read too rapidly to absorb what they are saying. Then Cain, furious,

> Smote him into the Midriff with a stone
> That beat out life; he fell, and deadly pale
> Groand out his Soul with gushing bloud effus'd.

The first two lines are wonderfully efficient and tonally correct; the last is too literary, with its noisy alliteration and assonance, falling rhythms, reference to Hebrew psychology in which the soul resided in the blood.[1] Of course it is less fluent than Bolingbroke's line about Abel in *Richard II*—"Sluic'd out his innocent soul through streams of blood" (I. i. 103)—for generic reasons; but the lack of fluency, the damming of "Smote him into the Midriff" naturalism with such a formalised conclusion, jerks back the reader's head. It is only one of many occasions, large and small in scale, in which Milton's verse behaves like Plato's charioteer managing the passionate horse.

But the meaner decorum prevails, and gives precision:

> So many grateful Altars I would reare
> Of grassie Terfe, and Pile up every Stone
> Of lustre from the brook,
>
> (XI. 323)

"Stone of lustre" is acutely observed. Hebrew history makes many passages pastoral, and it is real Old Testament pastoral—"A herd of Beeves" (xi. 647).

The efficiency of the writing here (and in much of *Paradise Regained*)—its combining vividness with cool objective reflection in historical perspective—was new to English at the time, and was not surpassed in verse perhaps until *Four Quartets*: beside it, Augustan verse is too mannered, rapid, versy, and the varieties of 19th-century reflective blank verse, however much they owe to Milton, much more introspective, and flaccid. It could have become, but didn't, a model of how in a scientific world to respond realistically to the actual without losing the apperceptive control of poetic wit.

[1] Cf. Hooker, referring to Cain, "effusion of blood" (*Ecc. Pol.* I. x. 3). The Vulgate simply has "interfecit eam".

Even the description of potentially "sublime" material is realistic. At the Flood, curt, mundane words put us in the place of a drowning man—"Ceeling . . . Rain . . . beaked prow . . . tilting . . . whelp'd And stabl'd . . . one small bottom". When Paradise is destroyed the rhythm is grand:

> then shall this Mount
> Of Paradise by might of Waves be moovd
> Out of his place, pushd by the horned floud,
> With all his verdure spoil'd, and Trees adrift
> Down the great River to the op'ning Gulf,
> And there take root an Iland salt and bare,
> The haunt of Seales and Orcs, and Sea-mews clang.

But the words are nearly all monosyllabic; "Verdure" alone represents the classical, epic splendour of Paradise as it was once. The "Iland salt and bare", essence of the fallen world, also has the geographical realism of the original Paradise. Travellers found huge logs floating down the Euphrates,[1] and often described islands of whales ("orcs") and seals. The only relief of this naturalism is the end of the Flood, when

> the Clouds were fled,
> Drivn by a keen North-winde, that blowing drie
> Wrinkl'd the face of Deluge, as decai'd;
> And the cleer Sun on his wide watrie Glass
> Gaz'd hot, and of the fresh Wave largely drew,
> As after thirst, which made thir flowing shrink
> From standing lake to tripping ebbe, that stole
> With soft foot towards the deep, who now had stopt
> His Sluces, as the Heav'n his windows shut.

The return to Elizabethan conceits and Paradisal animism presents the Flood's abatement as a new start, almost a second Creation; Michael pauses there, "Betwixt the world destroy'd

[1] Arnold used this phenomenon, as reported by travellers *c.* 1800, for "Sohrab and Rustum": see my essay on "Milton and Arnold", *EC*, VI (1956), for a discussion of their different kinds of realism. Leo Africanus wrote about a whole string of islands like this off the coast of Africa, such as "Mazua in forme like to an halfe moone" (*Geog. Hist.* p. 86), "The island of salt, being destitute of all other liuing things, saue onely wild gotes" (p. 98), and "the isle of Tristan d'Acunna . . . full of birds, and especially of sea-crowes or cormorants" (p. 92). In the Persian Gulf itself Ormus stood on an island "barren of all necessaries except salt wherewith their very rocks are covered" (Heylyn, *Cosmog.* iii. 142-3).

and world restor'd" (XII. 3)—Paradise nearly regained. In fact things still go from bad to worse and the style falls back into the even greyer tones of Book XII.

This one intrusion of Paradise into the fallen world makes more noticeable the pervasive presence of Hell before and soon after the Flood. The Flood itself comes like Sin and Death, "with black wings Wide hovering" (XI. 734). It is a bursting in of Chaos—"Sea cover'd Sea, Sea without shoar". Man's fallen activities ape the devils': Tubal Cain, with his "liquid Ore . . . dreind Into fit moulds" (XI. 570) recalls the building of Pandemonium. Human warfare is devilish:

> Part wield thir Arms, part courb the foaming Steed,
> Single or in Array of Battel rang'd
>
> (XI. 639)

> Part curb thir fierie Steeds . . .
> or fronted Brigads form.
>
> (II. 531)

After the war, the politicians imitate the devils in council. The Tower of Babel, ikon for Satan and Pandemonium, becomes the actuality of Book XII; its bricks are made of the bitumen that "Boiles out from under ground" at one of the traditional mouths of Hell (XII. 42). The imagery of Hell turns into the reality of "A darksom Cloud of Locusts" (XII. 185), the "potent Rod" of Moses, "Palpable darkness". Antagonism to God brings down on Pharaoh the climate of Hell, "Thunder mixt with Haile, Haile mixt with fire". "The tossing of these fiery waves" (I. 184) and "everlasting groans" of Hell (II. 184) are re-created on Earth in the lazar-house, that hospital endowed by the ruined millionaire where "Dire was the tossing, deep the groans" (XI. 489). The idolatrous orgies of lust and art that figured in Book I are repeated in the "Soft amorous Ditties" of the daughters of men (XI. 584) and in the palatial luxury, the music and the technological civilisation that the Flood overwhelms.

These linkages do much to focus ethic in aesthetic. The poem's image of Hell is revealed as the actuality of the fallen world. A steady religious gaze lights on human achievement. The technology of Tubal and the art of Jubal Cain are magnificent but unsanctified:

> studious they appere
> Of Arts that polish Life, Inventers rare,
> Unmindful of thir Maker, though his Spirit
> Taught them, but they his gifts acknowledg'd none.

Their selfishness destroys community,[1] as do the amours of the sons of God with the daughters of men. The antediluvian civilisation ruins itself by civil dissension which invites nomadic aggression. Milton's analysis of the situation is masterly, and his sketch of the post-war period universal:

> All now was turn'd to jollitie and game,
> To luxurie and riot, feast and dance,
> Marrying or prostituting, as befell,
> Rape or Adulterie, where passing faire
> Allurd them; thence from Cups to civil Broiles.

Failing as seer, Milton succeeds as prophet—and intended to, for the sea-monsters whelping in the palace are from *Lamentations* (iv. 3) as well as Ovid; the Flood as Hell is from *Isaiah* xiii; the whole process of idolatry, adultery and civil war from the *Wisdom of Solomon* xiv.

The precepts that Michael and Adam draw from all this seem naïve: "now I see Peace to corrupt no less then Warr to waste" (XI. 779), for example. Others we might contradict: "The rule of not too much" (XI. 531) with Blake's "The road of excess leads to the palace of wisdom". In both cases we can only read historically. At the Renaissance, as in childhood, ethics consisted of general precepts and concepts, directed towards preserving public order. We really are more sophisticated; we have lived through the 18th and 19th Centuries and —by about 1920 anyway—had reached a point where the public and private censorship of behaviour both had become tyrannical; so we look to ethics for positive commands to self-fulfilment. If the kind of revolution in ecclesiastical, civil and

[1] Cf. Macmurray's chapter on "Art and the Future" in his *Reason and Emotion* (1935); and Brunner, *The Divine Imperative: A Study in Christian Ethics* (trans. O. Wyon, 1937), pp. 493-4, and p. 500: "When man forgets that even he, in spite of his freedom through knowledge, is himself a creature, then he misunderstands his connexion with the rest of the creation, above all his essential connexion with his fellow-man. He forgets that the world which surrounds him, and especially his fellow-men, cannot be known as they really are by an attitude of objective detachment, but only by recognising the fact that all share in the life of creation."

domestic liberties that Milton fought for had then been achieved he would not have given archangelic authority to Aristotle and we would not be so exasperated by the sermonising. Michael is in fact preaching a 17th-century sermon of the plain Puritan kind recommended in William Perkins's *Art of Prophesying*.[1] He takes a text, explains it, derives "close and natural" doctrine from it, and applies the doctrine "to the life and manners of men in a simple and plaine speech". "Be sure they will" he says at XII. 485, and:

> But still I see the tenor of Mans woe
> Holds on the same, from Woman to begin.
>   From Mans effeminate slackness it begins,
> Said th' Angel, who should better hold his place
> By wisdome, and superiour gifts receav'd.
> But now prepare thee for another Scene.
>
> (XI. 628)

Chappel, Milton's tutor at Christ's, had recommended the same kind of sermon in his *Methodus Conconiandi* (1648), translated in 1656 as *The Preacher, or the Art and Method of Preaching*. The title relates the Puritan sermon, and Milton's work here, to *Ecclesiastes* and Hebrew "wisdom" literature generally—ethical, not evangelistic, based on the dictum, "The fear of the Lord is the beginning of wisdom", and the mood of *vanitas vanitatum omnia vanitas*:

> There is an evil among all things that are done under the sun, that there is one event unto all: yea, also, the heart of the sons of men is full of evil and madness is in their heart while they live, and after that they go to the dead.
>
> (*Ecc.* ix. 3)

Chappel recognised two directions in which doctrine might be applied: to the mind, to instruct or refute it; and to the heart, with reference to the present (reprehension or consolation) and to the future (exhortation to good, dissuasion from evil). Michael does all this for Adam, but he does not move the reader's heart. We may object to this as poetical failure, but the avoidance of excitement was deliberate. This kind of Puritan sermon operated at a much higher level than the modern evangelistic harangue, and left free the will to make its own decision.

[1] See Mitchell, *English Pulpit Oratory*, pp. 99 ff.

Baxter and Cotton explicitly rejected Metaphysical wit, with all its poetic associations, as speculative and thin. Cotton, asked to preach before the University at Great St Mary's, decided "That it was his Duty to preach with such a Plainness, as became the Oracles of God, which are intended for the Conduct of Men in the *Paths of Life*, and not for *Theatrical* Ostentations and Entertainments, and the Lord needed not any *Sin* of ours to maintain his own Glory". This is why Milton's "vision" is disappointing. He treats even mythical history as data for a prejudicial ethic, so that the inherent signficance of the stories is obscured. It is here, as Cassirer notes, that the ideal of Puritan religion and empirical philosophy ran together: "In both cases knowledge was looked upon as the organ of the will and defined as such. It was less for the sake of quiet contemplation than for the attainment of material ends . . . even though God is to be sought in absolute sublimity, above everything worldly; yet it is only in this world that man can truly serve God".[1] It was not of course an exclusively Puritan approach: Lancelot Andrewes preached on *Genesis* with the same intention. The question is whether it has any place in poetry. Hobbes said, epic : history :: fancy : judgement. This confines judgement to certain genres, such as Pope's imitations of Horace, Johnson's of Juvenal; yet we feel morals strike home more directly through the fancy of *The Rape of the Lock*. We regard Aeschylus' expansion into contemporaneity of the Atreides legend and Shakespeare's of the Leir chronicle as more deeply instructive than any plain "lessons from history". Coleridge made the point:

> What shall we say to his [*sc.* Shakespeare's] Moral conceptions? Not made up of miserable clap-traps, and the tag-ends of mawkish Novels and endless sermonizing;—but furnishing lessons of profound meditation to frail and fallible Human Nature.[2]

Shakespeare's characters of course sermonise the prevailing moral sentiments of his time. When we speak of Shakespeare's moral effect we mean our vicarious experience through the play as a whole of how men behave; we recognise our sins and omissions in them. We also mean the communal tonic of partici-

[1] Cassirer, *Platonic Renaissance in England* (trans. J. Pettegrove, 1953), pp. 68-9.

[2] *Treatise on Method* (ed. Snyder, 1934), p. 33.

pating in complicated movements and miracles of verbal expression—we experience a vicarious confidence in human genius, allied, in the case of tragedy, to pride in man's power to suffer. The play does not instruct us to behave well but encourages us to, by revealing the potentials of virtue and vice, removing the anxious ground of sin for a while, and injecting us with confidence. Our will is made more powerful not by our being shown where our duty lies, but by our self-regarding sentiment being made more capacious to absorb what we already know to be our duty. Coleridge commended Milton's Books XI and XII, but they don't do this: the lack of dramatic immediacy (Adam himself not aloof from the action) prevents the introjection of his responses into ours. The complaint is historical, though. It rests on the post-Romantic notion of poetry as a specially emotive form of communication. The energies we put into literary and cultural criticism, the higher broadcasting and journalism, had fewer media in the 17th Century, and none of them was yet specialised. When tragedy lost its Shakespearean catholicity even fewer media were left. The dilution of drama coincided with the specialisation of verse satire, essay, novel, sermon. If Milton had been able to write "Adam Unparadis'd" as a drama the "mask of all the evils of this life & world" planned for the last act might have been more stimulating but it would have been less trenchant than the epic's survey. As it is, the "vision" belongs to *Paradise Lost*; the sermons cannot belong in any poem for us, because for us "The tygers of wrath are wiser than the horses of instruction"; but they could belong in the poetry of a less expert age. Perhaps for some of Milton's earlier readers they were useful in a way that we, whose cultural and moral education is provided in so many other more efficient ways, cannot appreciate.

3. *Providence*

In his commentary on *Genesis*, Calvin had said:

> though Moses begins, in this Book, with the Creation of the World, he nevertheless does not confine us to this subject. For these things ought to be connected together, that the world was founded by God, and that man . . . fell by his own fault . . . but he soon adds the history of his restoration, where Christ shines forth with the

> benefit of redemption. From this point he not only relates continuously the singular Providence of God in governing and preserving the Church, but also commends us to the true worship of God; teaches wherein the salvation of man is placed, and exhorts us, from the example of the Fathers [*sc.* the Patriarchs], to constancy in enduring the cross.[1]

All constructs of this kind are attempts to transcend history. To establish the past in a rational pattern significant to me and my interests now, myth is made dogma. To direct the future to an end in which I will participate among the sheep and my enemies be destroyed with the goats, church history is run into eschatology. These are symptoms of *Angst* and manifestations of *ὕβρις*, but art can redeem them—loosen the pretensions to intellectual coherence, and make the motives sympathetic by offering beautifully a symbol of what they aim at. Yeats, in despite of his own attempts to make the inchoate cohere, could do it by the transmutation of a myth and the poetic conjunction of finite with eternal, as in "Leda" and "The Second Coming". It is not the gyres that matter but the concatenation of "A shudder in the loins" with Agamemnon, of "slouches" with Bethlehem. To do it well the narrative form, to which intellectual pretensions most obviously adhere, must generally be abandoned, and the tone be innocent; otherwise the claim to authority will condemn itself as merely human, unable to support the cosmic construct: as Hooker's orthodoxy does, and Calvin's Biblicism, Hobbes's intellection.

Milton, trying in Book XII to make the connection between Fall and redemption, fails in the same way and his failure is the more objectionable because it occurs in art. He strives to assert by dogma truths which need subtler substantiation, and by epic mechanics to kindle hopes which only lyricism will ignite. Book XI was just able to accommodate the myths of *Genesis*: in Book XII the more factual history is so intractable anyway—as the shift from vision to narration admits—that the verse becomes arthritic. The history of Israel from Ur to Ai is contained in a single paragraph of 190 lines cramping the splendid stories of the patriarchs into copybook sentences void of meaning: "*Egypt*, divided by the River *Nile*" (157) is one of the worst lines of verse in English and demeans every previous reference

[1] *Commentaries on Genesis*, pp. 64-5.

in the poem to Pharaoh, the Nile, the Red Sea, Moses. He writes merely as he wrote in the *History of Britain*: "Fifteen years she governs in behalf of her son; then resigning to him at age, retires to her father's dominion" (v. 174)—Abraham falls together with the fables of Brutus. The whole thing had been done better by Du Bartas: more cheerfully, with consideration for his audience; unable to comprehend all, he communicated something.

The source is the crushed formal histories of Israel in the Apocrypha.[1] Written at a period of intense anxiety, these tended to project myths of origin (the Watchers cast into hell, etc.) into eschatology (future damnation of devils, sinners and enemies). It was Paul who first sketched the standard series of events for a new doctrinal purpose: the call of Abraham (election); subsequent Israelite history as a model for the relation between law and gospel; the lineage of David's house leading to the Messiah's ascent of "The Throne hereditarie" (XII. 370), with a warning that this is not a physical conquest of Satan but fulfilment of the law by atonement and imputed righteousness; the promise in incarnation, crucifixion and resurrection of a better world, "far happier place Then this of *Eden*, and far happier dayes" (464), with the final destruction of evil. Now as Arnold says,

> perfectly to seize another man's meaning, as it stood in his own mind, is not easy; especially when the man is separated from us by such differences of race, training, time, and circumstances as St Paul . . . terms which St Paul employs, in trying to follow with his analysis of such profound power and originality some of the most delicate, intricate, obscure, and contradictory workings and states of the human spirit, are detached and employed by Puritanism, not in the connected and fluid way in which St Paul employs them, and for which alone words are really meant, but in an isolated, fixed, mechanical way, as if they were talismans. . . .[2]

Of course it is not simply a Puritan abuse. The early Fathers, as much as later Protestant theologians, deformed the historicity of Christianity into an historical myth. The *City of God* standard-

[1] Cf. *Judith*, v. 5-21, with Milton's history of Abraham.
[2] *Culture and Anarchy*, chap. V.

ised the myth and, though in the Middle Ages the actual existence of an historic catholic Church kept the error in check (the mystery-plays humanised the cycle), Augustine's synthesis became the basis for Calvin's and Milton's. For the Reformation, needing to give itself a place in history, thought in more obtrusively historical terms than ever before of the individual Christian existing at a point somewhere between Eden (or Ur) and the Last Judgement. This horizontal conception devalues myth at one end and eschatology at the other; and reduces its religion to an ethic not superior to the classical ethic it had to compete with. The claim of Christianity as an historical religion to continuing apprehension of the point of intersection of the timeless with time, is obscured by the megalomaniac effort to comprehend all time *sub specie aeternitatis*, and to know virtue.[1]

The prevailing ethic of Book XII is stoic. Michael recommends retreat from outward Hell into an inner condition which is not so much the kingdom of heaven within you, or the promised paradise, as indifference. His description of the incarnation is feeble as could be; and there is no answering experience of incarnation in Adam. Promised his happier Eden, Adam rejoices at *felix culpa* but quickly asks what will happen to the just in an unjust world. Michael mentions the Comforter, expatiates on the corruption of the Church (omitting the Reformation[2]) and ends with another general conflagration and another new world. Adam asserts his satisfaction and is recommended to a

[1] The Cambridge Platonists underplayed the gospel (see Willey, *17th-century Background*, p. 152) and Neo-Platonists generally did not regard the descent into the world as a fall for the soul. But their mysticism was a private substitute for a public gospel.

[2] Even at the time of *Areo.* (ii. 90) Milton had realised that so long as the Kingdom of Heaven is not actually at hand reform of institutions has only limited effect and cannot be salvific. But here he has reached Hooker's position (*Ecc. Pol.* pref. iii. 7): "The next thing hereunto is, to impute all faults and corruptions, wherewith the world aboundeth, unto the kind of ecclesiastical government established . . . whereas in truth unto the form even of Jewish government which the Lord himself (they all confess) did establish, with like shew of reason they might impute those faults which the prophets condemn in the governors of that commonwealth, as to the English kind of regiment ecclesiastical (whereof also God himself though in another sort is author,) the stains and blemishes found in our state; which springing from the root of human frailty and corruption, not only are, but have been always more or less, yea, and (for anything we know to the contrary) will be till the world's end complained of, what form of government soever take place."

final list of virtues taken from *II Peter*, i. 5-7 (on which Andrewes had also delivered a course of sermons). The Petrine epistles are dangerously concerned with ethics, conscience, temptation, lust and the corruptions of the world, the flesh and the devil: but they are saved by occasional flashes of faith and joy which make Adam and Michael seem all the drearier for the reference: "For we have not followed cunningly devised fables, when we made known unto you the power and coming of our Lord Jesus Christ, but were eyewitnesses of his majesty" (*II Pet.* i. 16). This is just what Michael and Adam are not.

Some readers take *felix culpa* to be the mainspring of *Paradise Lost*. But as Lovejoy admits,[1] Milton treats it less sharply and less joyfully than Du Bartas. Yet *felix culpa* was a liturgical expression of joy, appropriate as a carol for the night before Christ's resurrection:

> O certe necessarium Adae peccatum, quod Christi morte deletum est! O felix culpa, quae talem ac tantem meruit habere redemptorem!

It is by nature lyrical rather than doctrinal:

> Adam lay I-bowndyn, bowndyn in a bond,
> fowre þousand wynter þowt he not to long;
> And al was for an appil, an appil þat he tok,
> As clerkis fyndyn wretyn in here book.
>
> Ne hadde þe appil take ben, þe appil taken ben,
> ne hadde neuer our lady a ben heuene qwen;
> Blyssid be þe tyme þat appil take was,
> þer-fore we mown syngyn, "deo gracias!"

Adam's version shows what happens when this becomes an epic theme in the 17th Century:

> O goodness infinite, goodness immense!
> That all this good of evil shall produce,
> And evil turn to good; more wonderful
> Then that which by creation first brought forth
> Light out of darkness! full of doubt I stand,
> Whether I should repent me now of sin

[1] "Milton and the Paradox of the Fortunate Fall", *ELH*, IV (1937), repr. in his *Essays in the History of Ideas* (Baltimore, 1948).

> By mee done and occasiond, or rejoyce
> Much more, that much more good thereof shall spring,
> To God more glory, more good will to Men
> From God, and over wrauth grace shall abound. (469)

The lyric impulse is geared down into mechanics—"That all this good of evil shall produce, And evil turn to good"—as though the cosmos were a factory. In *De Doctrina* Milton seems faintly worried about this process (iv. 206) but does not elaborate. In *Paradise Lost* the wheels turn, in one direction or another, all over the poem; he makes more of it than any other hexemeral poet, but makes it a more mechanical and theoretical process than ever before. The transmutation is not accomplished in the poem, nor the hope of it celebrated as by Paul: "all things work together for good". Put so baldly, ethical value drains out of both elements, While Satan's embracing of evil has been shown, by the manner of its expression, to be a reversion to the primitive villainy of revenge tragedy, the final triumph of good is now asseverated in a way that projects it out of the cosmic theocracy of *Paradise Lost* into the mechanical universe of Newton and the *Essay on Man.* In his attempt to celebrate Christian culture, Milton has missed out on precisely that empirical knowledge of good and evil that inspired pagan and Renaissance literature. So far as evil is the condition of a fallen world, he faces it realistically; but so far as it is spiritual—the spiritual wickedness in high places which his poem is about—he does not really understand it. What he pits against it is not so much the faith that all things work together for good, but a stubborn Petrine determination to be unpolluted by evil. Thirty years before the Lady in *Comus* had believed that "all things ill Are but as slavish officers of vengeance" to "the Supreme good" (217), and the Elder Brother had established the Satanic metaphor of *Paradise Lost*:

> But evil on it self shall back recoyl,
> And mix no more with goodness, when at last
> Gather'd like scum, and setl'd to it self
> It shall be in eternal restless change
> Self-fed, and self-consum'd, if this fail,
> The pillar'd firmament is rott'nness,
> And earths base built on stubble. But com let's on.
> Against th'opposing will and arm of Heav'n

> May never this just sword be lifted up,
> But for that damn'd magician, let him be girt
> With all the greisly legions that troop
> Under the sooty flag of *Acheron*,
> *Harpyies* and *Hydra's*, or all the monstrous forms
> 'Twixt *Africa* and *Inde*, Ile find him out,
> And force him to restore his purchase back,
> Or drag him by the curls, to a foul death,
> Curs'd as his life.
>
> (593)

The Attendant Spirit wisely remarks that "the might of hellish charms" requires other weapons than such bold emprise; and the Lady and Sabrina demonstrate not so much the conquest of evil by good as the conquest of black magic by white, the triumph of spirit over nature. *Paradise Lost* shows no advance in the imaginative apprehension of good and evil; and offers no adequate representation of the bigger magic of Christianity. In a sense of course it is a pre-Christian poem, establishing the gospel's ground; but *Paradise Regained* does no more. Our demand for a vehemently supernatural Christianity is to countervail physical and mental sciences of a penetration Milton never dreamed of; and all his poems have great secular interest. But when all is said and done they do not justify the catholic divinity of their own terms. The paradise that Christ regains—rather, retains—is a private righteousness; while Samson, though ordering his relations with father, wife, persecutors and God, achieves the self-punitive revenge of personal phantasy: the choruses which represent it as a type of the crucifixion, a justification of the ways of God to men, seem false.

4. *The Wilderness*

Wonderfully the last hundred lines do much that the preceding 1500 had not. "For now too nigh Th' Archangel stood" shows with dramatic economy how alien the spirit world is now. The cherubim glister down the hill like *ignis lambens*,[1] reminiscent of Satan. The sword of God they brandish puts Hell—"with torrid heat, And vapour as the *Libyan* Air adust"—between man and Paradise. Michael seizes the hands of Adam

[1] See Svendsen, "Cosmological Lore in Milton", *ELH*, IX (1942), p. 220.

and Eve, erstwhile our grand parents, now children hastened down to the gate where Gabriel had sat awaiting night; "then disappeer'd", beyond their ken. Looking back they see "the Gate with dreadful Faces throng'd, and fierie Armes", like the war-time to come, "Cities of Men with lofty Gates and Towrs, Concours in Arms, fierce Faces threatning Warr" (XI. 636). "Som natural tears they drop'd, but wip'd them soon", weeping without Renaissance decoration. And they go.

The weakness of Book XII's gospel is confirmed when we notice that the great last lines—

> They hand in hand with wandring steps and slow,
> Through *Eden* took thir solitarie way.

—are beautiful and fit because they belong to *Paradise Lost* as a whole; but, as Bentley saw, they do not belong to Book XII. The distich, he says,

> *falls very much below the Passage foregoing.* It contradicts the Poet's own scheme; nor is the Diction unexceptionable. He tells us before, That *Adam*, upon hearing *Michael*'s predictions, was even *surcharg'd with Joy*, v. 372; was *replete with Joy and Wonder*, 468; was in doubt whether he should *repent of*, or *rejoice in his Fall*, 475; was *in great Peace of Thought*, 558: and *Eve* herself *not sad*, but *full of Consolation*, 620. Why then does this Distich dismiss our first Parents in Anguish, and the Reader in Melancholy? And how can the Expression be justified, *with wand'ring Steps and slow?* Why *wand'ring*? Erratic Steps? Very improper: when in the Line before, they were *guided by Providence.* And why *Slow*? when even *Eve* profess'd her Readiness and Alacrity for the Journey, 614;
>
> *But now lead on:*
> *In Me is no delay:*
>
> And why *their solitary Way*? All Words to represent a sorrowful Parting? When even their former Walks in Paradise were as solitary, as their Way now: there being no Body besides Them Two, both here and there. Shall I therefore, after so many prior Presumptions, presume at last to offer a Distich, as close as may be to the Author's Words, and entirely agreeable to his Scheme?
>
> THEN *hand in hand with* SOCIAL *steps their Way*
> *Through* Eden *took,* WITH HEAV'NLY COMFORT CHEER'D

Much of this is sentimental travesty in the worst 18th-century vein. Sad resignation is romanticised into "anguish" and "melancholy". Unfallen Paradise, though walked by God and "millions of spiritual creatures" (IV. 677) is felt to be distressingly uncivic, so that Milton's vision of the fallen world as a wilderness in which man must travel self-responsibly is tamed into a social *venu*, the heavenly comfort suggesting little more than a polite assumption of communal contentment. And Bentley misses entirely the point of "wandring", that it is one of the few poetic devices tying the last two books together and into the earlier books: the theme of Book XI is the hopeless errancy of man acting, like Eve, in a maze outside the directing will of God; Book XII is an attempt to show how direction and order may be restored and Christ

> bring back
> Through the worlds wilderness long wanderd man
> Safe to eternal Paradise of rest.
>
> (313)

But Bentley was right (and at least half-consciously so, I'm sure) in demonstrating that this dénouement is not amenable to what precedes, cannot be drawn dramatically out of Book XII despite the theological bonds.

12

CONCLUSION

THE final echo of sad error conforms to the personal devoutness of the invocations. The "adventrous Song" in between seems now adventitious to this Euripidean mood. The Metaphysicals were correctly cautious in restricting the *matériel* of *Genesis* to metaphor; Milton, expanding it heroically, produced (a paradox to be expected in English) an epic of mood. Coleridge made the point when he said that whereas Shakespeare "passes into all the forms of human character and passion", Milton "attracts all forms and things to himself, into the unity of his own ideal".[1]

The difficulty is that the personality consolidated in the poem is not easy to sympathise with, especially if you are bent on the construction of one for yourself, or have so far succeeded as to be qualified to contemn the flaws in Milton's. And the Miltonic "ideal" is not unified: reader after reader testifies to a split, chasm, dichotomy in the poem between ethic and aesthetic, process and sentiment. I will express it by saying that the "mood" of which this poem is the expression is itself dipolar: at the north, heroic (indeed megalomaniac and paranoiac) ambition to pursue things unattempted yet, to comprehend world and chaos, to write something for aftertimes they would not willingly let die; at the south, grave acceptance of the recalcitrant data of human existence. This is a common enough polarity of motive; but we expect art to reconcile the poles or anyway to release the power latent in the tension between them. *Paradise Lost* does not do this.

The first cause we may consider is the poet's centripetal force. We feel that he has accomplished a reconciliation of disparate ideals for himself in the very act of writing the poem: brought his mood's poles into contact at least, and as an example of detail sloughed off in the last books the heroic values established in the earlier ones. But this is for him, not given to us in the poem. In real life that is fair: as is shown in the poem by

[1] *Biog. Lit.* Chap. XV.

the difference between the actualised individual reconciliation of Adam and Eve, and the theoretical one made available to the world, we can reconcile only for ourselves. In expecting a symbol of it in art, demanding that art shall be "whole" (a New Testament word popular in psychology and aesthetics before the war) we are perhaps being soft. I shall attend a little more to that under a later cause; but here is one cause of dissatisfaction with the poem. I think Milton may have recognised it: all his larger poems end with abrupt dismission to the everyday while the poet or his persona steps off into privacy ("At last he rose, and twitch'd his Mantle blew"; "Home to his Mothers house private return'd") as though trying to disengage himself from the work's moodiness and relegate it to the reader's contemplation as an artifact. It appears the more, and for all its formality, as an excrescence of Milton's personality left looming like Ozymandias' statue on the shoals of time: "Look on my works, ye Mighty, and despair!" Each poem, more ominously than many an overt personal statement in the Metaphysical or Romantic mode, is a vast personification of the author. They are invested with a *mana* not referent so much to their aesthetic qualities as to their sheer existence. This gets in the way of reading, and provokes antagonism. We want to avenge ourselves on the gaunt patriarch for exposing us on the mountainside of his work. Even sympathetic readers like to think of Milton as de Hérédia's eagle:

> Quand l'aigle a dépassé les neiges éternelles,
> A sa vaste envergure il veut chercher plus d'air
> Et le soleil plus proche en un azur plus clair
> Pour échauffer l'éclat de ses mornes prunelles.
>
> Il s'enlève. Il aspire un torrent d'étincelles.
> Toujours plus haut, enflant son vol tranquille et fier,
> Il monte vers l'orage où l'attire l'éclair;
> Mais la foudre d'un coup a rompu ses deux ailes.
>
> Avec un cri sinistre, il tournoie, emporté
> Par la trombe, et, crispé, buvant, d'un trait sublime
> La flamme éparse, il plonge au fulgurant abîme.
>
> Heureux qui pour la Gloire ou pour la Liberté,
> Dans l'orgueil de la force et l'ivresse du rêve,
> Meurt ainsi d'une mort éblouissante et brève![1]

[1] *Les Trophées* (Cambridge, 1942).

Most poems about Milton have been written in terms of this myth even when honouring him:

> He pass'd the flaming bounds of Place and Time:
> The living Throne, the saphire-blaze,
> Where Angels tremble, while they gaze,
> He saw; but blasted with excess of light,
> Closed his eyes in endless night.

But you can't mythologise him into the suffering god. The nearest to a coherent myth about him, outside his own poems, is the Theban, and even there he has prevented us, seeing himself as Oedipus-Tiresias:

> Let then the calumniators of the divine goodness cease to revile, or to make me the object of their superstitious imaginations. Let them consider . . . that I am not depressed by any sense of the divine displeasure; that, on the other hand, in the most momentous periods, I have had full experience of the divine favour and protection . . . in short I am unwilling to exchange my consciousness of rectitude with that of any other person . . . in proportion as I am weak, I shall be invincibly strong; and in proportion as I am blind, I shall more clearly see. O! that I may thus be perfected by feebleness, and irradiated by obscurity! And, indeed, in my blindness, I enjoy in no inconsiderable degree the favour of the Deity, who regards me with more tenderness and compassion in proportion as I am able to behold nothing but himself. Alas! for him who insults me, who maligns and merits public execration! For the divine law not only shields me from injury, but almost renders me too sacred to attack; not indeed so much from the privation of my sight, as from the overshadowing of those heavenly wings, which seem to have occasioned this obscurity; and which, when occasioned, he is wont to illuminate with an interior light, more precious and more pure.
>
> (*2nd Def.* i. 235-40)

"Consciousness of rectitude . . . interior light": this is the Milton in God and Abdiel, heroised thrice more in the last books as Enoch "The onely righteous in a World perverse" (XI. 701), Noah "the onely Son of light In a dark Age" (808), and Abraham "the one faithful man" (XII. 111). It was a traditional motif, but we can hear Milton, at the north pole of his mood, making the claim for himself. It is appalling; yet Coleridge felt that "the egotism of such a man is a revelation of Spirit".[1] At least we respond to *Paradise Lost*, violently one way or the other, because—like Milton, and his poem—we are sustained by our antagonisms.[2]

Related to this is a second cause, the lack of a catastrophe. In *Paradise Lost* (and elsewhere) this usual release from the plot is replaced by Milton's simply walking away and leaving his work on our hands. We participate in solemn dedication, exuberant struggle, argument, depiction, then there is a collapse into the mundane which is not so much an issue of the plot in which we are involved as a relinquishment of the effort the poet has been involved in, because for him the act has sufficed. For us it does not; and we are likely to join Blake and see in this structural peculiarity a symbol of "reason restraining desire to passivity", for it appears on the scale of phrasing too: the verse typically elevates into expectancy and then crushes flat or wanders quietly away ("With vain attempt"; "And with them comes a third of Regal port, But Faded splendor wan").[3]

Thirdly there is the very ambition to convince: we are surprised to find a gap between "the ways of God" and the justice demanded by men only when we are told it is going to be bridged. And when we are told that—as when we are offered logical proofs of God's existence, or jolly reasons for praying—we suspect the motives of the speaker. It was Milton's error to let his north pole take charge here, to attempt to reconcile the ideal with the given through the nexus of Christian mythology *in extenso*. But here there have been sharp historical changes in sensibility as well, partly beyond Milton's control. They lead to some of the most interesting arguments for which the poem is still used as a prism so I want to consider them more at length, as a fourth cause of our discomfort.

There is no avoiding the explicit and for all essentials orthodox Theism which the poem's sequentia are founded on. I

[1] *Table Talk*, 18 Aug. 1833 (*ed. cit.* p. 279).

[2] The phrase is Kenneth Burke's. *P.L.* is particularly amenable, as an exercise in personal anthropology, to Burkeian interpretation.

[3] Cf. R. M. Adams, *Ikon: J. M. and the Modern Critics* (Ithaca, N.Y., 1955), pp. 196-7. This is typically Fifty-ish response to Milton, witty and learned. Adams is able to demolish a great deal of New Criticism (as well as old scholarship) with complete cheerfulness because (I assume) he has escaped or transcended the socio-moral complexes that underly it. It is much easier for Americans to do this than English; this is the chief cause of critical disagreement between them.

have quoted Augustine and Hooker, as well as Calvin, Brunner and Niebuhr, to interpret it; the most influential book on it is by an Augustinian Anglican; the chapter on Milton in the recent Pelican Guide seems to be written by a Roman Catholic priest; and Sister Miriam Joseph has concluded an essay on the poem's orthodoxy by claiming that "an intelligent Catholic reader can enjoy in *Paradise Lost* the expression of dogmatic, moral, and philosophical truths impregnated with a power peculiar to poetry."[1] So the poem is still subject to all the criticisms of orthodoxy from Montaigne through Blake to Kathleen Nott: chiefly, that the Christian mythology is crude and inadequate, and the Church's interpretation of it, in spite of reformations inside and revolts without, has tended to moral bullying, obscurantism and sentimentality, when it ought to have encouraged the will, enlightened the mind and purified the heart. This criticism can be made of any human institution, and Milton charged it more strongly than most against the church he knew. But just for that reason his reliance in *Paradise Lost* on all the major doctrines of Christianity, and the poem's directive that we should "to the hand of Heav'n submit, However chast'ning" (XI. 373), is felt as a betrayal, like Winston Smith's[2]; alternatively, as unconscious doublethink—Milton "was a true Poet and of the Devil's party without knowing it."

It is sometimes forgotten that Blake's meaning depends on his preliminary inversion of the qualities he supposed to belong to Satan (energy, passion, and so on) as good, and those belonging to God (rationality, legalism) as evil. This was because he saw 18th-century orthodoxy as a tyranny of false rationality over true feeling. His prophecy is perennially valid, more, or less, according to historical circumstances: in Milton's time, and ours after the war, rather less than in his own. So there is not a great deal of point in arguing with his epigram as a philosophical statement. We may note, though, that it is sometimes restated

[1] "Orthodoxy in *P.L.*", *Laval Théologique et Philosophique*, VIII (1952), repr. in *Centenary Publications*, St Mary's College, Notre Dame, Ia., 1954. She admits, though, that "In treating the differences between corporeal and incorporeal beings as one of degree rather than of kind Milton goes beyond that necessary accommodation to the human mind by which even Scripture, and *a fortiorio* a poem, attributes bodily characteristics to spirits". This confirms my chap. 7.

[2] He "loved Big Brother". The point is Empson's.

in the form, by saying "*Paradise Lost* is neither a majestic failure to justify God, nor a psychopathologically accidental justification of satanic man, but in itself a criticism of the theology it postulates". Now the poem had for Milton himself this characteristic of true myth, that it legitimises by controlled expression the conflicts inherent in its fable; but it does not legitimise them for us because—another detailed cause—the criticism is of the wrong kind. The criticism we are thinking of here is the rebellious energy of Satan, the fine poetry which silences God's voice, and the final mood of the poem, for example. But these seem not to be unified with that which they criticise; the work remains split, in a way which other self-critical works are not: *Troilus and Cressida* and the courtly code, or *Henry IV* and kingship, wherethe criticism is a subtle irony consistent with its objects in every area of work.

The alternative theory, of a betrayal to Theism, has been inflated by historical pressures till Milton became a symbol of the Establishment mouthing its pinstriped insincerities. He was an eminent victim of the French Symbolist cry, "Prends l'éloquence et de lui le cou torques!"[1] Then, English literature becoming material for examinations, the content of *Paradise Lost* was swamped by Verity's footnotes and its nature as a poem left hanging in the scales of antithetical exam questions of the Raleigh type.[2] To escape this, and to give undergraduates

[1] On the relation between the Symbolist poetic and anti-Milton criticism see Kermode's *Romantic Image* (1957). He has not dealt with the sociological causes, though.

[2] Forty-five years after the publication of *P.L.* Addison was uneasy about its references. Newton remarked that Milton "sometimes writes as though he had a mind to make work for commentators". In 1770 a Gentleman of Oxford published in Aberdeen a version of *P.L.* which he had turned into prose from a French translation: "No poem has had greater, or juster praise from the most eminent judges of literature . . . but being wrote in the highest stile of heroick poetry, and the thoughts many of them express'd by figures of grammar and rhetoric, being full of digressions and sentences transposed, as well as difficult terms in the mathematicks, history, astronomy, astrology, geography, architecture, navigation, anatomy, alchymy, divinity, and all other human arts and sciences, it hath so happened that many readers have been unable to see the beauties of the poem. . . . Besides which it is necessary they should understand the Hebrew, Chaldean, Arabic, Syriac, Phoenician, and Egyptian, and all the dead languages, with the living and modern ones, in all their different dialects: So that it has been a frequent complaint of the readers of MILTON, that he has not calculated his poem for common eyes . . ." By the 1830s it was being published

power to dispose of a large syllabus, "practical criticism" was applied to bits of the poem. The rhythm was shown to be monotonous, the diction abstract and generalised, the underlying sensibility therefore crude, and the myth poor. Such local judgements are not enforceable overall, but they seem to be so when the deductions made from them and the assumptions implicit in them are welcome for non-literary reasons. Thus, a good many objections to Milton's verse were really projections of some other controversy: in the thirties it was necessary to gag dilettanti from maundering about the Grand Style now that more precise terms of criticism were available, and to clear the ground for a modern poetic. The structure of *Paradise Lost*, which is symphonic, was blamed for not being dramatic, and called mechanical or lithic, so symbolising an objectionable social structure, and various manifestations of mechanicalness which seemed to threaten new life—actual machinery, and the mechanical ethic which Ibsen and Freud and Lawrence had been protesting against. Coarse British propaganda in the first war disgusted sensitive men[1]; after the war it went on in other forms, for the first time apparently encouraged by the Establishment—political promises, economic deceptions, the cozening complacency of newspapers and magazines, the amoral suasion of advertising, all megaphoning through mass media, inviting men to compensatory phantasy, the word taken for flesh, gesture usurping action. Hence the critical insistence on the organic, particularised, concrete, sincere. These were proper anxieties and it looked at one time as though they might be allayed, by literature itself, by psychology, experimental education, and by the second war and the revolution of 1945. But the troubles are still with us, as they were with Wordsworth:

as a schoolbook. Masson's (1874) was the last ed. annotated for the "general" grown-up reader as distinct from the student preparing a set book. Much recent literary iconoclasm is the result of teachers' taking their pupils' side against an antiquarian interest in literature which, so long as it remained amateur, was quite legitimate (though footnotes may be shored against the ruins of the editor's personality, and the kind of readerly curiosity they satisfy is likely to exclude more profitable kinds); but which, as a professional attitude, used to educate and examine youth, was clearly inadequate and deadening. Unfortunately the grounds of "practical criticism", never explicit, are now getting lost in history and people practise it without knowing why.

[1] See cartoons in *Punch*, 1915-18, and E. M. Forster in *Abinger Harvest*.

> a multitude of causes, unknown to former times, are now acting with a combined force to blunt the discriminating powers of the mind, and, unfitting it for all voluntary exertion, to reduce it to a state of almost savage torpor. The most effective of these causes are the great national events which are daily taking place, and the increasing accumulation of men in cities, where the uniformity of their occupations produces a craving for extraordinary incident, which the rapid communication of intelligence hourly gratifies. To this tendency of life and manners the literature and theatrical exhibitions of the country have conformed themselves. The invaluable works of our elder writers, I had almost said the works of Shakespeare and Milton, are driven into neglect by frantic novels, sickly and stupid German Tragedies, and deluges of idle and extravagant stories in verse.[1]

Indeed, they are the same troubles that worried Milton; but the main virtue he recommends is perseverance; the literacy he demands is founded on book-learning, an interest in language as such, and a stamina that will respond to curious musical rhythms; the religious feeling that imbues the poem is the dignified sombre realism of a Jew or a Christian Humanist. There is no need to prove how publicly desirable these virtues were at the time Milton wrote; that they were distorted and impoverished in the 18th Century, making Blake's revolution necessary, only emphasises the superiority of Milton and his culture to the Augustans and theirs. But, prejudice apart, they were virtues less desirable in the 1930s. That also was a time of revolution, needing a more positive ethic, wanting to rescue literature from the brown libraries of great houses and the oak desks of public schools, anxious to train its generation in a more supple kind of poetry than the traditional classico-romantic, a kind which would release them towards a millennium.

Complaints of this kind stem, of course, from the Romantic notions that there is a possible world of poetry's own making, and that poetry itself should be therapeutic, ease the agony of human hearts; from what Eliot called in Arnold "the educator's view of literature", the belief that poetry is itself a means of grace; and from a softness in our idea of the spiritual (we still

[1] Pref. to *Lyrical Ballads* (1800). This, and Coleridge's remarks on the renovating power of linguistic study in his chap. on the beauties of Wordsworth's poetry in *Biog. Lit.*, and Arnold's remarks on literature as a criticism of life in his essay on Wordsworth, are the originating documents of 20th-century socio-moral criticism.

view all past literature through the sensitivity of the great Edwardians, not yet through the sterner, more passionate and concrete eyes of Lawrence, Yeats and Eliot). So it is probably a false criticism philosophically, but just aesthetically. Milton did fail to realise, in both senses, his spiritual materials: in spite of their enormous and ready-made potential, his symbols and personifications of evil and good do not reach nearly as far down or up as even the human materials of Shakespeare and some great novelists.

This is not of course to put him in an inconsiderable rank; and I want to conclude by examining the more satisfactory south pole of his mood. It is a characteristic of *Paradise Lost*, and a cause of the deplorable quantity of Miltoniana, that there are exactly two sides to every issue it poses. So it is possible, if we abandon our Romantic demands on poetry, and admit the poem's relatively crude presentation of good and evil, to hold that its dichotomy of mood, this split between sentiment and process, is more valuable as symbolic prophecy, because more realistic, than the aesthetic satisfaction of a more balanced, unified and complex work of art. Doing this, we alter the metaphor and regard the south pole of Milton's mood as the ground from which the northern ambitions spring: they are indeed not unified with the ground, always aspiring beyond it and always being pulled back to it by a gravitational force which represents the earth-binding conditions of fallen human life. The effect then of checking the heroic or idealising verse, as of flattening the structure, is not to symbolise the restraint of desire by reason but the circumscription of life by sin.

This is why, when we look in *Paradise Lost* for a poetic vision which will symbolise perfection of the inner spiritual life whatever the outer hell we are trapped in, we can't find it. There are moments of human love and insight, but they only flicker like "the human face divine" and "chearful waies of men" cut off from Milton by his blindness. There are moments when divine power and love blaze out

> the Son
> On his great Expedition now appeer'd,
> Girt with Omnipotence, with Radiance crown'd
> Of Majestie Divine, Sapience and Love
> Immense, and all his Father in him shon. (VII. 192)

But they blaze alone in the sky, not striking the earth. There seems to be no conductor between God and man, and a high resistance between poet and reader. Wilson Knight makes the point about melopoeia: "The result is, too often, a thin, wavering time-stream rather than a created world".[1] Leavis remarks that Milton quite fails to subtilise and fuse the elements of his world into the "almost inconceivably close and delicate organic wholeness" of a Shakespeare play.[2] Our resentment is confirmed at the poem's end, where Michael is so emphatic of "the knowledge of sin" which is law, and not poetically adequate to the liberating "law of the Spirit of life in Christ Jesus" (*Rom.* iii. 20; viii. 2). The poem refuses to "be still and still moving Into another intensity For a further union, a deeper communion . . ." But it is Eliot (whose later work is criticised for the same reasons as Milton's) who may assist in recognising some validity in the judicious sanctity of Milton's mood. Milton leaves us at the stage of "Not fare well, But fare forward, voyagers".

He cannot give Eliot's careful explanations of why this must be (the effects of action cannot be foreseen so we must merely trust, etc.), and Eliot's considered rejection of other sources of grace ("The infirm glory of the positive hour. . . . The one veritable transitory power", for example). But Eliot having written and, in *Four Quartets*, written so Miltonically, we are able to see now much of the ground for Milton's grave south-polar mood which he had taken for granted.

Intellectually this ground may be described as a quite unhysterical recognition, in Satan and man, of sin, carefully defined with reference to the public world Milton knew as well as to the Bible and, accidentally, his own temperament. It is a sin issuing typically in discord, chaos and tyranny. We have lost that consciousness and definiteness for an agnostic irony about our motives, and the meanings of the words we use, and whose side we are supposed to be on.[3]

At the same time, without any nobilising such as one gets in Wordsworth and Shelley, and without the bombast of a Marlowe, a sense of the ideal dignity and responsibility of human life accrues from its being measured against a superhuman scale. Whereas in the more usual and popular verse of

[1] *Burning Oracle*, p. 99.
[2] *Revaluation*, pp. 60-61.
[3] Title of a poem by Auden.

the Metaphysical kind there is a counterpoint between metre (representing law, rationality, the ideal) and the speaking voice (nature, emotion, the actual) which asserts a balance, and sometimes symbolises the victory of nature over ideality, in Milton's verse the counterpoint is between the verse as it is and an ideal condition in which it would cease to be language and translate into the communication of angels. Arguments about abstract diction, vagueness, gigantic loftiness and so on are irrelevant. The effect in the poem is to suggest the power of reason to transcend its materials, to pitch close to its own ideal. It is of course an approval of "reason" in Milton's sense (more intuitive than ours or Blake's), and it is still open to the complaint that it does not subtly criticise itself: for this ambitious, cosmosophical pole of Milton's mood is bound to issue in what we now call rationalisation. But criticism of it, and a recognition of the natural and emotional basis of being, lie in the ground from which these heroics spring. The elevation is inconstant; especially at personal moments, and when similes (the ploughman, etc.) let the real world in, it drops to a simplicity which is more typically "Miltonic" than the other because unique: "They hand in hand . . ."

Acting together, then, Milton's two moods assert the ideal and admit the actual. Separately, the grave south polar mood, seeing things with simple sureness, corrects our loose ambivalencies. The north pole in isolation offers local "beauties" (Milton shines in a book of quotations); these have a value. Much of our reading now is professional and educative, aimed at extracting all sorts of infra-literary satisfactions from literature so as to justify our reading as work. To obtain full profit from Milton's art one has to approach it as an amateur, or after indulgence in impurer art, or with music (Handel, Bach, Haydn) in the mind's ear. Then one is content for a while, forgetting the flawed whole, with that local verbal artistry which as a professional one may regard as "mere". Then the judgement that the "Nativity Ode" is not so truly dedicated or devotional a poem as Herbert's stops mattering: it delights simply as ode, captivating and releasing the mind with its contrast in musical imagery of peace, rusticity, harmony, mourning vanity, angelic hosts. And *Paradise Lost*, freed from the cramps of context, displays an art more musical, and of course less human and semantic than the more nearly complete but, others having written too, identified and valued by that difference. At random one opens, unpropitiously enough in Book X:

> Hee ended, and the heav'nly Audience loud
> Sung Halleluia, as the sound of Seas,
> Through multitude that sung:
>
> (641)

The "loud" acting as adjective and adverb across two lines at once; the evocation of an oratorio with "Hallelujah!" sung against the exposition; the onomatopoeic collocation of "loud Sung . . . sound . . . sung" exhibiting the power to dispose language in mimetic pattern; the opportunity of metamorphosing a church congregation into an audience of angels—these effects are not subtle, or sensuous; but they are more competent than clever, and their competence temporarily sustains the mind with confidence and joy. Milton's "northern" verse is no measure of how far the imaginative intelligence may pierce into the recesses of natural and human being with language as both instrument and object; but it can act in a shuddering world as a criterion of what is chaotic, over-ripe, and not good enough.

The Paradise that Adam and Eve have lost was a potential spiritual majesty, uncertain and inconstant as the rest of the poem's ideal world. The one they have gained is the wary tolerance of litotes ("Dismiss them not disconsolate"), antithesis ("so send them forth, though sorrowing, yet in peace") and oxymoron ("new hope to spring Out of despaire, joy, but with fear yet linkt"; XI. 113, 117, 138). But it is made positive by the love they have regained for each other, and so for living: "Both in one Faith unanimous though sad" (XII. 603). The consolidating impulse of this line is unexciting but it represents a true virtue of the fallen life, once the inevitability of its being fallen is accepted.

INDEX

INDEX

INDEX

INDEX

INDEX